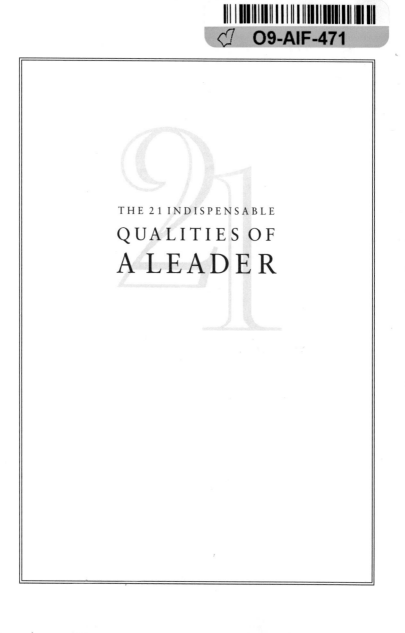

THE 21 INDISPENSABLE

QUALITIES OF

A LEADER

JOHN C. MAXWELL

THE 21 INDISPENSABLE
QUALITIES OF
A LEADER

Becoming the

Person Others Will

Want to Follow

THOMAS NELSON PUBLISHERS®
Nashville

Published in Nashville, Tennessee, by Thomas Nelson, Inc.

ISBN 0-7852-7440-5 (HC)
ISBN 0-7852-6795-6 (SE)
ISBN 0-7852-6796-4 (IE)

Printed in the United States of America.
1 2 3 4 5 6 BVG 04 03 02 01 00

Contents

ACKNOWLEDGMENTS

I want to thank all of the people at Thomas Nelson who always work so hard and do such a fine job on my books.

I'd like to thank INJOY Group staff members—Linda Eggers, my administrative assistant; Brent Cole, my research assistant; and Stephanie Wetzel, my proofreader—all of whom make me better than I am.

And I must thank Charlie Wetzel, my writer, who multiplies my time and influence through his work.

INTRODUCTION

What makes people want to follow a leader? Why do people reluctantly comply with one leader while passionately following another to the ends of the earth? What separates leadership theorists from successful leaders who lead effectively in the real world? The answer lies in the character qualities of the individual person.

My friend, do you know whether you have what it takes to become a great leader, the kind who attracts people and makes things happen? I mean, if you took the time to really look at yourself deep down, would you find the qualities needed to live out your boldest dreams, the ones so big that you've never shared them with anybody? That's a question each of us must have the courage to honestly ask—and answer—if we want to achieve our real potential.

I've written this book to help you recognize, develop, and refine the personal characteristics needed to be a truly effective leader, the kind people *want* to follow. If you've already read

The 21 Irrefutable Laws of Leadership, then you understand that becoming a leader takes time. The Law of Process says that leadership develops daily, not in a day. Part of a leader's development comes from learning the laws of leadership, for those are the tools that teach how leadership works. But *understanding* leadership and actually *doing* it are two different activities.

Recently I talked to a friend named Bill Freeman. He is the president of Watkins Associated Industries, Inc., the largest privately owned trucking company in America. Bill is an excellent executive, and like all good leaders, he is continually looking for ways to learn and grow.

"I'm about halfway through your book," he told me, meaning *The 21 Irrefutable Laws of Leadership.* "It's making quite an impact on me." Then he said something that made quite an impact on *me.* "Let me tell you how I'm going through it," he said. "Each morning I read a chapter of the book. And all through the day, I think about that law. As I work, I look at myself and ask, How am I doing with this leadership law? I watch the people in the office, looking to see whether they practice it. I measure our whole company against it, observing, assessing, reflecting. Every morning it's a different law. It's an eye-opener."

Bill really got my juices flowing. In fact, his comments prompted me to write this book. He is approaching his own leadership development from the inside out, as he should. Leaders are effective because of who they are on the inside—in the qualities that make them up as people. And to go to the highest level of leadership, people have to develop these traits from the inside out.

After talking to Bill, I took some time to reflect on the characteristics of the best leaders I know, the ones who people really want to follow. I looked for common themes. I talked to other leaders and heard their impressions. And I examined leaders who have impacted history. I settled on a list of 21 qualities possessed by all great leaders. These traits are described and illustrated in this book, meant to be a complementary companion to *The 21 Irrefutable Laws of Leadership*.

As you dive into the book, you may find that you are able to easily breeze through several chapters at a time. You may even be able to knock out the whole book in one sitting. *Don't do it. The 21 Indispensable Qualities of a Leader* is designed to be absorbed the same way Bill Freeman approaches a book: strategically and methodically.

I want to encourage you to live with this book for a while. Read a chapter, and then give it some time. Use it to reflect, review, and renew. If the quality you're studying is a weak area in your life, spend some time addressing it before you move on to the next chapter. You may even want to repeat this process several times over the course of a year, cementing each trait into your character.

Everything rises and falls on leadership. And leadership truly develops from the inside out. If you can become the leader you *ought* to be on the *inside,* you will be able to become the leader you *want* to be on the *outside.* People will want to follow you. And when that happens, you'll be able to tackle anything in this world.

CHARACTER:

BE A PIECE OF THE ROCK

Leadership is the capacity and will
to rally men and women to a common purpose
and the character which inspires confidence.

—Bernard Montgomery,
British Field Marshal

Never "for the sake of peace and quiet"
deny your own experience or convictions.

—Dag Hammarskjöld,
Statesman and Nobel Peace Prize Winner

PUTTING IT ALL ON THE LINE

If you've traveled through smaller airports or have much experience flying in corporate aircraft, you've probably seen or flown in a Lear Jet. I've had the opportunity to fly in one a couple of times, and it's quite an experience. They're small—capable of carrying only five or six passengers—and very fast. It's like climbing into a narrow tube with jet engines strapped to it.

I have to admit, the whole experience of riding in a Lear Jet is pretty exhilarating. But by far the most amazing thing to me about it is the time it saves. I've traveled literally millions of miles on airlines, and I'm accustomed to long drives to airports, car rental returns, shuttles, terminal congestion, and seemingly endless delays. It can be a nightmare. Flying on a Lear Jet can easily cut travel time in half.

The father of this amazing airplane was a man named Bill Lear. An inventor, aviator, and business leader, Lear held more than 150 patents, including those of the automatic pilot, car radio, and eight-track tapes (you can't win them all). Lear was a pioneer in his thinking, and in the 1950s, he could see the potential for the manufacture of small corporate jets. It took him several years to make his dream a reality, but in 1963, the first Lear Jet made its maiden voyage, and in 1964 he delivered his first production jet to a client.

Lear's success was immediate, and he quickly sold many aircraft. But not long after he got his start, Lear learned that two aircraft he'd built had crashed under mysterious circumstances. He was devastated. At that time, fifty-five Lear Jets were privately owned, and Lear immediately sent word to all of the owners to ground their planes until he and his team could determine what had caused the crashes. The thought that more lives might be lost was far more important to him than any adverse publicity that action might generate in the media.

As he researched the ill-fated flights, Lear discovered a potential cause, but he couldn't verify the technical problem on the ground. There was only one sure way to find out whether he had diagnosed the problem correctly. He would have to try to re-create it personally—in the air.

It was a dangerous process, but that's what he did. As he flew the jet, he nearly lost control and almost met the same fate as the other two pilots. But he did manage to make it through the tests, and he was able to verify the defect. Lear developed a new part to correct the problem and fitted all fifty-five planes with it, eliminating the danger.

Grounding the planes cost Lear a lot of money. And it planted seeds of doubt in the minds of potential customers. As a result, he needed two years to rebuild the business. But Lear never regretted his decision. He was willing to risk his success, his fortune, and even his life to solve the mystery of those crashes—but not his integrity. And that takes character.

FLESHING IT OUT

How a leader deals with the circumstances of life tells you many things about his character. Crisis doesn't necessarily make character, but it certainly does reveal it. Adversity is a crossroads that makes a person choose one of two paths: character or compromise. Every time he chooses character, he becomes stronger, even if that choice brings negative consequences. As Nobel prize-winning author Alexander Solzhenitsyn noted, "The meaning of earthly existing lies, not as we have grown used to thinking, in prospering, but in the development of the soul." The development of character is at the heart of our development not just as leaders, but as human beings.

What must every person know about character?

1. Character Is More than Talk

Anyone can *say* that he has integrity, but action is the real indicator of character. Your character determines who you are. Who you are determines what you see. What you see determines what you do. That's why you can never separate a leader's character from his actions. If a leader's actions and intentions are continually working against each other, then look to his character to find out why.

2. Talent Is a Gift, but Character Is a Choice

We have no control over a lot of things in life. We don't get to choose our parents. We don't select the location or circumstances of our birth and upbringing. We don't get to pick our talents or IQ. But we do choose our character. In fact, we create it every time we make choices—to cop out or dig out of a hard situation, to bend the truth or stand under the weight of it, to take the easy money or pay the price. As you live your life and make choices today, you are continuing to create your character.

3. Character Brings Lasting Success with People

True leadership always involves other people. (As the leadership proverb says, if you think you're leading and no one is following you, then you're only taking a walk.) Followers do not trust leaders whose character they know to be flawed, and they will not continue following them.

4. Leaders Cannot Rise Above the Limitations of Their Character

Have you ever seen highly talented people suddenly fall apart when they achieved a certain level of success? The key to that phenomenon is character. Steven Berglas, a psychologist at Harvard Medical School and author of *The Success Syndrome,* says that people who achieve great heights but lack the bedrock character to sustain them through the stress are headed for disaster. He believes they are destined for one or more of the four A's: *arrogance,* painful feelings of *aloneness,* destructive *adventure-seeking,* or *adultery.* Each is a terrible price to pay for weak character.

R E F L E C T I N G   O N   I T

If you've found yourself being sucked in by one of the four A's that Berglas identifies, call a time-out. Do what you must to step away from some of the stress of your success, and seek professional help. Don't think that the valley you're in will pass with time, more money, or increased prestige. Unaddressed cracks in character only get deeper and more destructive with time.

If you're not struggling in any of these four areas, you should still examine the condition of your character. Ask yourself whether your words and actions match—all the time. When you say you'll finish an assignment, do you always follow through? If you tell your children that you'll make it to their recital or ball game, are you there for it? Can people trust your handshake as they would a legal contract?

As you lead others at home, at work, and in the community, recognize that your character is your most important asset. G. Alan Bernard, president of Mid Park, Inc., stated, "The respect that leadership must have requires that one's ethics be without question. A leader not only stays above the line between right and wrong, he stays well clear of the 'gray areas.'"

BRINGING IT HOME

To improve your character, do the following:

- *Search for the cracks.* Spend some time looking at the major areas of your life (work, marriage, family, service, etc.), and identify anywhere you might have cut corners, compromised, or let people down. Write down every instance you can recall from the past two months.

- *Look for patterns.* Examine the responses that you just wrote down. Is there a particular area where you have a weakness, or do you have a type of problem that keeps surfacing? Detectable patterns will help you diagnose character issues.

- *Face the music.* The beginning of character repair comes when you face your flaws, apologize, and deal with the consequences of your actions. Create a list of people to whom you need to apologize for your actions, then follow through with sincere apologies.

- *Rebuild.* It's one thing to face up to your past actions. It's another to build a new future. Now that you've identified any areas of weakness, create a plan that will prevent you from making the same mistakes again.

D A I L Y   T A K E - A W A Y

A man took his young daughter to a carnival, and she immediately ran over to a booth and asked for cotton candy. As the attendant handed her a huge ball of it, the father asked, "Sweetheart, are you sure you can eat all that?"

"Don't worry, Dad," she answered, "I'm a lot bigger on the inside than on the outside."

That's what real character is—being bigger on the inside.

CHARISMA:

THE FIRST IMPRESSION CAN

SEAL THE DEAL

How can you have charisma? Be more concerned
about making others feel good about themselves than
you are making them feel good about you.

—Dan Reiland,
Vice President of Leadership Development, INJOY

I have yet to find the man,
however exalted his station, who did not
do better work and put forth greater effort under a
spirit of approval than under a spirit of criticism.

—Charles Schwab, Industrialist

T H E   C L E V E R E S T   I N   E N G L A N D

During the second half of the nineteenth century, two strong men vied for leadership of Great Britain's government: William Gladstone and Benjamin Disraeli. The two politicians were intense rivals. You can detect how they felt about each other based on a comment once made by Disraeli: "The difference between a misfortune and a calamity? If Gladstone fell into the Thames [River], it would be a misfortune. But if someone dragged him out again, it would be a calamity."

Many people believe that Gladstone, leader of the Liberal Party for three decades, personified the best qualities of Victorian England. A career public servant, he was a great orator, a master of finance, and a staunchly moral man. He was made prime minister of the United Kingdom four different times, the only person in the nation's history to achieve that honor. Under his leadership, Great Britain established a national education system, instituted parliamentary reform, and saw the vote given to a significant number of people in the working classes.

Benjamin Disraeli, who served twice as prime minister, had a different kind of background. In his thirties, he entered politics and built a reputation as a diplomat and social reformer. But his greatest accomplishment was masterminding Great Britain's purchase of shares in the Suez Canal.

Though both men accomplished much for Britain, what really separated them as leaders was their approach to people. The difference can be best illustrated by a story told by a young woman who dined with the two rival statesmen on consecutive nights. When asked her impression of them, she said, "When I left the dining room after sitting next to Mr. Gladstone, I thought he was the cleverest *man* in England. But after sitting next to Mr. Disraeli, I thought I was the cleverest *woman* in England." Disraeli possessed a quality that drew people to him and made them want to follow him. He had charisma.

FLESHING IT OUT

Most people think of charisma as something mystical, almost undefinable. They think it's a quality that comes at birth or not at all. But that's not true. Charisma, plainly stated, is the ability to draw people to you. And like other character traits, it can be developed.

To make yourself the kind of person who attracts others, you need to personify these pointers:

1. Love Life

People enjoy leaders who enjoy life. Think of the people you want to spend time with. How would you describe them? Grumpy? Bitter? Depressed? Of course not. They're celebrators, not complainers. They're passionate about life. If you want to attract people, you need to be like the people you enjoy being with. Eighteenth-century evangelist John Wesley recognized that, saying, "when you set yourself on fire, people love to come and see you burn."

2. Put a "10" on Every Person's Head

One of the best things you can do for people—which also attracts them to you—is to expect the best of them. I call it putting a "10" on everyone's head. It helps others think more highly of themselves, and at the same time, it also helps you. According to Jacques Wiesel, "A survey of one hundred self-made millionaires showed only one common denominator. These highly successful men and women could only see the good in people."

Benjamin Disraeli understood and practiced this concept, and it was one of the secrets of his charisma. He once said, "The greatest good you can do for another is not just to share your riches but to reveal to him his own." If you appreciate others, encourage them, and help them reach their potential, they will love you for it.

3. Give People Hope

French General Napoleon Bonaparte characterized leaders as "dealers in hope." Like all great leaders, he knew that hope is the greatest of all possessions. If you can be the person who bestows that gift on others, they will be attracted to you, and they will be forever grateful.

4. Share Yourself

People love leaders who share themselves and their life journeys. As you lead people, give of yourself. Share wisdom, resources, and even special occasions. That's one of my favorite things to do. For example, I recently went to an annual storytelling festival in Jonesborough, Tennessee. It was something I had wanted to do for years, and when I was finally able to work it into my schedule, my wife, Margaret, and I took two leaders from my staff and their wives. We had a wonderful time, and more important, I was able to add value to their lives by spending special time with them.

When it comes to charisma, the bottom line is othermindedness. Leaders who think about others and their concerns before thinking of themselves exhibit charisma.

REFLECTING ON IT

How would you rate yourself when it comes to charisma? Are other people naturally attracted to you? Are you well liked? If not, you may possess one of these roadblocks to charisma:

Pride. Nobody wants to follow a leader who thinks he is better than everyone else.

Insecurity. If you are uncomfortable with who you are, others will be too.

Moodiness. If people never know what to expect from you, they stop expecting anything.

Perfectionism. People respect the desire for excellence, but dread totally unrealistic expectations.

Cynicism. People don't want to be rained on by someone who sees a cloud around every silver lining.

If you can stay away from these qualities, you can cultivate charisma.

B R I N G I N G I T H O M E

To improve your charisma, do the following:

- *Change your focus.* Observe your interaction with people during the next few days. As you talk to others, determine how much of your conversation is concentrated on yourself. Determine to tip the balance in favor of focusing on others.

- *Play the first impression game.* Try an experiment. The next time you meet someone for the first time, try your best to make a good impression. Learn the person's name. Focus on his interests. Be positive. And most important, treat him as a "10." If you can do this for a day, you can do it every day. And that will increase your charisma overnight.

- *Share yourself.* Make it your long-term goal to share your resources with others. Think about how you can add value to five people in your life this year. They can be family members, colleagues, employees, or friends. Provide resources to help them grow personally and professionally, and share your personal journey with them.

D A I L Y T A K E - A W A Y

Perle Mesta, the greatest Washington hostess since Dolley Madison, was asked the secret of her success in getting so many rich and famous people to attend her parties.

"It's all in the greetings and good-byes," she replied. When a guest arrived, she met him, saying, "At last you're here!" and as each left, she said, "I'm sorry you have to leave so soon!" Her agenda was to focus on others, not herself. That's charisma.

Commitment:

It Separates Doers from Dreamers

People do not follow uncommitted leaders.
Commitment can be displayed in a full range of
matters to include the work hours you choose to maintain,
how you work to improve your abilities, or what you
do for your fellow workers at personal sacrifice.

—Stephen Gregg,
Chairman and CEO of Ethix Corp.

He who has done his best
for his own time has lived for all times.

—Johann von Schiller, Playwright

OLD BEFORE HIS TIME

A couple of years ago, my wife, Margaret, and I had the opportunity to vacation in Italy. Our two greatest priorities were food and art. To find the finest food, we talked to friends who had been there. To see the finest artwork, we enlisted the help of a fantastic guide who is a buyer for New York's Metropolitan Museum of Art. During that tour we saw many great pieces of artwork. But none struck me the way Michelangelo's *David* did. That's when I understood why it is called a masterpiece.

Michelangelo lived an incredible life. Possibly the greatest artist of Western civilization—and certainly the most influential—he was born to sculpt. He once said that when he drank his wet nurse's milk as a baby, along with it came a love for the stonecutter's tools. He sculpted his first mature masterpiece at age twenty-one. He completed his *Pietà* and *David* before age thirty.

In his early thirties, Michelangelo was summoned to Rome by Pope Julius II to sculpt a magnificent papal tomb, but was then asked to work on a painting project instead. At first Michelangelo wanted to refuse, having no desire to paint a dozen figures on the ceiling of a small chapel in the Vatican. Though as a boy he had been trained to paint, his passion was sculpture. But when the pope pressed him, he reluctantly accepted the assignment.

Scholars believe Michelangelo's rivals pushed for him to get the job, hoping he would refuse it and lose favor with the pope, or take it and discredit himself. But once Michelangelo accepted the assignment, he thoroughly committed himself to it, expanding the project from a simple depiction of the twelve apostles to include more then four hundred figures and nine scenes from the book of Genesis.

For four grueling years, the artist lay on his back painting the ceiling of the Sistine Chapel. And he paid a great price. The work permanently damaged his eyesight and wore him down. Michelangelo said, "After four tortured years, more than four hundred over-life-sized figures, I felt as old and as weary as Jeremiah. I was only thirty-seven, yet friends did not recognize the old man I had become."

The impact of Michelangelo's commitment was far-reaching. He pleased his benefactor, the pope, and received other commissions from the Vatican. But more important, he made a huge impact in the artistic community. His Sistine Chapel frescoes were so boldly painted, so original, so exquisitely executed that they caused many fellow artists, including the gifted painter Raphael, to alter their style. Art historians maintain that Michelangelo's masterpiece forever changed the course of painting in Europe. And it laid a foundation for his equally important impact on sculpture and architecture.

Undoubtedly Michelangelo's talent created the potential for greatness, but without commitment, his influence would have been minimal. That level of commitment could be seen in his attention to the fine details as well as the overarching vision. When asked why he was working so diligently on a dark corner of the Sistine Chapel that no one would ever see, Michelangelo's simple reply was, "God will see."

FLESHING IT OUT

The world has never seen a great leader who lacked commitment. Ed McElroy of USAir spoke of its importance: "Commitment gives us new power. No matter what comes to us—sickness, poverty, or disaster—we never turn our eye from the goal."

What is commitment? To each person, it means something different:

To the boxer, it's getting off the mat one time more than you've been knocked down.

To the marathoner, it's running another ten miles when your strength is gone.

To the soldier, it's going over the hill, not knowing what's waiting on the other side.

To the missionary, it's saying good-bye to your own comfort to make life better for others.

To the leader, it's all that and more because everyone you lead is depending on you.

If you want to be an effective leader, you have to be committed. True commitment inspires and attracts people. It shows them that you have conviction. They will believe in you only if you believe in your cause. As the Law of Buy-In states, people buy into the leader, then the vision.

What is the true nature of commitment? Take a look at three observations.

1. Commitment Starts in the Heart

Some people want everything to be perfect before they're willing to commit themselves to anything. But commitment always precedes achievement. I am told that in the Kentucky Derby, the winning horse effectively runs out of oxygen after the first half mile, and he goes the rest of the way on heart. That's why all great athletes recognize its importance. NBA legend Michael Jordan explains that "heart is what separates the good from the great." If you want to make a difference in *other* people's lives as a leader, look into *your* heart to see if you're really committed.

2. Commitment Is Tested by Action

It's one thing to talk about commitment. It's another to do something about it. The only *real* measure of commitment is action. Arthur Gordon acknowledged, "Nothing is easier than saying words. Nothing is harder than living them day after day."

Someone told me about a newly elected judge who had won office in a special county election. During his acceptance speech, he said, "I wish to thank the 424 people who promised to vote for me. I wish to thank the 316 people who said that they did vote for me. I wish to thank the 47 people who came out last Thursday to vote, and I wish to thank the 26 folks who actually did vote for me." How are you doing when it comes to following through on your commitments?

3. Commitment Opens the Door to Achievement

As a leader, you will face plenty of obstacles and opposition—if you don't already. And there will be times when commitment is the only thing that carries you forward. David McNally commented, "Commitment is the enemy of resistance, for it is the serious promise to press on, to get up, no matter how many times you are knocked down." If you want to get anywhere worthwhile, you must be committed.

REFLECTING ON IT

When it comes to commitment, there are really only four types of people:

1. *Cop-outs.* People who have no goals and do not commit.

2. *Holdouts.* People who don't know if they can reach their goals, so they're afraid to commit.

3. *Dropouts.* People who start toward a goal but quit when the going gets tough.

4. *All-outs.* People who set goals, commit to them, and pay the price to reach them.

What kind of person are you? Have you been reaching your goals? Are you achieving all that you believe you can? Do people believe in you and follow you readily? If your answer to any of these questions is no, the problem may be your level of commitment.

To improve your commitment, do the following:

- *Measure it.* Sometimes we *think* we are committed to something, yet our actions indicate otherwise. Take out your calendar and your checkbook register. Spend a few hours tallying up how you spend your time and where you spend your money. Look at how much time you spend at work, in service, with family, in health and recreation activities, and so forth. Figure out how much money you spent on living expenses, entertainment, personal development, and giving. All these things are true measures of your commitment. You may be surprised by what you find.

- *Know what's worth dying for.* One of the questions every leader must ask himself is, What am I willing to die for? If it came down to it, what in life would you not be able to stop doing, no matter what the consequences were? Spend some time alone meditating on that thought. Write down what you discover. Then see if your actions match your ideals.

- *Use the Edison method.* If taking the first step toward commitment is a problem, try doing what Thomas Edison did. When he had a good idea for an invention, he would call a press conference to announce it. Then he'd go into his lab and invent it. Make your plans public, and you might be more committed to following through with them.

DAILY TAKE-AWAY

Former pro basketball player Bill Bradley attended a summer basketball camp at age fifteen conducted by "Easy" Ed Macauley. During that camp, Macauley made a statement that changed Bradley's life: "Just remember that if you're not working at your game to the utmost of your ability, there will be someone out there somewhere with equal ability. And one day you'll play each other, and he'll have the advantage." How do you measure up against that standard?

COMMUNICATION:

WITHOUT IT YOU TRAVEL ALONE

Developing excellent communication skills is
absolutely essential to effective leadership. The leader
must be able to share knowledge and ideas to transmit a
sense of urgency and enthusiasm to others. If a leader can't
get a message across clearly and motivate others to act
on it, then having a message doesn't even matter.

—Gilbert Amelio,
President and CEO of National Semiconductor Corp.

Educators take something simple
and make it complicated. Communicators take
something complicated and make it simple.

—John C. Maxwell

A GREAT COMMUNICATOR
IN ALL CIRCUMSTANCES

Many American presidents have made an impact on our country as great communicators. John F. Kennedy, Franklin D. Roosevelt, and Abraham Lincoln come to mind as outstanding examples. But only one president in our lifetime was called the Great Communicator, and that was Ronald Reagan.

Flashes of Reagan's talent for communication revealed themselves early in his career. He started out in radio. In his early twenties, Reagan quickly became one of the best-known announcers in the Midwest. He usually announced games live, but occasionally he would simulate the broadcast of a Chicago Cubs game using Western Union reports of each play. During one such game, the wire went dead while Augie Galan was at bat in a tough situation. Reagan deftly kept Galan fouling off pitch after imaginary pitch for *six minutes* until he could pick up the play-by-play again.

Throughout his career, Reagan displayed an uncommon ability to connect and communicate with people. Nowhere was that more evident than during his time leading up to and in the White House. While announcing his run for the presidency in 1980, he cast the vision for his campaign clearly and simply, saying, "At the heart of our message should be five simple familiar words. No big economic theories. No sermons on political philosophy. Just five short words: *family, work, neighborhood, freedom, peace*."

During his campaign, Reagan successfully debated incumbent Jimmy Carter. The former California governor came across as a relaxed, likable, competent middle American. He won easily. Afterward when asked if he had been nervous debating the president, Reagan answered, "No, not at all. I've been on the same stage with John Wayne."

Whether he was speaking to a group, looking into a camera, or connecting with someone one-on-one, Reagan was able to communicate with maximum effectiveness. Even when he was shot and was being wheeled into the operating room, his goal was to put others at ease. His comment to the surgeons was, "Please assure me that you are all Republicans."

Reagan was a good executive because he possessed a clear vision, made decisions easily, and delegated very effectively. But he was a great leader because of his uncanny ability to communicate. When it came to leading the country, people knew who he was, where he stood, and what he wanted, and they couldn't wait to get on board with him. Communication made him the kind of leader that people wanted to follow.

Fleshing It Out

Even if you don't have your sights set on leading the country, as Ronald Reagan did, you still need to possess the ability to communicate. The success of your marriage, job, and personal relationships depends greatly on it. People will not follow you if they don't know what you want or where you are going.

You can be a more effective communicator if you follow four basic truths.

1. Simplify Your Message

Communication is not just *what* you say. It's also how you say it. Contrary to what some educators teach, the key to effective communication is simplicity. Forget about impressing people with big words or complex sentences. If you want to connect with people, keep it simple. Napoleon Bonaparte used to tell his secretaries, "Be clear, be clear, be clear."

A story about a junior executive gives a blueprint for effective communication. The young man was invited to speak to a large group for the first time, so he approached his mentor for advice about giving a good speech. The older man said, "Write an exciting opening that will grab everybody in your audience. Then you write a dramatic summary and closing that will make the people want to act. Then put them as close together as possible."

2. See the Person

Effective communicators focus on the people with whom they're communicating. They know it is impossible to effectively communicate to an audience without knowing something about them.

As you communicate with people—whether individuals or groups—ask yourself these questions: Who is my audience? What are their questions? What needs to be accomplished? And how much time do I have? If you want to become a better communicator, become audience oriented. People believe in great communicators because great communicators believe in people.

3. *Show the Truth*
Credibility precedes great communication. There are two ways to convey credibility to your audience. First, believe in what you say. Ordinary people become extraordinary communicators when they are fired up with conviction. Field Marshal Ferdinand Foch observed, "The most powerful weapon on earth is the human soul on fire." Second, live what you say. There is no greater credibility than conviction in action.

4. *Seek a Response*
As you communicate, never forget that the goal of all communication is action. If you dump a bunch of information on people, you're not communicating. Every time you speak to people, give them something to feel, something to remember, and something to do. If you're successful in doing that, your ability to lead others will go to a new level.

REFLECTING ON IT

Danto Manquez Jr., president of MVM, Inc., has spoken to the issue of a leader's ability to communicate: "A leader must get things done through others, therefore the leader must have the ability to inspire and motivate, guide and direct, and listen. It's only through communication that the leader is able to cause others to internalize his or her vision and implement it."

How do you rate your ability to communicate with others? Is communication a priority for you? Can you inspire and motivate people? Do you express your vision in such a way that your people are able to understand, internalize, and implement it? When you talk to people one-on-one, are you able to connect with them? How about with groups? If you know in your heart that your vision is great, yet people still do not buy into it, your problem may be an inability to communicate effectively.

BRINGING IT HOME

To improve your communication, do the following:

- *Be clear as a bell.* Examine a letter, memo, or other item you've recently written. Are your sentences short and direct, or do they meander? Will your readers be able to grasp the words you've chosen, or will they have to scramble for a dictionary? Have you used the fewest words possible? To a communicator, your best friends are simplicity and clarity. Write your next piece of communication keeping both in mind.

- *Refocus your attention.* During the coming week, pay attention to your focus when you communicate. Is it on you, your material, or your audience? If it's not on people, you need to change it. Think about their needs, questions, and desires. Meet people where they are, and you will be a better communicator.

- *Live your message.* Are there any discrepancies between what you communicate and what you do? Talk to a few trustworthy people and ask them whether you are living your message. Your spouse, a mentor, or a close friend may be able to see things that you are blind to. Receive their comments without defensiveness. Then purpose to make changes in your life to be more consistent.

D A I L Y   T A K E - A W A Y

On April 7, 1865, President Abraham Lincoln made a burdensome decision, and he needed to communicate it to his general in the field. On it rested all his hopes and the entire weight of his leadership as president. Using all his considerable skill as a communicator, he wrote the following message:

Lieut. Gen. Grant,
Gen. Sheridan says, "If the thing is pressed, I think that Lee will surrender." Let the thing be pressed.
A. Lincoln

The president didn't allow the importance of a piece of communication to complicate its simplicity. Neither should we.

COMPETENCE:

IF YOU BUILD IT, THEY WILL COME

Competence goes beyond words.
It's the leader's ability to say it, plan it, and do it
in such a way that others know that you know how—
and know that they want to follow you.

—John C. Maxwell

The society which scorns excellence in plumbing
because plumbing is a humble activity and tolerates
shoddiness in philosophy because it is an exalted activity
will have neither good plumbing nor good philosophy.
Neither its pipes nor its theories will hold water.

—John Gardner, Author

FANFARE FOR A COMMON MAN

Benjamin Franklin always thought of himself as an ordinary citizen. One of seventeen children, Franklin was the son of a tradesman, a candlemaker, who was far from wealthy. He experienced a typical childhood. He attended school for only two years, and at age twelve, he was apprenticed to his brother in the printing trade.

Franklin worked hard and lived a simple life, governing his actions according to a set of thirteen virtues, upon which he graded himself daily. At age twenty he started his own printing business. Had Franklin been content to work at his trade, his name would be little more than a footnote in Philadelphia's history. Yet he lived an extraordinary life. He was one of the fathers of American independence and a great leader of the emerging nation. He coauthored the Declaration of Independence, and he later helped write the Treaty of Paris and the Constitution of the United States. (He was the only man who signed all three.) And he was selected to perform a difficult and dangerous secret diplomatic mission to Paris during the war to secure military and financial support for the Revolution.

What gave a northern tradesman the opportunity to exert so much influence among the wealthy, predominately southern landholders who headed the war for independence? I believe it was Franklin's incredible competence.

Benjamin Franklin excelled at everything he touched for seven decades. When he started his own printing business in 1726, people believed Philadelphia could not support a third printer, but Franklin quickly established a reputation as the most skilled and industrious printer in town. But the Philadelphia tradesman wasn't content with only that accomplishment.

Franklin's mind was curious, and he continually sought ways to improve himself and others. He expanded into publishing, his work including the noted *Poor Richard's Almanack*. He did extensive experiments with electricity and coined many of the terms still associated with its use. He invented numerous items such as the potbellied stove, the catheter, and bifocals. And when he traveled frequently across the Atlantic Ocean, he took it upon himself to chart the Gulf Stream. His attitude toward life could be seen in an aphorism he wrote for his almanac: "Hide not your talents. They for use were made. What's a sundial in the shade?"

The evidences of Franklin's talents were many. He helped establish Philadelphia's first library. He started the nation's first fire department. He developed the concept of daylight saving time. And he held many posts serving the government.

For the most part, Franklin was recognized for his ability. But sometimes he had to let his competence speak for itself. During a time when he was working on improvements in agriculture, he discovered that plaster made grains and grasses grow better, but he had a difficult time convincing his neighbors about the discovery. His solution? When spring arrived, he went to a field close to a path, dug out some letters into the dirt with his hands, put plaster into the ruts, and then sowed seed over the whole area. As people passed that way in following weeks, they could see green letters growing brighter than the rest of the field. They said simply, "This has been plastered." People got the message.

F L E S H I N G I T O U T

We all admire people who display high competence, whether they are precision craftsmen, world-class athletes, or successful business leaders. But the truth is that you don't have to be Fabergé, Michael Jordan, or Bill Gates to excel in the area of competence. If you want to cultivate that quality, here's what you need to do.

1. Show Up Every Day

There's a saying, "All things come to him who waits." Unfortunately sometimes it's just the leftovers from the people who got there first. Responsible people show up when they're expected. But highly competent people take it a step farther. They don't show up in body only. They come ready to play every day—no matter how they feel, what kind of circumstances they face, or how difficult they expect the game to be.

2. Keep Improving

Like Benjamin Franklin, all highly competent people continually search for ways to keep learning, growing, and improving. They do that by asking *why*. After all, the person who knows *how* will always have a job, but the person who knows *why* will always be the boss.

33

3. Follow Through with Excellence

I've never met a person I considered competent who didn't follow through. I bet it's the same for you. Willa A. Foster remarked, "Quality is never an accident; it is always the result of high intention, sincere effort, intelligent direction and skillful execution; it represents the wise choice of many alternatives."

Performing at a high level of excellence is always a choice, an act of the will. As leaders, we expect our people to follow through when we hand them the ball. They expect that and a whole lot more from us as their leaders.

4. Accomplish More than Expected

Highly competent people always go the extra mile. For them, good enough is never good enough. In *Men in Mid-Life Crisis,* Jim Conway writes that some people feel "a weakening of the need to be a great man and an increasing feeling of 'let's just get through this the best way we can.' Never mind hitting home runs. Let's just get through the ball game without getting beaned." Leaders cannot afford to have that kind of attitude. They need to do the job, and then some, day in and day out.

5. Inspire Others

Highly competent leaders do more than perform at a high level. They inspire and motivate their people to do the same. While some people rely on relational skills alone to survive, effective leaders combine these skills with high competence to take their organizations to new levels of excellence and influence.

Where do you stand when it comes to getting the job done? Do you attack everything you do with fervor and perform at the highest level possible? Or is good enough sometimes good enough for you?

When you think about people who are competent, you're really considering only three types of people:

1. Those who can see what needs to happen.

2. Those who can make it happen.

3. Those who can make things happen when it really counts.

When it comes to your profession, where do you consistently perform? Are you a thinker, a doer, or a clutch player? The better you are, the greater potential for influence you will have with your people.

B R I N G I N G   I T   H O M E

To improve your competence, do the following:

- *Get your head in the game.* If you've been mentally or emotionally detached from your work, it's time to reengage. First, rededicate yourself to your job. Determine to give it an appropriate amount of your undivided attention. Second, figure out why you have been detached. Do you need new challenges? Are you in conflict with your boss or coworkers? Are you in a dead-end job? Identify the source of the problem, and create a plan to resolve it.

- *Redefine the standard.* If you're not performing at a consistently high level, reexamine your standards. Are you shooting too low? Do you cut corners? If so, hit your mental reset button, and outline more demanding expectations for yourself.

- *Find three ways to improve.* Nobody keeps improving without being intentional about it. Do a little research to find three things you can do to improve your professional skills. Then dedicate the time and money to follow through on them.

DAILY TAKE-AWAY

I read an editorial in *Texas Business* not long ago that said, "We are truly the lost generation, huffing and puffing down the fast track to nowhere, always looking to the dollar sign for direction. That's the only standard we recognize. We have no built-in beliefs, no ethical boundaries."

You're only as good as your private standards. When was the last time you gave a task your absolute best even though nobody but you would know about it?

COURAGE:

ONE PERSON WITH COURAGE

IS A MAJORITY

Courage is rightly esteemed the
first of human qualities . . . because it is the
quality which guarantees all others.

—*Winston Churchill, British Prime Minister*

Courage is fear that has said its prayers.

—*Karl Barth, Swiss Theologian*

THE ACE OF ACES

What do these three men have in common: the auto racer who set the world speed record at Daytona in 1914, the pilot who recorded the highest number of victories in aerial combat against the Germans in World War I, and the secretary of war's special adviser who survived a plane crash and twenty-two days on a raft in the Pacific during World War II? They all lived through dangerous circumstances. They all displayed courage and steely nerves under duress. And they all happen to be the same person—Eddie Rickenbacker.

Meeting a challenge was never a big problem for Eddie Rickenbacker, whether it was physical, mental, or economic. When he was twelve, his father died, and he quit school to become the family's primary breadwinner. He sold newspapers, eggs, and goat's milk. He worked in a glass factory, brewery, shoe factory, and foundry. Then as a teenager, he started working as a race car mechanic, and at age twenty-two, he began racing. Two years later he set the world speed record.

When the United States entered World War I, Rickenbacker tried to enlist as an aviator, but he was overage and undereducated. So instead he entered as a chauffeur and then talked his superiors into sending him to flight training. Despite not fitting in with his college-educated fellow aviators, he excelled as a pilot. And by the time the war was over, he had logged 300 combat hours (the most of any American pilot), survived 134 aerial encounters with the enemy, claimed 26 kills, and earned the

Medal of Honor, eight Distinguished Service Crosses, and the French Legion of Honor. He was also promoted to captain and put in command of his squadron.

Rickenbacker's prowess in the air caused the press to dub him the "American Ace of Aces." When asked about his courage in combat, he admitted that he had been afraid. "Courage," he said, "is doing what you're afraid to do. There can be no courage unless you're scared."

That courage served the Ace of Aces well after World War I. In 1933, he became the vice president of Eastern Air Transport (later Eastern Airlines). Back then all airlines existed only because they were subsidized by the government. But Rickenbacker thought they should be self-sufficient. He decided to completely change the way the company did business. Within two years he made Eastern profitable, a first in aviation history. And when the president of the United States canceled all commercial carriers' air mail contracts, Rickenbacker took him on— and won. Rickenbacker led Eastern successfully for thirty years and retired at age seventy-three. When he died ten years later, his son, William, wrote, "If he had a motto, it must have been the phrase I've heard a thousand times: 'I'll fight like a wildcat!'"

FLESHING IT OUT

When you look at the life of someone like Eddie Rickenbacker, you cannot help seeing great courage. It's easy to see in war heroes, but it's also present in every great leader in business, government, and the church. Whenever you see significant progress in an organization, you know that the leader made courageous decisions. A leadership position doesn't give a person courage, but courage can give him a leadership position. That was true for Captain Eddie Rickenbacker.

Larry Osborne offers this observation: "The most striking thing about highly effective leaders is how little they have in common. What one swears by, another warns against. But one trait stands out: the willingness to risk."

As you approach the tough decisions that challenge you, recognize these truths about courage:

1. Courage Begins with an Inward Battle

Every test you face as a leader begins within you. The test of courage is no different. As psychotherapist Sheldon Kopp notes, "All the significant battles are waged within self." Courage isn't an absence of fear. It's doing what you are afraid to do. It's having the power to let go of the familiar and forge ahead into new territory. That was true for Rickenbacker, and it can be true for you.

2. Courage Is Making Things Right, Not Just Smoothing Them Over

Civil rights leader Martin Luther King Jr. declared, "The ultimate measure of a man is not where he stands in moments of comfort and convenience, but where he stands at times of challenge and controversy." Great leaders have good people skills, and they can get people to compromise and work together. But they also take a stand when needed.

Courage deals with principle, not perception. If you don't have the ability to see when to stand up and the conviction to do it, you'll never be an effective leader. Your dedication to potential must remain stronger than your desire to appease others.

3. Courage in a Leader Inspires Commitment from Followers

"Courage is contagious," asserts evangelist Billy Graham. "When a brave man takes a stand, the spines of others are stiffened." A show of courage by any person encourages others. But a show of courage by a leader inspires. It makes people want to follow him. My friend Jim Mellado explains, "Leadership is the expression of courage that compels people to do the right thing."

4. Your Life Expands in Proportion to Your Courage

Fear limits a leader. Roman historian Tacitus wrote, "The desire for safety stands against every great and noble enterprise." But courage has the opposite effect. It opens doors, and that's one of its most wonderful benefits. Perhaps that's why British theologian John Henry Newman said, "Fear not that your life will come to an end but that it will never have a beginning." Courage not only gives you a good beginning, but it also provides a better future.

What's ironic is that those who don't have the courage to take risks and those who do, experience the same amount of fear in life. The only difference is that those who don't take chances worry about trivial things. If you're going to have to overcome your fear and doubts anyway, you might as well make it count.

R E F L E C T I N G   O N   I T

Eleanor Roosevelt acknowledged, "You gain strength, courage, and confidence by every experience in which you really stop to look fear in the face. You are able to say to yourself, 'I lived through this horror. I can take the next thing that comes along.' You must do the thing you think you cannot do."

How do you tend to handle fear? Do you embrace it? Are stretching experiences a regular part of your daily life? Or have you retreated so far into your comfort zone that you don't ever even feel fear? How must you change to develop a spirit of courage in your life?

B R I N G I N G   I T   H O M E

To improve your courage, do the following:

- *Face the music.* Go out and do something stretching simply for the sake of growing in courage. Skydive. Speak in front of an audience (most people's greatest fear). Perform in a play. Go white-water rafting. Rock climb. It doesn't matter what you do as long as it causes you to face a genuine fear.

- *Talk to* that *person.* Most people are avoiding confrontation with someone in their lives—an employee, a relative, or a coworker. If that's true for you, talk to that person this week. Don't dump on him or abuse him. Speak the truth in love. (You won't be so afraid to do it if you've already sky-dived rafted, etc.)

- *Take a giant step.* Maybe you've been afraid to make a career move. If you've known in your heart that you should have changed jobs or started that new business, now is the time to face up to it. Take the time to really look at it. Talk to your spouse, your mentor, and a trusted friend or two. If it's the right thing to do, then *do it*.

Daily Take-Away

A nineteenth-century circuit-riding preacher named Peter Cartwright was preparing to deliver a sermon one Sunday when he was warned that President Andrew Jackson was in attendance, and he was asked to keep his remarks inoffensive. During that message, he included these statements: "I have been told that Andrew Jackson is in this congregation. And I have been asked to guard my remarks. What I must say is that Andrew Jackson will go to hell if he doesn't repent of his sin."

After the sermon, Jackson strode up to Cartwright. "Sir," the president said, "if I had a regiment of men like you, I could whip the world."

A courageous act often brings unexpected positive results.

DISCERNMENT:

PUT AN END TO UNSOLVED MYSTERIES

Smart leaders believe only half of what they hear.
Discerning leaders know *which* half to believe.

—*John C. Maxwell*

The first rule of holes:
When you're in one, stop digging.

—*Molly Ivins, Columnist*

A L W A Y S   A T   T H E
H E A R T   O F   T H E   M A T T E R

Marya Sklodowska always wanted to get to the heart of things. As a child growing up in Poland, she loved school and learning. When her parents lost their teaching jobs and took in boarders to survive, she spent endless hours helping with the chores. But that didn't stop her from finishing first in her high school class—and her exams were in Russian!

Since higher education wasn't available to her, she became a governess and tutor. Somehow she managed to save enough money to send her older sister through medical school in Paris. Then she also moved to France to study at the Sorbonne. Two years later she finished first in her class in physics. Another year of study earned her a master's degree in mathematics.

It was then that she turned her attention full time to research, conducting experiments for a French industrial society. But her real passion was searching for the secret to uranium's rays.

While looking for a better laboratory, Marya met the man who would become her husband and research partner, Pierre. You've probably heard of Marya Sklodowska, but it's likely that you learned the name she preferred after she married Pierre Curie in 1895: she called herself Madame Marie Curie.

Madame Curie went on to do groundbreaking work in the field of radioactivity (a term she coined), and she opened the door to the study of nuclear physics and modern medical radiology. And when Pierre died in an accident in 1906, Marie Curie › continued the work and made many additional breakthroughs.

"Life is not easy for any of us," she once said. "But what of that? We must have perseverance and above all confidence in ourselves. We must believe that we are gifted for something and that this thing must be attained." Her research brought her great recognition: fifteen gold medals, nineteen degrees, and two Nobel prizes (one in physics and one in chemistry).

Curie's tenacity was evident not only in her desire to know, but also in her practical application of her research. During World War I, she noted what was happening on the battlefields and recognized that the technology she had discovered could help save lives. She and her daughter Irene (who would later also win a Nobel prize) developed X-radiography and then led a movement to equip ambulances with X-ray equipment. And Curie trained 150 technicians to use it. Curie also helped found the Radium Institute at the University of Paris. Not only did she oversee the building of its laboratories, but she raised funds and materials in Europe and the United States to equip it.

Curie observed, "Nothing in life is to be feared. It is only to be understood." Her intelligence and discernment allowed her to understand and discover many things that have made a positive impact on our world. Unfortunately keen discernment did not extend to her health. Because she was on the cutting edge of research with radioactive materials, she did not protect herself from the effects of radiation. Her work slowly killed her. Rather suddenly, her health declined, and in 1934, she died of leukemia at age sixty-six.

FLESHING IT OUT

Discernment can be described as the ability to find the root of the matter, and it relies on intuition as well as rational thought. Effective leaders need discernment, although even good leaders don't display it all the time. For example, read these comments made by leaders, which I like to think of as famous last words:

"I tell you Wellington is a bad general, the English are bad soldiers; we will settle the matter by lunch time."
—*Napoleon Bonaparte at breakfast with his generals preceding the Battle of Waterloo (1815)*

"I think there is a world market for about five computers."
—*Thomas J. Watson, chairman of IBM (1943)*

"I don't need bodyguards."
—*Jimmy Hoffa, one month before his disappearance (1975)*

Discernment is an indispensable quality for any leader who desires to maximize effectiveness. It helps to do several important things:

1. Discover the Root Issues

Leaders of large organizations must cope with tremendous chaos and complexity every day. They are never able to gather enough information to get a complete picture of just about anything. As a result, they have to rely on discernment. Researcher Henry

Mintzberg of McGill University stated, "Organizational effectiveness does not lie in that narrowminded concept called rationality. It lies in the blend of clearheaded logic and powerful intuition." Discernment enables a leader to see a partial picture, fill in the missing pieces intuitively, and find the real heart of a matter.

2. Enhance Your Problem Solving

If you can see the root issue of a problem, you can solve it. The closer a leader is to his area of gifting, the stronger his intuition and ability to see root causes. If you want to tap into your discernment potential, work in your areas of strength.

3. Evaluate Your Options for Maximum Impact

Management consultant Robert Heller has this advice: "Never ignore a gut feeling, but never believe that it's enough." Discernment isn't relying on intuition alone, nor is it relying only on intellect. Discernment enables you to use both your gut and your head to find the best option for your people and your organization.

4. Multiply Your Opportunities

People who lack discernment are seldom in the right place at the right time. Although great leaders often appear to be lucky to some observers, I believe leaders create their own "luck" as the result of discernment, that willingness to use their experience and follow their instincts.

Are you a discerning leader? When faced with complex issues, can you readily identify the heart of the matter? Are you able to see root causes of difficult problems without having to get every bit of information? Do you trust your intuition and rely on it as much as you do your intellect and experience? If not, you need to cultivate it. Value nontraditional thinking. Embrace change, ambiguity, and uncertainty. Broaden your horizons experientially. Your intuition will only increase with use.

B R I N G I N G   I T   H O M E

To improve your discernment, do the following:

- *Analyze past successes.* Look at some problems you solved successfully in the past. What was the root issue in each problem? What enabled you to succeed? If you can capture the heart of the matter in a few words, you can probably learn to do it with future issues.

- *Learn how others think.* Which great leaders do you admire? Pick some whose profession or gifting is similar to yours, and read their biographies. By learning how other discerning leaders think, you can become more discerning.

- *Listen to your gut.* Try to recall times when your intuition "spoke" to you and was correct (you may or may not have listened to it at the time). What do those experiences have in common? Look for a pattern that may give you insight into your intuitive ability.

DAILY TAKE-AWAY

For a long time, the Swiss had a lock on watchmaking. They built the best watches money could buy, and by the 1940s, they produced 80 percent of all watches worldwide. In the late 1960s, when an inventor presented an idea for a new type of watch to the leaders of a Swiss watch company, they rejected it. In fact, every Swiss company he approached had the same negative reaction.

Believing his design had merit, the man took it to a company in Japan. The name of the organization was Seiko, the design of the watch was digital, and today, 80 percent of all watches use a digital design. One discernment-driven decision can change the entire course of your destiny.

FOCUS:

THE SHARPER IT IS,

THE SHARPER YOU ARE

If you chase two rabbits, both will escape.

—*Unknown*

What people say, what people do, and
what they say they do are entirely different things.

—*Margaret Mead, Anthropologist*

A D I F F E R E N T K I N D
O F O N E - T R A C K M I N D

In 1998, the Atlanta Braves and the San Diego Padres played for major-league baseball's National League pennant, and I had the privilege of attending several of the games. Back when I lived in San Diego, I was a die-hard Padres fan, but when I moved to Atlanta in 1997, I changed my allegiance to the Braves. I rooted for them all season long—until they faced San Diego in the play-offs. Why did I change? I could not bring myself to root against Tony Gwynn.

Tony Gwynn is the greatest hitter in the last fifty years—the best since Ted Williams. He has won an incredible eight batting titles. (Only Ty Cobb has won more.) In his career, he has batted a tremendous .339. It's always a joy to watch Gwynn play. He is surely destined for the Hall of Fame in Cooperstown, New York.

If you saw Tony Gwynn on the street and didn't know who he was, you might not guess he was a professional ballplayer. At five feet eleven inches and 220 pounds, he doesn't look the part of the star athlete the way someone like Mark McGwire does. But make no mistake: Gwynn is a talented athlete, having been drafted out of college for baseball and basketball. And though he has tremendous talent, the real key to his success is focus.

Tony Gwynn loves hitting a baseball, and he *devotes* himself to it. Several times each season, he reads Ted Williams's *The Science of Hitting,* a book he first discovered and read while in college. He watches countless hours of videotape. At home he has a library of hitting tapes, continually fed by his five VCRs that record games via satellite dish. He even reviews tape on the road. When he travels for games, he takes two VCRs so that he can tape and edit every one of his at bats. And when he is not swinging the bat or watching tape, he is talking about hitting constantly—with teammates, at the All-Star Game, with great players such as Ted Williams.

Gwynn just can't get enough. Hitting is his joy. He has been known to arrive at social events with a batting glove sticking out of his pocket, having stopped to hit a few. And even when not practicing, watching tape, or talking to other hitters, he can be found playing Ping-Pong or doing activities to improve his eye-to-hand coordination. Even his decision to remain in San Diego his whole career has improved his game. "One of my strengths is knowing how much I can handle," Gwynn says. "There are few distractions in San Diego. There isn't a lot of media hoopla. That helps me be consistent."

Consistent is right. Gwynn has batted over .300 in every season as a professional except one—his first. Columnist George Will maintains that people who are great at what they do, such as Gwynn, have "cultivated a kind of concentration unknown to most people."

F L E S H I N G   I T   O U T

What does it take to have the focus required to be a truly effective leader? The keys are priorities and concentration. A leader who knows his priorities but lacks concentration knows what to do but never gets it done. If he has concentration but no priorities, he has excellence without progress. But when he harnesses both, he has the potential to achieve great things.

I frequently meet people in leadership positions who seem to major in minor things. That just doesn't make sense. It would be the equivalent of Tony Gwynn spending all his time studying base stealing. Now, Gwynn *can* steal bases. He has stolen more than three hundred in his career, but it's not his strength. And dedicating all his time to that instead of hitting would be a waste of his time and talent.

So the important question is, How should you focus your time and energy? Use these guidelines to help you:

Focus 70 Percent on Strengths
Effective leaders who reach their potential spend more time focusing on what they do well than on what they do wrong. Leadership expert Peter Drucker notes, "The great mystery isn't that people do things badly but that they occasionally do a few things well. The only thing that is universal is incompetence. Strength is always specific! Nobody ever commented, for example, that the great violinist Jascha Heifetz probably couldn't play the trumpet very well." To be successful, focus on your strengths and develop them. That's where you should pour your time, energy, and resources.

Focus 25 Percent on New Things
Growth equals change. If you want to get better, you have to keep changing and improving. That means stepping out into new

areas. Gwynn modeled that several years ago after he had a conversation with Ted Williams. The old pro suggested that learning to hit inside pitches would make Gwynn a better player. Gwynn, who preferred outside balls, worked on it, and his average went up significantly. If you dedicate time to new things related to areas of strength, then you'll grow as a leader. Don't forget: in leadership, if you're through growing, you're through.

Focus 5 Percent on Areas of Weakness

Nobody can entirely avoid working in areas of weakness. The key is to minimize it as much as possible, and leaders can do it by delegating. For example, I delegate detail work to others. A team of people at The INJOY Group handles all the logistics of my conferences. That way when I'm there, I stick to the things I do best, such as the actual speaking.

REFLECTING ON IT

How would you rate yourself in the area of focus? Have you been majoring in minor things? Have you spent so much time shoring up your weaknesses that you've failed to build up your strengths? Do the people with the least potential monopolize your time? If so, you've probably lost focus.

To get back on track with your focus, do these things:

Work on yourself. You are your greatest asset or detriment.
Work at your priorities. You will have to fight for them.

Work in your strengths. You can reach your potential.

Work with your contemporaries. You can't be effective alone.

B R I N G I N G   I T   H O M E

To improve your focus, do the following:

- *Shift to strengths.* Make a list of three or four things you do well in your job. What percentage of your time do you spend doing them? What percentage of your resources is dedicated to these areas of strength? Devise a plan to make changes, allowing you to dedicate 70 percent of your time to your strengths. If you can't, it may be time to reassess your job or career.

- *Staff your weaknesses.* Identify three or four activities necessary for your job that you don't do well. Determine how you can delegate the jobs to others. Will it require hiring staff? Can you partner with a coworker to share responsibilities? Develop a plan.

- *Create an edge.* Now that you've looked at priorities, think about concentration. What would it take for you to go to the next level in your main area of strength? What new tools do you need? Rethink how you do things, and be willing to make sacrifices. Time and money spent to take you to the next level are the best investment you can make.

Experienced animal trainers take a stool with them when they step into a cage with a lion. Why a stool? It tames a lion better than anything—except maybe a tranquilizer gun. When the trainer holds the stool with the legs extended toward the lion's face, the animal tries to focus on all four legs at once. And that paralyzes him. Divided focus always works against you.

GENEROSITY:

YOUR CANDLE LOSES NOTHING

WHEN IT LIGHTS ANOTHER

No person was ever honored for what he received.
Honor has been the reward for what he gave.

—Calvin Coolidge, American President

Giving is the highest level of living.

—John C. Maxwell

IT STARTS IN THE HEART

When you think of generous people, who comes to mind? Do you picture millionaire philanthropists from the turn of the century such as Andrew Carnegie, J. P. Morgan, and Andrew Mellon? Do you think of contemporary givers such as Joan Kroc or Bill Gates? Those people have given away millions of dollars. But I want to acquaint you with another giver. She is someone you've probably never heard of, yet she typifies the deepest kind of giving, the kind that can come only from the heart.

Her name is Elisabeth Elliot. In the early 1950s, she accompanied a group of missionaries to Ecuador with the hope of reaching the Quichua Indians. Among that group was a young man named Jim, who had been courting her since 1947. While they worked together and gave their lives to serving the Ecuadoran Indians, they finally decided to give themselves to each other and were married.

They had been together about two years and had a ten-month-old daughter named Valerie when Jim and four other missionaries felt compelled to make contact with another small group of Indians living in the area called the Auca. The Indians had a fierce reputation. The earliest record of any contact with them was of their killing a priest in the 1600s. Since then, they had attacked every outsider who came their way. Even the other Ecuadoran Indians avoided them because of their brutality.

As Jim and the others prepared to make contact, Elisabeth knew that the five men would be putting themselves in danger, but she was resolute. The two of them had given their lives to this mission. For several weeks, a missionary pilot flew a small plane over an Aucan village and dropped supplies and other items as gifts. They even included pictures of themselves to prepare the tribespeople for their first contact.

A few weeks later, Jim and four others landed on a small stretch of beach on the Curaray River and set up camp. There they made contact with three Aucans—a man and two women—who seemed to be friendly and receptive. And in following days, they met with several others. They told their wives by radio that they seemed to be making significant progress in befriending the tribe.

But then a few days later, the men failed to check in with the base camp at an appointed time. Their wives waited in vain to hear from them. Minutes passed, then hours, and then a day. Elisabeth and the others feared the worst.

A search party went out to look for the men and radioed back bad news. They had spotted the body of a white man floating in the river. The searchers found the men, one by one. With each it was the same: he had been slashed with Aucan spears. All five of the men were dead.

Under those circumstances, many people in Elisabeth Elliot's shoes would have gone home. It's one thing to be willing to give up a comfortable life in the United States to help other people; it's quite another to give up your spouse. But Elliot had a truly generous heart. Despite her terrible loss, she still wanted to help the people of Ecuador. She stayed and served the Quichuans with whom she was living.

What happened after that is even more remarkable. Other missionaries continued trying to make contact with an Aucan village. And after a couple of years, they succeeded. Immediately Elisabeth Elliot rushed to the village. Was it to seek revenge? No, it was to work with the people there and serve them. Elliot lived and worked among the Aucan people for two years, and many of them gladly accepted the message of God's love she carried—including two of the seven men who had killed her husband.

F L E S H I N G   I T   O U T

Nothing speaks to others more loudly or serves them better than generosity from a leader. True generosity isn't an occasional event. It comes from the heart and permeates every aspect of a leader's life, touching his time, money, talents, and possessions. Effective leaders, the kind that people want to follow, don't gather things just for themselves; they do it in order to give to others. Cultivate the quality of generosity in your life. Here's how:

1. Be Grateful for Whatever You Have

It's hard for a person to be generous when he is not satisfied with what he has. Generosity rises out of contentment, and that doesn't come with acquiring more. Millionaire John D. Rockefeller admitted, "I have made millions, but they have brought me no happiness." If you're not content with little, you won't be content with a lot. And if you're not generous with little, you won't suddenly change if you become wealthy.

2. Put People First

The measure of a leader is not the number of people who serve him, but the number of people he serves. Generosity requires putting others first. If you can do that, giving becomes much easier.

3. Don't Allow the Desire for Possessions
to Control You

According to my friend Earle Wilson, people can be divided into three groups: "Haves, have-nots, and have not paid for what they have." More and more people are becoming enslaved to the desire to acquire. Author Richard Foster writes, "Owning things is an obsession in our culture. If we own it, we feel we can control it; and if we can control it, we feel it will give us more pleasure. The idea is an illusion." If you want to be in charge of your heart, don't allow possessions to take charge of you.

4. Regard Money as a Resource

Someone once said that when it comes to money, you can't win. If you focus on making it, you're materialistic. If you try to but don't make any, you're a loser. If you make a lot and keep it, you're a miser. If you make it and spend it, you're a spendthrift. If you don't care about making any, you're unambitious. If you make a lot and still have it when you die, you're a fool—for trying to take it with you.

The only way to really win with money is to hold it

loosely—and be generous with it to accomplish things of value. As E. Stanley Jones said, "Money is a wonderful servant but a terrible master. If it gets on top and you get under it, you will become its slave."

5. *Develop the Habit of Giving*

In 1889, millionaire industrialist Andrew Carnegie wrote an essay called "Gospel of Wealth." In it he said that the life of a wealthy person should have two periods: a time of acquiring wealth and one of redistributing it. The only way to maintain an attitude of generosity is to make it your habit to give—your time, attention, money, and resources. Richard Foster advises, "Just the very act of letting go of money, or some other treasure, does something within us. It destroys the demon greed." If you're enslaved by greed, you cannot lead.

R E F L E C T I N G   O N   I T

Are you a generous leader? Do you continually look for ways to add value to others? Are you giving money to something greater than yourself? And to whom are you giving your time? Are you pouring your life into others? Are you helping those who cannot help you or give anything in return? Writer John Bunyan affirmed, "You have not lived today until you have done something for someone who can never repay you." If you aren't giving in the small areas of your life, you're probably not as generous a leader as you could be.

BRINGING IT HOME

To improve your generosity, do the following:

- *Give something away.* Find out what kind of hold your possessions have on you. Take something you truly value, think of someone you care about who could benefit from it, and give it to him. If you can do it anonymously, even better.

- *Put your money to work.* If you know someone with the vision to do something really great—something that will positively impact the lives of others—provide resources for him to accomplish it. Put your money to work for something that will outlive you.

- *Find someone to mentor.* Once you reach a certain level in your leadership, the most valuable thing you have to give is yourself. Find someone to pour your life into. Then give him time and resources to become a better leader.

DAILY TAKE-AWAY

When popular French author Dominique Lapierre first traveled to India to do research for a new book, he went in style—in a Rolls-Royce Silver Shadow he had just purchased with a book advance. While he was there, he got what he needed for his book *The City of Joy*. But he also received something else: a passion to help the poor and miserable people he discovered there. That discovery has changed his life forever. Now he divides his time between writing, fund-raising, and donating time and money to help the people. His attitude can be summed up by the words of Indian poet Rabindranath Tagore, which are printed on the back of Lapierre's business card: "All that is not given is lost." What are you currently losing by holding on to it?

INITIATIVE:

YOU WON'T LEAVE HOME WITHOUT IT

Success seems to be connected with action.

Successful people keep moving.

They make mistakes, but they don't quit.

—*Conrad Hilton, Hotel Executive*

Of all the things a leader should fear,

complacency should head the list.

—*John C. Maxwell*

JUST ANOTHER STEP FORWARD

Kemmons Wilson has always been an initiator. He started working when he was seven years old and hasn't stopped since. He began by selling magazines, newspapers, and popcorn. In 1930 at the ripe old age of seventeen, he decided to try a salaried job for the first time, working for a cotton broker. He made $12 a week writing figures on the broker's price board.

When a bookkeeper's job paying $35 a week opened up, Wilson applied for it and got it. But when he received his pay, it was still only $12. He requested a raise and got one. The next week he received an additional $3. When he asked why he didn't get the same $35 as the other bookkeeper, he was told the company wouldn't pay that kind of money to a seventeen-year-old kid. Wilson gave his notice. That was the last time in more than seventy-five years that he took a salaried job.

Wilson made money in a variety of businesses after that: pinball machines, soft drink distribution, and vending machines. And he was able to save enough money to build his mother a house. That's when he realized home building had a lot of potential. So he went into the business in Memphis and made a fortune, capitalizing on the postwar building boom.

Wilson's initiative made him a lot of money, but it didn't make an impact on the world—not until 1951, that is. That was the year the Memphis businessman took his family on vacation to Washington, D.C. On that trip, he learned about the sorry state of hotel lodging in the United States. Motels had sprung up all over the country since the 1920s. Some were nice family places. Others rented beds by the hour. The problem was a traveler didn't know which he would find.

"You never could tell what you were getting," Wilson recalled later. "Some of the places were too squalid for words. And they all charged for children. That made my Scottish blood boil." A guy like Wilson who had five children really took a beating. Motels charged $4 to $6 a night for a room *plus* $2 per child. It tripled his bill.

Most people would have complained and then forgotten about it. But Wilson, always the initiator, decided to take action and do something about it. "Let's go home and start a chain of family hotels," he said to his wife, "hotels with a name you could trust." His goal was to build four hundred hotels. His wife just laughed.

When Wilson returned to Memphis, he hired a draftsman to help him design his first hotel. He wanted it to be clean, simple, and predictable. And he wanted it to have all the things he and his family had missed, such as a television in every room and a pool. The next year he opened his first hotel on the outskirts of Memphis. Its name flashed out front on a huge fifty-three-foot-tall sign. It was called the Holiday Inn.

It took Wilson longer than he expected to reach four hundred hotels. By 1959, he had one hundred. But when he decided to franchise them, that boosted the openings. By 1964, there were five hundred Holiday Inns. In 1968, there were one thousand. And by 1972, a Holiday Inn opened somewhere in the world every seventy-two hours. The chain was still growing in 1979 when Wilson stepped down from the company's leadership after a heart attack.

"I was so hungry when I was young," Wilson said, "I just had to do something to make a living. And when I retired after my heart attack, I went home to smell the roses. That lasted about a month." It's just too hard for an initiator to stop making things happen.

FLESHING IT OUT

In *The 21 Irrefutable Laws of Leadership,* I pointed out that leaders are responsible for initiating a connection with their followers. But that's not the only area where leaders must show initiative. They must always look for opportunities and be ready to take action.

What qualities do leaders possess that enable them to make things happen? I see at least four.

1. They Know What They Want

Humorous pianist Oscar Levant once joked, "Once I make up my mind, I'm full of indecision." Unfortunately, that's the way many people actually operate. But no one can be both indecisive and effective. As Napoleon Hill says, "The starting point of all achievement is desire." If you are going to be an effective leader, you've got to know what you want. That's the only way you'll recognize opportunity when it comes.

2. They Push Themselves to Act

There's an old saying: "You can if you will." Initiators don't wait for other people to motivate them. They knew it is their responsibility to push themselves beyond their comfort zone. And they make it a regular practice. That's why someone such as President Theodore Roosevelt, one of the great initiating leaders of the twentieth century, was able to say, "There is nothing brilliant or outstanding in my record, except perhaps this one thing: I do the things that I believe ought to be done . . . And when I make up my mind to do a thing, I act."

3. They Take More Risks

When leaders know what they want and can push themselves to act, they still have one more hurdle. That's willingness to take risks. Proactive people always take risks. But one of the reasons good leaders are willing to take risks is that they recognize there is a price for not initiating too. President John F. Kennedy asserted, "There are risks and costs to a program of action, but they are far less than the long-range risks and costs of comfortable inaction."

4. They Make More Mistakes

The good news for initiators is that they make things happen. The bad news is that they make lots of mistakes. IBM founder Thomas J. Watson recognized that when he remarked, "The way to succeed is to double your failure rate."

Even though initiating leaders experience more failure, they don't let it bother them. The greater the potential, the greater the chance for failure. Senator Robert Kennedy summed it up: "Only those who dare to fail greatly can ever achieve greatly." If you want to achieve great things as a leader, you must be willing to initiate and put yourself on the line.

REFLECTING ON IT

Are you an initiator? Are you constantly on the lookout for opportunity, or do you wait for it to come to you? Are you willing to take steps based on your best instincts? Or do you endlessly analyze everything? Former Chrysler chairman Lee Iacocca said, "Even the right decision is the wrong decision if it is made too late." When was the last time you initiated something significant in your life? If you haven't pushed yourself lately and gotten out of your comfort zone, you may need to jump-start your initiative.

BRINGING IT HOME

To improve your initiative, do the following:

- *Change your mind-set.* If you lack initiative, recognize that the problem comes from the inside, not from others. Determine why you hesitate to take action. Does risk scare you? Are you discouraged by past failures? Do you not see the potential that opportunity offers? Find the source of your hesitation, and address it. You won't be able to move forward on the outside until you can move forward on the inside.

- *Don't wait for opportunity to knock.* Opportunity doesn't come to the door knocking. You've got to go out and look for it. Take stock of your assets, talents, and resources. Doing that will give you an idea of your potential. Now, spend every day for a week looking for opportunities. Where do you see needs? Who is looking for expertise you have? What unreached group of people is practically dying for what you have to offer? Opportunity is everywhere.

- *Take the next step.* It's one thing to see opportunity. It's another to do something about it. As someone once quipped, everyone has a great idea in the shower. But only a few people step out, dry off, and do something about it. Pick the best opportunity you see, and take it as far as you can. Don't stop until you've done everything you can to make it happen.

DAILY TAKE-AWAY

In 1947, Lester Wunderman was arbitrarily fired from his advertising job in New York. But the young man knew he could learn a lot from the head of the agency, Max Sackheim. The next morning, Wunderman went back to his office and worked just as he had before—but without pay.

Sackheim ignored him for a month, but finally walked up to Wunderman and said, "Okay, you win. I never saw a man who wanted a job more than he wanted money."

Wunderman went on to become one of the most successful advertising men of the century. He is known as the father of direct marketing. It will take a bold step from you today to reach your potential tomorrow.

LISTENING:

TO CONNECT WITH THEIR HEARTS,

USE YOUR EARS

The ear of the leader
must ring with the voices of the people.

—*Woodrow Wilson, American President*

A good leader encourages followers to tell him
what he needs to know, not what he wants to hear.

—*John C. Maxwell*

A S   M U C H   A S   S H E   T A L K S ,
S H E   L I S T E N S   M O R E

Who would you include in a list of the most influential people in the United States? Certainly the president would make that list. So would Alan Greenspan. Michael Jordan might make it—his is the most recognized face on the planet. You could argue for Bill Gates to be on it. Stop for a moment and think about the people you would include. Now I want you to add a name that you might not have considered: Oprah Winfrey.

In 1985, Winfrey was practically unknown. She appeared in Steven Spielberg's *The Color Purple,* and she was the host of a local morning talk show, which she had been doing in Chicago for a year. What success she had achieved could be attributed to her ability to talk. "Communicating with people is how I always developed any kind of value about myself," explains Winfrey. And she received praise for it early in life. "I remember being two years old and speaking in church and hearing people say, 'That child sure can talk. That is one talking child.'"

But Winfrey also did more than her share of listening. In fact, the ability to listen has been a chief characteristic of her life. She is an inveterate learner, and her listening ability got its start as she absorbed the wisdom of writers. She devoured fiction and biographies, learning about how other people feel and think—and in the process she also learned about herself.

That bent toward listening has served her well in every

aspect of her career. Its application is obvious for her television show. She is constantly observing and listening to find issues to address on the air. And when she brings celebrities, authors, or experts on her show, she genuinely listens to what they have to say. Music star Madonna said about her, "She has been in the public eye for so long, yet she has this amazing rapport with people. I don't know how she does it." She does it through listening.

Oprah Winfrey's ability to listen has been rewarded with remarkable success and incredible influence. She is the highest paid entertainer in the world and is worth nearly half a billion dollars. Each week, thirty-three million people in the United States alone watch her show.

Despite her show's success, she recently gave thought to discontinuing it. But instead she decided to revamp it. How did she decide what changes to make? She asked her staff.

"It doesn't have to be work," she told them. "Making changes in this show is like making changes in our lives. It can be fun to do. So let's stretch. What can we do to make it more fun?"

She had a lot of doubts about one of the ideas her people came up with. But she also had enough wisdom to listen to it—and give it a try. The idea was for a book club. As you probably know, its success has been phenomenal. Hundreds of thousands of people are learning and growing by reading, some for the first time. And Winfrey is delighted. Her goal in life is to add value to people. And she succeeds because she listens.

F L E S H I N G   I T   O U T

In *The 21 Irrefutable Laws of Leadership,* I point out that leaders touch a heart before they ask for a hand. That's the Law of Connection. But before a leader can touch a person's heart, he has to know what's in it. He learns that by listening.

An unwillingness to listen is too common among poor leaders. Peter Drucker, the father of American management, believes that 60 percent of all management problems are the result of faulty communications. I would say that the overwhelming majority of communication problems come from poor listening.

A lot of voices are clamoring out there for your attention. As you think about how to spend your listening time, keep in mind that you have two purposes for listening: to connect with people and to learn. For that reason, you should keep your ear open to these people:

1. Your Followers

Good leaders, the kind that people want to follow, do more than conduct business when they interact with followers. They take the time to get a feel for who each one is as a person. Philip Stanhope, the earl of Chesterfield, believed, "many a man would rather you heard his story than granted his request." If you're in the habit of listening only to the facts and not the person who expresses them, change your focus—and really listen.

2. Your Customers

A Cherokee saying states, "Listen to the whispers and you won't have to hear the screams." I am amazed by the leaders who are so caught up in their own ideas that they never hear their customers' concerns, complaints, and suggestions. In his book *Business @ the Speed of Thought,* Microsoft CEO Bill Gates said, "Unhappy customers are always a concern. They're also your greatest opportunity." Good leaders always make it a priority to keep in contact with the people they're serving.

3. Your Competitors

Sam Markewich announced, "If you don't agree with me, it means you haven't been listening." Though he was no doubt making a joke, the sad truth is that when a leader sees another organization as competition, he focuses his attention on building his own case or championing his cause and forgets to learn from what the other group is doing.

Larry King says, "I remind myself every morning: nothing I say this day will teach me anything. So if I'm going to learn, I must do it by listening." As a leader, you don't want to base your actions on what the other guy is doing, but you should still listen and learn what you can to improve yourself.

4. Your Mentors

No leader is so advanced or experienced that he can afford to be without a mentor. I've learned so much from leaders who have more experience than I have, people such as Melvin Maxwell (my father), Elmer Towns, Jack Hayford, Fred Smith, and J. Oswald Sanders. If you don't already have a mentor, go out and find one. If you can't get someone to help you in person, begin the process by reading books. That's where I got started. The main thing is to get the process under way.

R E F L E C T I N G   o n   I t

Are you a good listener? I know when I started in leadership, I wasn't. I was too busy doing my own thing and trying to make things happen. But once I slowed down and paid greater attention to what was going on around me, I found that my activity had sharper focus and accomplished more.

When was the last time you really paid close attention to people and what they have to say? Do more than just grab onto facts. Start listening not only for words, but also for feelings, meanings, and undercurrents.

B R I N G I N G   I t   H O M E

To improve your listening, do the following:

- *Change your schedule.* Do you spend time listening to your followers, customers, competitors, and mentors? If you don't have all four groups on your calendar regularly, you're probably not giving them enough attention. Pencil in time for each of them on a daily, weekly, or monthly basis.

- *Meet people on their turf.* A key to being a good listener is to find common ground with people. The next time you meet with an employee or a customer, discipline yourself to ask four or five questions about him as a person. Get to know who he is, and seek common ground to build your connection with him.

- *Listen between the lines.* As you interact with people, you certainly want to pay attention to the factual content of the conversation. But don't ignore the emotional content. Sometimes you can learn more about what's really going on by reading between the lines. Spend time in the coming days and weeks listening with your heart.

DAILY TAKE-AWAY

President Theodore Roosevelt was a man of action, but he was also a good listener, and he appreciated that quality in other people. Once at a gala ball, he grew tired of meeting people who returned his remarks with stiff, mindless pleasantries. So he began to greet people with a smile, saying, "I murdered my grandmother this morning." Most people, so nervous about meeting him, didn't even hear what he said. But one diplomat did. Upon hearing the president's remark, he leaned over and whispered to him, "I'm sure she had it coming to her!" The only way to find out what you're missing is to start listening.

12

PASSION:

TAKE THIS LIFE AND LOVE IT

When a leader reaches out in passion,
he is usually met with an answering passion.

—*John C. Maxwell*

Anyone can dabble, but once you've made that
commitment, your blood has that particular thing in it,
and it's very hard for people to stop you.

—*Bill Cosby, Comedian*

PIZZA SAUCE IS IN HIS BLOOD

In *The 21 Irrefutable Laws of Leadership,* I tell the story of Papa John's Pizza and how the company, founded in 1984 by John Schnatter, grew from 1 to 46 stores in its first seven years and then from 46 to 1,600 in the seven years after that. The phenomenal success the company experienced in the second half was due to the Law of Explosive Growth, which says, "To add growth, lead followers—to multiply, lead leaders." But what was the key to Papa John's success in the first half?

The answer is passion. John Schnatter not only eats Papa John's Pizza; he breathes, sleeps, and lives it. It is always his predominating thought. Lehman Brothers analyst Michael Speiser said of him in *Success* magazine, "Pizza is Schnatter's life, and he takes it very seriously."

Schnatter's philosophy is simple and straightforward. "Concentrate on what you do well," he advises, "and do it better than anybody else." What he does well is lead the fastest-growing business of its kind in the world. And he enjoys it so much that he is always in the thick of things.

Recently he went to visit a franchise owned by his wife, Annette, in downtown Louisville and found that the store was unexpectedly swamped with orders. What did he do? He jumped in and helped make pizzas for an hour and a half. It's something he loves doing. He visits stores four or five times a week—often unannounced—just to make sure everything is on track.

"Talking about my dreams for a pizza business at age twenty-two, people thought I was crazy," Schnatter has said. "Vendors, bankers and even some friends just laughed when I told them I'd be opening five or six stores a month." Now he regularly opens an amazing *thirty* stores a month—a new store every day of the year.

And he wants to increase that. A franchise opened in Mexico, and Schnatter has plans to expand into Venezuela, Puerto Rico, and other foreign markets. He doesn't intend to stop until he leads the largest seller of pizza in the world. He just might do it because he loves it and gives it everything he's got.

FLESHING IT OUT

Experts spend a lot of time trying to figure out what makes people successful. They often look at people's credentials, intelligence, education, and other factors. But more than anything else, passion makes the difference. David Sarnoff of RCA maintains that "nobody can be successful unless he loves his work."

If you look at the lives of effective leaders, you will find that they often don't fit into a stereotypical mold. For example, more than 50 percent of all CEOs of Fortune 500 companies had C or C– averages in college. Nearly 75 percent of all U.S. presidents were in the bottom half of their school classes. And more than 50 percent of all millionaire entrepreneurs never finished college. What makes it possible for people who might seem ordinary to achieve great things? The answer is passion. Nothing can take the place of passion in a leader's life.

Take a look at four truths about passion and what it can do for you as a leader:

1. *Passion Is the First Step to Achievement*

Your desire determines your destiny. Think of great leaders, and you will be struck by their passion: Gandhi for human rights, Winston Churchill for freedom, Martin Luther King Jr. for equality, Bill Gates for technology.

Anyone who lives beyond an ordinary life has great desire. It's true in any field: weak desire brings weak results, just as a small fire creates little heat. The stronger your fire, the greater the desire—and the greater the potential.

2. *Passion Increases Your Willpower*

It is said that a dispassionate young man approached the Greek philosopher Socrates and casually stated, "O great Socrates, I come to you for knowledge."

The philosopher took the young man down to the sea, waded in with him, and then dunked him under the water for thirty seconds. When he let the young man up for air, Socrates asked him to repeat what he wanted.

"Knowledge, O great one," he sputtered. Socrates put him under the water again, only that time a little longer. After repeated dunkings and responses, the philosopher asked, "What do you want?" The young man finally gasped, "Air. I want air!"

"Good," answered Socrates. "Now, when you want knowledge as much as you wanted air, you shall have it."

There is no substitute for passion. It is fuel for the will. If you want anything badly enough, you can find the willpower to achieve it. The only way to have that kind of desire is to develop passion.

3. Passion Changes You

If you follow your passion—instead of others' perceptions—you can't help becoming a more dedicated, productive person. And that increases your ability to impact others. In the end, your passion will have more influence than your personality.

4. Passion Makes the Impossible Possible

Human beings are so made that whenever anything fires the soul, impossibilities vanish. A fire in the heart lifts everything in your life. That's why passionate leaders are so effective. A leader with great passion and few skills always outperforms a leader with great skills and no passion.

R E F L E C T I N G   O N   I T

Despite the power of passion, many people in our culture seem to believe that passion is something to be suspicious about. Sociologist Tony Campolo has observed, "We are caught up at a particular stage in our national ethos in which we're not only materialistic but worse than that; we're becoming emotionally dead as people. We don't sing, we don't dance, we don't even commit sin with much enthusiasm."

Is passion a characteristic of your life? Do you wake up feeling enthusiastic about your day? Is the first day of the week your favorite, or do you live from weekend to weekend, sleepwalking through your everyday routine? How long has it been since you couldn't sleep because you were too *excited* by an idea?

If passion is not a quality in your life, you're in trouble as a leader. The truth is that you can never lead something you don't care passionately about. You can't start a fire in your organization unless one is first burning in you.

Bringing It Home

To increase your passion, do the following:

- *Take your temperature.* How passionate are you about your life and work? Does it show? Get an honest assessment by querying several coworkers and your spouse about your level of desire. You won't become passionate until you believe passion can be the difference maker in your life.

- *Return to your first love.* Many people allow life and its circumstances to get them off track. Think back to when you were just starting out in your career—or even farther back to when you were a child. What really turned your crank? What could you spend hours and hours doing? Try to recapture your old enthusiasm. Then evaluate your life and career in light of those old loves.

- *Associate with people of passion.* It sounds hokey, but birds of a feather really do flock together. If you've lost your fire, get around some firelighters. Passion is contagious. Schedule some time with people who can infect you with it.

D A I L Y   T A K E - A W A Y

General Billy Mitchell, a career army officer, was assigned to an aviation section in 1916. That's where he learned to fly, and it became the passion of his life. Though aircraft played a minor role in World War I, he could see the military potential of air power. After the war, he began a campaign to convince the military to create an air force. He provided demonstration after demonstration of what airplanes could do, but he met strong resistance. Frustrated, he forced the army to court-martial him in 1925. A year later he resigned. Only after World War II was Mitchell exonerated—and posthumously awarded the Medal of Honor. He was willing to pay any price to do what he knew was right. How about you?

POSITIVE ATTITUDE:

IF YOU BELIEVE YOU CAN, YOU CAN

The greatest discovery of my generation
is that human beings can alter their lives by
altering their attitude of mind.

—William James, Psychologist

A successful man is one who can lay a firm foundation
with the bricks others have thrown at him.

—David Brinkley, Television Journalist

M O R E   T H A N   P E R S P I R A T I O N
A N D   I N S P I R A T I O N

Life magazine named him the number one man of the millennium. The number of things he invented is astounding—1,093. He held more patents than any other person in the world, having been granted at least one every year for sixty-five consecutive years. He also developed the modern research laboratory. His name was Thomas Edison.

Most people credit Edison's ability to creative genius. He credited it to hard work. "Genius," he declared, "is ninety-nine percent perspiration and one percent inspiration." I believe his success was also the result of a third factor: his positive attitude.

Edison was an optimist who saw the best in everything. "If we did all the things we were capable of doing," he once said, "we would literally astound ourselves." When it took him ten thousand tries to find the right materials for the incandescent light bulb, he didn't see them as that many failures. With each attempt he gained information about what didn't work, bringing him closer to a solution. He never doubted that he would find a good one. His belief could be summarized by his statement: "Many of life's failures are people who did not realize how close they were to success when they gave up."

Probably the most notable display of Edison's positive attitude can be seen in the way he approached a tragedy that occurred when he was in his late sixties. The lab he had built in West Orange, New Jersey, was world famous. He called the fourteen-building complex his invention factory. Its main building was massive—greater than three football fields in size. From that base of operations, he and his staff conceived of inventions, developed prototypes, manufactured products, and shipped them to customers. It became a model for modern research and manufacturing.

Edison loved the place. He spent every minute he could there. He even slept there, often on one of the lab tables. But on a December day in 1914, his beloved lab caught fire. As he stood outside and watched it burn, he is reported to have said, "Kids, go get your mother. She'll never see another fire like this one."

Most people would have been crushed. Not Edison. "I am sixty-seven," he stated after the tragedy, "but not too old to make a fresh start. I've been through a lot of things like this." He rebuilt the lab, and he kept working for another seventeen years. "I am long on ideas, but short on time," he commented. "I expect to live to be only about a hundred." He died at age eighty-four.

Fleshing It Out

If Edison hadn't been such a positive person, he never would have achieved such success as an inventor. If you look at the lives of people in any profession who achieve lasting success, you will find that they almost always possess a positive outlook on life.

If you desire to be an effective leader, having a positive attitude is essential. It not only determines your level of contentment as a person, but it also has an impact on how others interact with you. To learn more about what it means to be positive, think on these things:

1. Your Attitude Is a Choice

The average person wants to wait for someone else to motivate him. He perceives that his circumstances are responsible for the way he thinks. But which comes first—the attitude or the circumstances? That's really a chicken-or-the-egg kind of question. The truth is that it doesn't matter which came first. No matter what happened to you yesterday, your attitude is your choice today.

Psychologist Victor Frankl believed, "The last of our human freedoms is to choose our attitude in any given circumstances." He knew the truth of that statement. Frankl survived imprisonment in a Nazi death camp, and throughout his ordeal, he wouldn't allow his attitude to deteriorate. If he could maintain a good attitude, so can you.

2. Your Attitude Determines Your Actions

Family life expert Denis Waitley addresses this issue: "The winner's edge is not in a gifted birth, a high IQ, or in talent. The winner's edge is all in the attitude, not aptitude. Attitude is the criterion for success." Your attitude is crucial because it determines how you act.

3. Your People Are a Mirror of Your Attitude

I am constantly amazed by people who display a poor attitude, yet expect their people to be upbeat. But the Law of Magnetism really is true: who you are is who you attract.

If you look at Edison's life, you can see that his positive attitude and enthusiasm not only fueled him but also inspired his people to keep pressing on until they succeeded. He purposely tried to pass on that quality to others. He once remarked, "If the only thing we leave our kids is the quality of enthusiasm, we will have given them an estate of incalculable value."

4. *Maintaining a Good Attitude Is Easier Than Regaining One*

In *Earth and Altar,* Eugene H. Peterson wrote, "Pity is one of the noblest emotions available to human beings; self-pity is possibly the most ignoble . . . [It] is an incapacity, a crippling emotional disease that severely distorts our perception of reality . . . a narcotic that leaves its addicts wasted and derelict."

If you already have a positive attitude, I want to encourage you to keep it up. On the other hand, if you have a difficult time expecting the best of yourself and others, don't despair. Because you choose your attitude, you can change it.

REFLECTING ON IT

English heart surgeon Martyn Lloyd-Jones asserted, "Most unhappiness in life is due to the fact that you are listening to yourself rather than talking to yourself." What kind of voices do you hear? When you meet people, do you tell yourself they'll let you down? When you face new experiences, does a voice in your head say you're going to fail? If you're hearing negative messages, you need to learn to give yourself positive mental pep talks. The best way to retrain your attitude is to prevent your mind from going down any negative forks in the road.

Bringing It Home

To improve your attitude, do the following:

- *Feed yourself the right "food."* If you've been starved of anything positive, then you need to start feeding yourself a regular diet of motivational material. Read books that encourage a positive attitude. Listen to motivational tapes. The more negative you are, the longer it will take to turn your attitude around. But if you consume a steady diet of the right "food," you can become a positive thinker.

- *Achieve a goal every day.* Some people get into a rut of negativity because they feel they're not making progress. If that describes you, then begin setting achievable daily goals for yourself. A pattern of positive achievement will help you develop a pattern of positive thinking.

- *Write it on your wall.* We all need reminders to help us keep thinking right. Alex Haley used to keep a picture in his office of a turtle on a fence post to remind him that everybody needed the help of others. As incentive, people put up awards they've won, inspirational posters, or letters they've received. Find something that will work for you and put it on your wall.

DAILY TAKE-AWAY

When you look at any professional athlete, you see great talent. But the mind is what elevates the best to the highest level. For example, look at Chris Evert. One of the greatest female athletes of all time, she holds 18 grand slam titles and an overall win-loss record of 1,309 and 146. In her seventeen-year career, she never ranked below number four. She commented, "The thing that separates good players from great ones is mental attitude. It might only make a difference of two or three points in an entire match but how you play those key points often makes the difference between winning and losing. If the mind is strong you can do almost anything you want." Is your mind "conditioned" to win the key points ahead of you?

PROBLEM SOLVING:

YOU CAN'T LET YOUR PROBLEMS

BE A PROBLEM

You can measure a leader by the problems he tackles.
He always looks for ones his own size.

—*John C. Maxwell*

The measure of success is not
whether you have a tough problem to deal with,
but whether it is the same problem you had last year.

—*John Foster Dulles, Former Secretary of State*

THE SMALL-TOWN MERCHANT
WHO COULD

The founder of Wal-Mart, Sam Walton, has been called many things, including enemy of small-town America and destroyer of Main Street merchants. "Quite a few smaller stores have gone out of business during the time of Wal-Mart's growth," conceded Walton. "Some people have tried to turn it into this big controversy, sort of a 'Save the Small Town Merchants' deal, like they were whales or whooping cranes or something." The truth is that Walton *was* a small-town, Main Street merchant of the type he is criticized for displacing. The only difference is that he was an excellent leader who was able to solve problems and change rather than go out of business.

Sam Walton was born in Kingfish, Oklahoma, and grew up in Columbia, Missouri. He demonstrated leadership in high school when he was elected student-body president, led his football team to an undefeated season and state championship as its quarterback, and then performed the same feat with the basketball team as its five-foot-nine-inch floor leader.

After graduating from college and working for a few years, Walton served in the army during World War II. When he got out, he selected a career in retail, the field he loved, and along with his wife picked the small town of Bentonville, Arkansas, in which to live. That's where they opened a Walton's Five and Dime Variety Store.

The business did well, partly because of Walton's hustle, but also because he had shown foresight in making his store self-service, a new concept at the time. He worked hard and continued to expand. By 1960, he had fifteen stores. But that was also about the time when competitor Herb Gibson brought discount stores into northwest Arkansas. They competed directly with Walton's variety stores.

"We really had only two choices," said Walton, "stay in the variety store business and be hit hard by the discounting wave, or open a discount store. So I started running all over the country, studying the concept . . . We opened Wal-Mart Number 1 on July 2, 1962, in Rogers, Arkansas, right down the road from Bentonville."

Walton soon added additional stores. His Wal-Mart chain was small compared to some of the others begun around the same time—Kmart, Target, and Woolco—but it was going strong. And that led to the next problem. Walton realized that he needed to improve the stores' planning and distribution. He and his people solved the problem by creating central distribution centers. That, along with computerization, allowed them to order in bulk, keep track of each store's needs, and distribute to them quickly and efficiently. And when the outlay for new equipment and buildings for the new distribution centers created a heavy debt load, it was merely another problem to be solved. Walton did it by taking the company public in 1970.

When he died in 1992, the company operated more than 1,700 stores in forty-two states and Mexico. Sam Walton, the small-town variety store owner, had become America's number one retailer. And since his death, the company has continued strongly, its leadership still solving problems as they arise and keeping Wal-Mart and the other retail chain, Sam's Club, moving forward.

FLESHING IT OUT

Effective leaders, like Sam Walton, always rise to a challenge. That's one of the things that separates winners from whiners. While other retailers complained about the competition, Walton rose above it by solving his problems with creativity and tenacity.

No matter what field a leader is in, he will face problems. They are inevitable for three reasons. First, we live in a world of growing complexity and diversity. Second, we interact with people. And third, we cannot control all the situations we face.

Leaders with good problem-solving ability demonstrate five qualities:

1. They Anticipate Problems

Since problems are inevitable, good leaders anticipate them. Anyone who expects the road to be easy will continually find himself in trouble. I heard a story about David Livingstone, the missionary to Africa, that illustrates the kind of attitude leaders need. A mission organization wanted to send helpers to Dr. Livingstone, so its leader wrote, "Have you found a good road to where you are? If so, we want to send other men to join you."

Livingstone replied, "If you have men who will come *only* if they know there is a good road, I don't want them. I want men who will come even if there is no road at all." If you keep your attitude positive but plan for the worst, you'll find yourself in a good position to solve problems that come your way.

2. They Accept the Truth

People respond to problems in these ways: they refuse to accept them; they accept them and then put up with them; or they accept them and try to make things better. Leaders must always do the latter.

Broadcaster Paul Harvey said, "In times like these it is good to remember that there have always been times like these." No leader can simultaneously have his head in the sand and navigate his people through troubled waters. Effective leaders face up to the reality of a situation.

3. They See the Big Picture

Leaders must continually see the big picture. They cannot afford to be overwhelmed by emotion. Nor can they allow themselves to get so bogged down in the details that they lose sight of what's important. Author Alfred Armand Montapert wrote, "The majority see the obstacles; the few see the objectives; history records the successes of the latter, while oblivion is the reward of the former."

4. They Handle One Thing at a Time

Richard Sloma has this advice: "Never try to solve all the problems at once—make them line up for you one-by-one." The leaders who get into trouble most often are the ones who are overwhelmed by the sheer size or volume of their troubles and then dabble at problem solving. If you're faced with lots of problems, make sure you really solve the one you're working on before moving on to the next one.

5. They Don't Give Up a Major Goal When They're Down

Effective leaders understand the peak-to-peak principle. They make major decisions when they are experiencing a positive swing in their leadership, not during the dark times. As NFL fullback Bob Christian says, "I never decide whether it's time to retire during training camp." He knows not to give up when he is in the valley.

REFLECTING ON IT

Author George Matthew Adams stated, "What you think means more than anything else in your life. More than what you earn, more than where you live, more than your social position, and more than what anyone else may think about you." Every problem introduces you to yourself. It shows you how you think and what you're made of.

When you come face-to-face with a problem, how do you react? Do you ignore it and hope it will go away? Do you feel powerless to solve it? Have you had such bad experiences trying to solve problems in the past that you've just given up? Or do you tackle them willingly? The ability to solve problems effectively comes from experience facing and overcoming obstacles. Each time you solve another problem, you get a little better at the process. But if you never try, fail, and try again, you'll never be good at it.

B R I N G I N G   I T   H O M E

To improve your problem solving, do the following:

- *Look for trouble.* If you've been avoiding problems, go out looking for them. You'll only get better if you gain experience dealing with them. Find situations that need fixing, come up with several viable solutions, and then take them to a leader with good problem-solving experience. You'll learn from his decisions how he thinks when handling difficulties.

- *Develop a method.* Some people have a hard time solving problems because they don't know how to tackle them. Try using the TEACH process:

  > T IME—spend time to discover the real issue.
  >
  > E XPOSURE—find out what others have done.
  >
  > A SSISTANCE—have your team study all angles.
  >
  > C REATIVITY—brainstorm multiple solutions.
  >
  > H IT IT—implement the best solution.

- *Surround yourself with problem solvers.* If you aren't a good problem solver, bring others onto your team who are. They will immediately complement your weaknesses, and you will also learn from them.

DAILY TAKE-AWAY

Boxer Gene Tunney won the world heavyweight championship by beating Jack Dempsey. Most people don't know that when Tunney started his boxing career, he was a power puncher. But before turning pro, he broke both hands. His doctor and manager told him he would never be a world champion as a result. But that didn't deter him.

"If I can't become a champion as a puncher," he said, "I'll make it as a boxer." He learned and he became one of the most skillful boxers ever to become champion. Never allow others to put obstacles in the pathway to your dreams.

Relationships:

If You Get Along, They'll Go Along

The most important single ingredient
in the formula of success is knowing how
to get along with people.

—*Theodore Roosevelt, American President*

People don't care how much you know,
until they know how much you care.

—*John C. Maxwell*

THE BEST MEDICINE

If you're not a physician, you've probably never heard the name William Osler. He was a doctor, university professor, and author who practiced medicine and taught until his death at age seventy in 1919. His book, *Principles and Practice of Medicine,* influenced the preparation of physicians for more than forty years in the entire English-speaking world, China, and Japan. Yet that was not his greatest contribution to the world. Osler worked on putting the human heart back into the practice of medicine.

Osler's penchant for leadership became apparent while he was still a child. He was a natural ringleader and the most influential student in his school. He always showed an uncanny ability with people. Everything Osler did spoke to the importance of building relationships. As he grew older and became a doctor, he founded the Association of American Physicians so that medical professionals could come together, share information, and support one another. As a teacher, he changed the way medical schools functioned. He brought students out of dry lecture halls and into the hospital wards to interact with patients. He believed that students learn first and best from the patients themselves.

But Osler's passion was to teach doctors compassion. He told a group of medical students,

> There is a strong feeling abroad among people—you see it in the newspapers—that we doctors are given over nowadays to science; that we care much more for the disease

and its scientific aspects than for the individual . . . I would urge upon you in your own practice, to care more particularly for the individual patient . . . Dealing as we do with poor suffering humanity, we see the man unmasked, exposed to all the frailties and weaknesses, and you have to keep your heart soft and tender lest you have too great a contempt for your fellow creatures.

Osler's ability to show compassion and build relationships can be capsulized by his treatment of a patient during the 1918 epidemic of influenzal pneumonia. Osler usually limited his work to hospitals, but because of the magnitude of the epidemic, he treated many patients in their homes. The mother of a little girl recounted how Osler visited her child twice a day, speaking to her gently and playing with her to entertain her and gather information about her symptoms.

Knowing the child was nearing death, Osler arrived one day with a beautiful red rose wrapped in paper, the last rose of the summer, grown in his own garden. He presented it to her, explaining that even roses couldn't stay as long as they wanted in one place, but had to go to a new home. The child seemed to take comfort from his words and the gift. She died a few days later.

Osler died the next year. One of his British colleagues said of him,

So passed into history, untimely, even though he had attained unto the allotted span, the greatest physician in history . . .

And above all it is as a friend that during his lifetime we regarded Osler; as one who possessed the genius of friendship to a greater degree than anyone of our generations. It was his wonderful interest in all of us that was the outstanding feature . . . It was from his humanity, his extraordinary interest in his fellows, that all his other powers seemed to flow.

FLESHING IT OUT

The ability to work with people and develop relationships is absolutely indispensable to effective leadership. According to the May 1991 issue of *Executive Female* magazine, a survey was taken of employers asking for the top three traits they desired in employees. Number one on the list was the ability to relate to people: 84 percent responded that they sought good interpersonal skills. Only 40 percent listed education and experience in their top three. And if *employees* need good people skills, think about how much more critical those skills are for *leaders*. People truly do want to go along with people they get along with. And while someone can have people skills and not be a good leader, he cannot be a good leader without people skills.

What can a person do to manage and cultivate good relationships as a leader? It requires three things:

1. Have a Leader's Head—Understand People
The first quality of a relational leader is the ability to understand how people feel and think. As you work with others, recognize

that all people, whether leaders or followers, have some things in common:

> They like to feel special, so sincerely compliment them.
> They want a better tomorrow, so show them hope.
> They desire direction, so navigate for them.
> They are selfish, so speak to their needs first.
> They get low emotionally, so encourage them.
> They want success, so help them win.

Recognizing these truths, a leader must still be able to treat people as individuals. The ability to look at each person, understand him, and connect with him is a major factor in relational success. That means treating people differently, not all the same as one another. Marketing expert Rod Nichols notes that in business, this is particularly important: "If you deal with every customer in the same way, you will only close 25 percent to 30 percent of your contacts, because you will only close one personality type. But if you learn how to effectively work with all four personality types, you can conceivably close 100 percent of your contacts."

This sensitivity can be called the soft factor in leadership. You have to be able to adapt your leadership style to the person you're leading.

2. Have a Leader's Heart—Love People

President and CEO of Difinitive Computer Services Henry Gruland captures this idea: "Being a leader is more than just wanting to lead. Leaders have empathy for others and a keen ability to find the best in people . . . not the worst . . . by truly caring for others."

You cannot be a truly effective leader, the kind that people *want* to follow, unless you love people. Physicist Albert Einstein put it this way: "Strange is our situation here upon earth. Each of us comes for a short visit, not knowing why, yet sometimes seeming to divine a purpose. From the standpoint of daily life, however, there is one thing we do know: that man is here for the sake of other men."

3. Extend a Leader's Hand—Help People

Le Roy H. Kurtz of General Motors said, "The fields of industry are strewn with the bones of those organizations whose leadership became infested with dryrot, who believed in taking instead of giving . . . who didn't realize that the only assets that could not be replaced easily were the human ones." People respect a leader who keeps their interests in mind. If your focus is on what you can put into people rather than what you can get out of them, they'll love and respect you—and these create a great foundation for building relationships.

REFLECTING ON IT

How are your people skills? Do you mix well with strangers? Do you interact well with all kinds of people? Can you find common ground readily? What about long-term interaction? Are you able to sustain relationships? If your relational skills are weak, your leadership will always suffer.

BRINGING IT HOME

To improve your relationships, do the following:

- *Improve your mind.* If your ability to understand people needs improvement, jump-start it by reading several books on the subject. I recommend works written by Dale Carnegie, Alan Loy McGinnis, and Les Parrott III. Then spend more time observing people and talking to them to apply what you've learned.

- *Strengthen your heart.* If you're not as caring toward others as you could be, you need to get the focus off yourself. Make a list of little things you could do to add value to friends and colleagues. Then try to do one of them every day. Don't wait until you feel like it to help others. Act your way into feeling.

- *Repair a hurting relationship.* Think of a valued long-term relationship that has faded. Do what you can to rebuild it. Get in touch with the person and try to reconnect. If you had a falling out, take responsibility for your part in it, and apologize. Try to better understand, love, and serve that person.

DAILY TAKE-AWAY

In a short story titled "The Capitol of the World," Nobel prize–winning author Ernest Hemingway tells about a father and a teenage son, Paco, whose relationship breaks down. After the son runs away from home, the father begins a long journey in search of him. Finally as a last resort, the man puts an ad in the local newspaper in Madrid. It reads, "Dear Paco, meet me in front of the newspaper office tomorrow at noon . . . all is forgiven . . . I love you." The next morning in front of the newspaper office were eight hundred men named Paco, desiring to restore a broken relationship. Never underestimate the power of relationships on people's lives.

RESPONSIBILITY:

IF YOU WON'T CARRY THE BALL, YOU CAN'T LEAD THE TEAM

Success on any major scale requires you
to accept responsibility . . . In the final analysis,
the one quality that all successful people have
is the ability to take on responsibility.

—Michael Korda,
Editor-in-chief of Simon & Schuster

A leader can give up anything—
except final responsibility.

—John C. Maxwell

THE ALAMO REVISITED

In late 1835, a group of Texas rebels lay siege to a small mission-turned-fort in San Antonio, Texas. By the end of the year, the Mexican soldiers in it surrendered and headed south, leaving the fort in the rebels' hands. The name of the old church building was the Alamo.

That action set the stage for one of the great heroic events in United States history. The battle that occurred there in February and March of the following year is a story of valor and incredible responsibility.

The battle at the Alamo between American settlers and the Mexican army was inevitable. For twenty-five years, the citizens of Texas repeatedly attempted to gain their independence from the Mexican government. And each time Mexican troops were promptly dispatched to suppress the rebellion. But this time it was different. The fort was manned by a resolute group of 183 volunteers, including seasoned soldiers and frontiersmen William Travis, Davy Crockett, and Jim Bowie. Their motto was "Victory or Death."

In late February, several thousand Mexican soldiers under the command of Antonio Lopez de Santa Anna marched on San Antonio and lay siege to the Alamo. When the Mexicans offered them terms for surrender, the rebel defenders held firm. And when the enemy told them they would be given no quarter if they fought, the Americans would not be moved.

When it became certain that battle was inevitable, the

Texans sent a young man out to try to bring back reinforcements from the Texas army. His name was James Bonham. He slipped out of the old mission at night and made his way ninety-five miles to Goliad for help. But when he arrived, he was told that no troops were available.

For eleven days Santa Anna pounded away at the Alamo. And on the morning of March 6, 1836, the Mexican army stormed the old mission. At the end of the battle, not a single man of the 183 defenders lived. But they had managed to take six hundred enemy soldiers to the grave with them.

And what happened to James Bonham, the messenger who had been sent to Goliad? It would have been easy for Bonham to simply ride away. But his sense of responsibility was too great. Instead he rode back to the Alamo, made his way through enemy lines, and joined his comrades so that he could stand, fight, and die with them.

Though the Americans were defeated at the Alamo, that battle was the turning point in the war with Mexico. "Remember the Alamo" became the cry in subsequent battles, rallying support against General Santa Anna and his troops. Less than two months later, Texas secured its independence.

FLESHING IT OUT

Rarely in American culture today do you see the kind of responsibility displayed by James Bonham and his companions. People now focus more on their rights than on their responsibilities.

Reflecting on current attitudes, my friend Haddon Robinson observes, "If you want to get rich, invest in victimization. It is America's fastest growing industry." He points out that millions of people are becoming rich by identifying, representing, interviewing, treating, insuring, and counseling victims.

Good leaders never embrace a victim mentality. They recognize that who and where they are remain their responsibility—not that of their parents, their spouses, their children, the government, their bosses, or their coworkers. They face whatever life throws at them and give it their best, knowing that they will get an opportunity to lead the team only if they've proved that they can carry the ball.

Take a look at the following characteristics of people who embrace responsibility:

1. They Get the Job Done

In a study of self-made millionaires, Dr. Thomas Stanley of the University of Georgia found that they all have one thing in common: they work hard. One millionaire was asked why he worked twelve to fourteen hours a day. He answered, "It took me fifteen years, working for a large organization, to realize that in our society you work eight hours a day for survival, and if you work only eight hours a day, all you do is survive . . . Everything over eight hours is an investment in your future." No one can do the minimum and reach his maximum potential.

How do people maintain a get-it-done attitude? They think of themselves as self-employed. If you want to achieve more and build your credibility with followers, adopt that mind-set. It can take you far.

2. They Are Willing to Go the Extra Mile

Responsible people never protest, "That's not my job." They're willing to do whatever it takes to complete the work needed by the organization. If you want to succeed, be willing to put the organization ahead of your agenda.

3. They Are Driven by Excellence

Excellence is a great motivator. People who desire excellence—and work hard to achieve it—are almost always responsible. And when they give their all, they live at peace. Success expert Jim Rohn says, "Stress comes from doing less than you can." Make high quality your goal, and responsibility will naturally follow.

4. They Produce Regardless of the Situation

The ultimate quality of a responsible person is the ability to finish. In *An Open Road,* Richard L. Evans writes, "It is priceless to find a person who will take responsibility, who will finish and follow through to the final detail—to know when someone has accepted an assignment that it will be effectively, conscientiously completed." If you want to lead, you've got to produce.

R E F L E C T I N G   O N   I T

Gilbert Arland offers this advice: "When an archer misses the mark he turns and looks for the fault within himself. Failure to hit the bull's-eye is never the fault of the target. To improve your aim, improve yourself."

Are you on target when it comes to responsibility? Do others see you as a finisher? Do people look to you to carry the ball in pressure situations? Are you known for excellence? If you haven't been performing at the highest level, you may need to cultivate a stronger sense of responsibility.

BRINGING IT HOME

To improve your responsibility, do the following:

- *Keep hanging in there.* Sometimes an inability to deliver despite difficult circumstances can be due to a persistence problem. The next time you find yourself in a situation where you're going to miss a deadline, lose a deal, or fail to get a program off the ground, stop and figure out how to succeed. Think outside the lines. Can you work through the night? Can you call a colleague to help you? Can you hire a staff member or find a volunteer to help? Creativity can bring responsibility to life.

- *Admit what's not good enough.* If you have trouble achieving excellence, maybe you've lowered your standards. Look at your personal life for places where you've let things slip. Then make changes to set higher standards. It will help you to reset the bar of excellence for yourself.

- *Find better tools.* If you find that your standards are high, your attitude is good, and you consistently work hard—and you still don't achieve the way you'd like—get better equipped. Improve your skills by taking classes, reading books, and listening to tapes. Find a mentor. Do whatever it takes to become better at what you do.

D A I L Y   T A K E - A W A Y

An inmate at Butte County Jail in California explained his absence from jail to sheriff's deputies in this way: "I was playing pole vault and I got too close to the wall and I fell over the wall. When I regained my senses, I ran around to try and find a way back in, but being unfamiliar with the area, got lost. Next thing I knew I was in Chico." People seldom realize how weak *their* excuses are until they hear some from others.

SECURITY:

COMPETENCE NEVER COMPENSATES

FOR INSECURITY

You can't lead people if you need people.

—John C. Maxwell

No man will make a great leader
who wants to do it all himself or get
all the credit for doing it.

—Andrew Carnegie, Industrialist

A C O N S T I T U T I O N O F I R O N A N D
S E C U R I T Y T O M A T C H

During the term of President Ronald Reagan, leaders of seven industrial nations were meeting at the White House to discuss economic policy. Reagan has recounted that during the meeting he came across Canadian Prime Minister Pierre Trudeau strongly upbraiding British Prime Minister Margaret Thatcher, telling her that she was all wrong and that her policies wouldn't work. She stood there in front of him with her head up, listening until he was finished. Then she walked away.

Following the confrontation, Reagan went up to her and said, "Maggie, he should never have spoken to you like that. He was out of line, just entirely out of line. Why did you let him get away with that?"

Thatcher looked at Reagan and answered, "A woman must know when a man is being simply childish."

That story surely typifies Margaret Thatcher. It takes a strong, secure person to succeed as a world leader. And that is especially true when the person is a woman.

Margaret Thatcher has continually swum upstream throughout her life. As a student at Oxford University, she majored in chemistry, a field dominated by men, and she became the first woman president of the Oxford University Conservative Association. A few years later, she qualified as a lawyer and practiced as a tax specialist.

In 1959, Thatcher entered politics, another overwhelmingly

male profession, when she was elected a member of Parliament. Analytical, articulate, and calm under fire, she was frequently asked by her party to face opponents in debate. Her skill and conviction may have been fired by an attitude she learned from her father, who told her, "You don't follow the crowd; you make up your own mind."

Her strong resolve and high competence earned her several government posts. It was during her tenure as secretary of state for education and science that she was referred to as "the most unpopular woman in Britain." But Thatcher didn't waver under the criticism. She continued working hard and gaining people's respect. Her reward was being named the first female prime minister in the history of Britain.

In that position, she continued to face criticism. She weathered abuse for privatizing state-owned industries, reducing the role of organized labor, sending troops to the Falkland Islands, and maintaining conservative policies against the Soviet Union. But no matter how severely she was criticized, she remained secure in her convictions and maintained her self-respect. She once said, "To me consensus seems to be the process of abandoning all beliefs, principles, values, and policies in search of something in which no one believes . . . What great cause would have been fought and won under the banner, 'I stand for consensus'?"

Thatcher stood for conviction in leadership. And as a result, the "Iron Lady," as she was called, was elected to three consecutive terms as prime minister. She is the only British leader of the modern era to achieve that.

F L E S H I N G I T O U T

Margaret Thatcher appeared to have no doubts about herself or her beliefs—and she was absolutely secure in her leadership as a result. That is the case for all great leaders. No one can live on a level inconsistent with the way he sees himself. You may have observed that in people. If someone sees himself as a loser, he finds a way to lose. Anytime his success surpasses his security, the result is self-destruction. That's not only true for followers, but it's also true for leaders.

Insecure leaders are dangerous—to themselves, their followers, and the organizations they lead—because a leadership position amplifies personal flaws. Whatever negative baggage you have in life only gets more difficult to bear when you're trying to lead others.

Insecure leaders have several common traits:

1. They Don't Provide Security for Others

An old saying states, "You cannot give what you do not have." Just as people without skill cannot impart skill to others, people without security cannot make others feel secure. And for a person to become an effective leader, the kind that others *want* to follow, he needs to make his followers feel good about themselves.

2. They Take More from People than They Give

Insecure people are on a continual quest for validation, acknowledgment, and love. Because of that, their focus is on finding security, not instilling it in others. They are primarily takers rather than givers, and takers do not make good leaders.

3. They Continually Limit Their Best People

Show me an insecure leader, and I'll show you someone who cannot genuinely celebrate his people's victories. He might even prevent them from realizing any victories. Or he might take credit personally for the best work of his team. As I mention in *The 21 Irrefutable Laws of Leadership,* only secure leaders give power to others. That's the Law of Empowerment. But an insecure leader hoards power. In fact, the better his people are, the more threatened he feels—and the harder he will work to limit their success and recognition.

4. They Continually Limit the Organization

When followers are undermined and receive no recognition, they become discouraged and eventually stop performing at their potential. And when that happens, the entire organization suffers.

In contrast, secure leaders are able to believe in others because they believe in themselves. They aren't arrogant; they know their own strengths and weaknesses and respect themselves. When their people perform well, they don't feel threatened. They go out of their way to bring the best people together and then build them up so that they will perform at the highest level. And when a secure leader's team succeeds, it brings him great joy. He sees that as the highest compliment he can receive for his leadership ability.

How well do you understand and respect yourself? Do you know your strengths and feel good about them? Have you recognized your weaknesses and accepted the ones you can't change? When a person realizes that he is created with a particular personality type and has unique gifts, he is better able to appreciate the strengths and successes of others.

How secure are you as a leader? When a follower has a great idea, do you support it or suppress it? Do you celebrate your people's victories? When your team succeeds, do you give the members credit? If not, you may be dealing with insecurity, and it could be limiting you, your team, and your organization.

To improve your security, do the following:

- *Know yourself.* If you are the kind of person who is not naturally self-aware, take time to learn about yourself. Take a personality test, such as the ones created by Myers-Briggs or Florence Littauer. Ask several people who know you well to name your three greatest talents and your three greatest weaknesses. Don't defend yourself when you hear their answers; gather the information and then reflect on it.

- *Give away the credit.* You may not believe that you can succeed if others receive the praise for the job your team is doing. Try it. If you assist others and acknowledge their contributions, you will help their careers, lift their morale, and improve the organization. And it will make you look like an effective leader.

•   *Get some help.* If you cannot overcome feelings of insecurity on your own, seek professional help. Get to the root of your problems with the assistance of a good counselor, not only for your own benefit but also for that of your people.

DAILY TAKE-AWAY

French novelist Honoré de Balzac was a keen observer of human nature, and he sought to capture a complete picture of modern civilization in his huge work *The Human Comedy*. He once observed, "Nothing is a greater impediment to being on good terms with others than being ill at ease with yourself." Don't let insecurity prevent you from reaching your potential.

SELF-DISCIPLINE:

THE FIRST PERSON YOU LEAD IS YOU

The first and best victory is to conquer self.

—*Plato, Philosopher*

A man without decision of character
can never be said to belong to himself . . .
He belongs to whatever can make captive of him.

—*John Foster, Author*

KING OF THE HILL

It's a tough road to the top. Not many people ever reach the place where they are considered one of the best at their work. And even fewer are believed to be *the* best—ever. Yet that's what Jerry Rice has achieved. He is called the best person ever to play wide receiver in football. And he has got the records to prove it.

People who know him well say he is a natural. Physically his God-given gifts are incredible. He has everything a coach would want in a receiver. Hall of Fame football coach Bill Walsh said, "I don't think there's been a guy equal to him physically." Yet that alone has not made him great. The real key to his success has been his self-discipline. He works and prepares—day in and day out—unlike anyone else in professional football.

The story of Rice's ability to push himself can be told in his experiences conquering hills. The first came in high school. At the end of each practice, B. L. Moor High School Coach Charles Davis used to have his players sprint twenty times up and down a forty-yard hill. On a particularly hot and muggy Mississippi day, Rice was ready to give up after eleven trips. As he sneaked toward the locker room, he realized what he was doing. "Don't quit," he told himself. "Because once you get into that mode of quitting, then you feel like it's okay." He went back and finished his sprints, and he has never been a quitter since.

As a professional player, he has become famous for his ability to sprint up another hill. This one is a rugged 2.5-mile park trail in San Carlos, California, that Rice makes a regular part of his workout schedule. Other top players try to keep up with him on it, but they fall behind, astounded by his stamina. But that's only a part of Rice's regular routine. Even in the off-season, while other players are fishing or lying around enjoying downtime, Rice is working, his normal exercise routine lasting from 7:00 A.M. to noon. Someone once joked, "He is so well-conditioned that he makes Jamie Lee Curtis look like James Earl Jones."

"What a lot of guys don't understand about Jerry is that with him, football's a twelve-month thing," says NFL cornerback Kevin Smith. "He's a natural, but he still works. That's what separates the good from the great."

Rice recently climbed another hill in his career: he made a comeback from a devastating injury. Prior to that, he had never missed a game in nineteen seasons of football, a testament to his disciplined work ethic and absolute tenacity. When he blew out his knee on August 31, 1997, people thought he was finished for the season. After all, only one player had ever had a similar injury and come back in the same season—Rod Woodson. He had rehabilitated his knee in four and a half months. Rice did it in three and a half—through sheer grit, determination, and incredible self-discipline. People had never seen anything like it before, and they might not again. And Rice continues to build his records and his reputation while helping his team win.

FLESHING IT OUT

Jerry Rice is a perfect example of the power of self-discipline. No one achieves and sustains success without it. And no matter how gifted a leader is, his gifts will never reach their maximum potential without the application of self-discipline. It positions a leader to go to the highest level and is a key to leadership that lasts.

If you want to become a leader for whom self-discipline is an asset, follow these action points:

1. Develop and Follow Your Priorities

Anyone who does what he must only when he is in the mood or when it's convenient isn't going to be successful. Nor will people respect and follow him. Someone once said, "To do important tasks, two things are necessary: a plan and not quite enough time." As a leader, you already have too little time. Now all you need is a plan. If you can determine what's really a priority and release yourself from everything else, it's a lot easier to follow through on what's important. And that's the essence of self-discipline.

2. Make a Disciplined Lifestyle Your Goal

Learning about any highly disciplined person, such as Jerry Rice, should make you realize that to be successful, self-discipline can't be a one-time event. It has to become a lifestyle.

One of the best ways to do that is to develop systems and routines, especially in areas crucial to your long-term growth and success. For example, because I continually write and speak, I read and file material for future use every day. And since my heart attack in December 1998, I exercise every morning. It's not something I'll do just for a season. I'll do it every day for the rest of my life.

3. Challenge Your Excuses

To develop a lifestyle of discipline, one of your first tasks must be to challenge and eliminate any tendency to make excuses. As French classical writer François La Rochefoucauld said, "Almost all our faults are more pardonable than the methods we think up to hide them." If you have several reasons why you can't be self-disciplined, realize that they are really just a bunch of excuses—all of which need to be challenged if you want to go to the next level as a leader.

4. Remove Rewards Until the Job Is Done

Author Mike Delaney wisely remarked, "Any business or industry that pays equal rewards to its goof-offs and its eager-beavers sooner or later will find itself with more goof-offs than eager-beavers." If you lack self-discipline, you may be in the habit of having dessert before eating your vegetables.

A story illustrates the power of withholding rewards. An older couple had been at a campground for a couple of days when a family arrived at the site next to them. As soon as their sport-utility vehicle came to a stop, the couple and their three kids piled out. One child hurriedly unloaded ice chests, backpacks, and other items while the other two quickly put up tents. The site was ready in fifteen minutes.

The older couple was amazed. "You folks sure do work great together," the elderly gentleman told the dad admiringly.

"You just need a system," replied the dad. "Nobody goes to the bathroom until camp's set up."

5. Stay Focused on Results
Anytime you concentrate on the difficulty of the work instead of its results or rewards, you're likely to become discouraged. Dwell on it too long, and you'll develop self-pity instead of self-discipline. The next time you're facing a must-do task and you're thinking of doing what's convenient instead of paying the price, change your focus. Count the benefits of doing what's right, and then dive in.

REFLECTING ON IT

Author H. Jackson Brown Jr. quipped, "Talent without discipline is like an octopus on roller skates. There's plenty of movement, but you never know if it's going to be forward, backwards, or sideways." If you know you have talent, and you've seen a lot of motion—but little concrete results—you may lack self-discipline.

Look at last week's schedule. How much of your time did you devote to regular, disciplined activities? Did you do anything to grow and improve yourself professionally? Did you engage in activities promoting good health? Did you dedicate part of your income to savings or investments? If you've been putting off those things, telling yourself that you'll do them later, you may need to work on your self-discipline.

B R I N G I N G   I T   H O M E

To improve your self-discipline, do the following:

- *Sort out your priorities.* Think about which two or three areas of life are most important to you. Write them down, along with the disciplines that you must develop to keep growing and improving in those areas. Develop a plan to make the disciplines a daily or weekly part of your life.

- *List the reasons.* Take the time to write out the benefits of practicing the disciplines you've just listed. Then post the benefits someplace where you will see them daily. On the days when you don't want to follow through, reread your list.

- *Get rid of excuses.* Write down every reason why you might not be able to follow through with your disciplines. Read through them. You need to dismiss them as the excuses they are. Even if a reason seems legitimate, find a solution to overcome it. Don't leave yourself any reasons to quit. Remember, only in the moment of discipline do you have the power to achieve your dreams.

DAILY TAKE-AWAY

A nursery in Canada displays this sign on its wall: "The best time to plant a tree is twenty-five years ago . . . The second best time is today." Plant the tree of self-discipline in your life today.

SERVANTHOOD:

TO GET AHEAD, PUT OTHERS FIRST

The true leader serves. Serves people.
Serves their best interests, and in so doing
will not always be popular, may not always impress.
But because true leaders are motivated by loving
concern rather than a desire for personal glory,
they are willing to pay the price.

—*Eugene B. Habecker, Author*

You've got to love your people
more than your position.

—*John C. Maxwell*

ON SHAKY GROUND

Not long ago Americans became acquainted with U.S. Army General H. Norman Schwarzkopf. He displayed highly successful leadership abilities in commanding the allied troops in the Persian Gulf War, just as he had done throughout his career, beginning in his days at West Point.

In *The 21 Irrefutable Laws of Leadership,* I wrote how in Vietnam he turned around a battalion that was in shambles. The First Battalion of the Sixth Infantry—known as the "worst of the sixth"—went from laughingstock to effective fighting force and were selected to perform a more difficult mission. That turned out to be an assignment to what Schwarzkopf described as "a horrible, malignant place" called the Batangan Peninsula. The area had been fought over for thirty years, was covered with mines and booby traps, and was the site of numerous weekly casualties from those devices.

Schwarzkopf made the best of a bad situation. He introduced procedures to greatly reduce casualties, and whenever a soldier *was* injured by a mine, he flew out to check on the man, had him evacuated using his chopper, and talked to the other men to boost their morale.

On May 28, 1970, a man was injured by a mine, and Schwarzkopf flew to the man's location. While the helicopter was evacuating the injured soldier, another soldier stepped on a mine, severely injuring his leg. The man thrashed around on the ground, screaming and wailing. That's when everyone realized the first mine hadn't been a lone booby trap. They were all standing in the middle of a minefield.

Schwarzkopf believed the injured man could survive and even keep his leg—but only if he stopped flailing around. There was only one thing he could do. He had to go after the man and immobilize him. Schwarzkopf wrote,

> I started through the minefield, one slow step at a time, staring at the ground, looking for telltale bumps or little prongs sticking up from the dirt. My knees were shaking so hard that each time I took a step, I had to grab my leg and steady it with both hands before I could take another . . . It seemed like a thousand years before I reached the kid.

The 240-pound Schwarzkopf, who had been a wrestler at West Point, then pinned the wounded man and calmed him down. It saved his life. And with the help of an engineer team, Schwarzkopf got him and the others out of the minefield.

The quality that Schwarzkopf displayed that day could be described as heroism, courage, or even foolhardiness. But I think the word that best describes it is *servanthood*. On that day in May, the only way he could be effective as a leader was to serve the soldier who was in trouble.

FLESHING IT OUT

When you think of servanthood, do you envision it as an activity performed by relatively low-skilled people at the bottom of the positional totem pole? If you do, you have a wrong impression. Servanthood is not about position or skill. It's about attitude. You have undoubtedly met people in service positions who have poor attitudes toward servanthood: the rude worker at the government agency, the waiter who can't be bothered with taking your order, the store clerk who talks on the phone with a friend instead of helping you.

Just as you can sense when a worker doesn't want to help people, you can just as easily detect whether a leader has a servant's heart. And the truth is that the best leaders desire to serve others, not themselves.

What does it mean to embody the quality of servanthood? A true servant leader:

1. Puts Others Ahead of His Own Agenda

The first mark of servanthood is the ability to put others ahead of yourself and your personal desires. It is more than being willing to put your agenda on hold. It means intentionally being aware of your people's needs, available to help them, and able to accept their desires as important.

2. Possesses the Confidence to Serve

The real heart of servanthood is security. Show me someone who thinks he is too important to serve, and I'll show you someone who is basically insecure. How we treat others is really a reflection of how we think about ourselves. Philosopher-poet Eric Hoffer captured that thought:

The remarkable thing is that we really love our neighbor as ourselves; we do unto others as we do unto ourselves. We hate others when we hate ourselves. We are tolerant toward others when we tolerate ourselves. We forgive others when we forgive ourselves. It is not love of self but hatred of self which is at the root of the troubles that afflict our world.

The Law of Empowerment says that only secure leaders give power to others. It's also true that only secure leaders exhibit servanthood.

3. Initiates Service to Others

Just about anyone will serve if compelled to do so. And some will serve in a crisis. But you can really see the heart of someone who initiates service to others. Great leaders see the need, seize the opportunity, and serve without expecting anything in return.

4. Is Not Position-Conscious

Servant leaders don't focus on rank or position. When Colonel Norman Schwarzkopf stepped into that minefield, rank was the last thing on his mind. He was one person trying to help another. If anything, being the leader gave him a greater sense of obligation to serve.

5. Serves Out of Love

Servanthood is not motivated by manipulation or self-promotion.

It is fueled by love. In the end, the extent of your influence depends on the depth of your concern for others. That's why it's so important for leaders to be willing to serve.

REFLECTING ON IT

Where is your heart when it comes to serving others? Do you desire to become a leader for the perks and benefits? Or are you motivated by a desire to help others?

If you really want to become the kind of leader that people want to follow, you will have to settle the issue of servanthood. If your attitude is to be served rather than to serve, you may be headed for trouble. If this is an issue in your life, then heed this advice:

Stop lording over people, and *start* listening to them.
Stop role-playing for advancement, and *start* risking for others' benefit.
Stop seeking your own way, and *start* serving others.

It is true that those who would be great must be like the least and the servant of all.

BRINGING IT HOME

To improve your servanthood, do the following:

- *Perform small acts.* When was the last time you performed small acts of kindness for others? Start with those closest to you: your spouse, children, parents. Find ways today to do small things that show others you care.

- *Learn to walk slowly through the crowd.* One of the greatest lessons I learned as a young leader came from my father. I call it walking slowly through the crowd. The next time you attend a function with a number of clients, colleagues, or employees, make it your goal to connect with others by circulating among them and talking to people. Focus on each person you meet. Learn his name if you don't know it already. Make your agenda getting to know each person's needs, wants, and desires. Then later when you go home, make a note to yourself to do something beneficial for half a dozen of those people.

- *Move into action.* If an attitude of servanthood is conspicuously absent from your life, the best way to change it is to start serving. Begin serving with your body, and your heart will eventually catch up. Sign up to serve others for six months at your church, a community agency, or a volunteer organization. If your attitude still isn't good at the end of your term, do it again. Keep at it until your heart changes.

D A I L Y   T A K E - A W A Y

Albert Schweitzer wisely stated, "I don't know what your destiny will be, but one thing I know: The ones among you who will be really happy are those who have sought and found how to serve." If you want to lead on the highest level, be willing to serve on the lowest.

TEACHABILITY:

TO KEEP LEADING, KEEP LEARNING

Value your listening and reading time at
roughly ten times your talking time. This will assure
you that you are on a course of continuous
learning and self-improvement.

—*Gerald McGinnis,*
President and CEO of Respironics, Inc.

It's what you learn after you know it all that counts.

—*John Wooden, Hall of Fame Basketball Coach*

SUCCESS DISGUISED AS A TRAMP

If you see the image of a little man sporting a tiny moustache, carrying a cane, and wearing baggy pants, big, clumsy shoes, and a derby hat, you know immediately that it's Charlie Chaplin. Just about everyone recognizes him. In the 1910s and 1920s, he was *the* most famous and recognizable person on the planet. If we looked at today's celebrities, the only person even in the same category as Chaplin in popularity would be Michael Jordan. And to measure who is the bigger star, we would have to wait another seventy-five years to find out how well everyone remembers Michael.

When Chaplin was born, nobody would have predicted great fame for him. Born into poverty as the son of English music hall performers, he found himself on the street as a small child when his mother was institutionalized. After years in workhouses and orphanages, he began working on the stage to support himself. By age seventeen, he was a veteran performer. In 1914, while in his mid-twenties, he worked for Mack Sennett at Keystone Studios in Hollywood making $150 a week. During that first year in the movie business, he made thirty-five films working as an actor, writer, and director. Everyone recognized his talent immediately, and his popularity grew. A year later, he earned $1,250 a week. Then in 1918, he did something unheard of. He signed the entertainment industry's first $1 million contract. He was rich; he was famous; and he was the most powerful filmmaker in the world—at the ripe old age of twenty-nine.

Chaplin was successful because he had great talent and incredible drive. But those traits were fueled by teachability. He continually strived to grow, learn, and perfect his craft. Even when he was the most popular and highest paid performer *in the world,* he wasn't content with the status quo.

Chaplin explained his desire to improve to an interviewer:

> When I am watching one of my pictures presented to an audience, I always pay close attention to what they don't laugh at. If, for example, several audiences do not laugh at a stunt I mean to be funny, I at once begin to tear that trick to pieces and try to discover what was wrong in the idea or in the execution of it. If I hear a slight ripple at something I had not expected to be funny, I ask myself why that particular thing got a laugh.

That desire to grow made him successful economically, and it brought a high level of excellence to everything he did. In those early days, Chaplin's work was hailed as marvelous entertainment. As time went by, he was recognized as a comic genius. Today many of his movies are considered masterpieces, and he is appreciated as one of the greatest filmmakers of all time. Screenwriter and film critic James Agee wrote, "The finest pantomime, the deepest emotion, the richest and most poignant poetry were in Chaplin's work."

If Chaplin had replaced his teachability with arrogant self-satisfaction when he became successful, his name would be right up there along with Ford Sterling or Ben Turpin, stars of silent films who are all but forgotten today. But Chaplin kept growing and learning as an actor, director, and eventually film executive. When he learned from experience that filmmakers were at the mercy of studios and distributors, he started his own organization, United Artists, along with Douglas Fairbanks, Mary Pickford, and D. W. Griffith. The film company is still in business today.

FLESHING IT OUT

Leaders face the danger of contentment with the *status quo*. After all, if a leader already possesses influence and has achieved a level of respect, why should he keep growing? The answer is simple:

> Your growth determines who you are.
> Who you are determines who you attract.
> Who you attract determines the success of your organization.

If you want to grow your organization, *you* have to remain teachable.

Allow me to give you five guidelines to help you cultivate and maintain a teachable attitude:

1. Cure Your Destination Disease
Ironically, lack of teachability is often rooted in achievement. Some people mistakenly believe that if they can accomplish a particular goal, they no longer have to grow. It can happen with almost anything: earning a degree, reaching a desired position, receiving a particular award, or achieving a financial goal.

But effective leaders cannot afford to think that way. The day they stop growing is the day they forfeit their potential—and the potential of the organization. Remember the words of Ray Kroc: "As long as you're green, you're growing. As soon as you're ripe, you start to rot."

2. Overcome Your Success

Another irony of teachability is that success often hinders it. Effective leaders know that what got them there doesn't keep them there. If you have been successful in the past, beware. And consider this: if what you did yesterday still looks big to you, you haven't done much today.

3. Swear Off Shortcuts

My friend Nancy Dornan says, "The longest distance between two points is a shortcut." That's really true. For everything of value in life, you pay a price. As you desire to grow in a particular area, figure out what it will really take, including the price, and then determine to pay it.

4. Trade In Your Pride

Teachability requires us to admit we don't know everything, and that can make us look bad. In addition, if we keep learning, we must also keep making mistakes. But as writer and expert craftsman Elbert Hubbard said, "The greatest mistake one can make in life is to be continually fearing you will make one." You cannot be prideful and teachable at the same time.

Emerson wrote, "For everything you gain, you lose something." To gain growth, give up your pride.

5. Never Pay Twice for the Same Mistake

Teddy Roosevelt asserted, "He who makes no mistakes, makes no progress." That's true. But the leader who keeps making *the same* mistakes also makes no progress. As a teachable leader, you will make mistakes. Forget them, but always remember what they taught you. If you don't, you will pay for them more than once.

REFLECTING ON IT

When I was a kid growing up in rural Ohio, I saw this sign in a feed store: "If you don't like the crop you are reaping, check the seed you are sowing." Though the sign was an ad for seeds, it contained a wonderful principle.

What kind of crop are you reaping? Do your life and leadership seem to be getting better day after day, month after month, year after year? Or are you constantly fighting just to hold your ground? If you're not where you hoped you would be by this time in your life, your problem may be lack of teachability. When was the last time you did something for the first time? When was the last time you made yourself vulnerable by diving into something for which you weren't the expert? Observe your attitude toward growing and learning during the next several days or weeks to see where you stand.

B R I N G I N G   I T   H O M E

To improve your teachability, do the following:

- *Observe how you react to mistakes.* Do you admit your mistakes? Do you apologize when appropriate? Or are you defensive? Observe yourself. And ask a trusted friend's opinion. If you react badly—or you make no mistakes at all—you need to work on your teachability.

- *Try something new.* Go out of your way today to do something different that will stretch you mentally, emotionally, or physically. Challenges change us for the better. If you really want to start growing, make new challenges part of your daily activities.

- *Learn in your area of strength.* Read six to twelve books a year on leadership or your field of specialization. Continuing to learn in an area where you are already an expert prevents you from becoming jaded and unteachable.

D A I L Y   T A K E - A W A Y

After winning his third world championship, bull rider Tuff Hedeman didn't have a big celebration. He moved on to Denver to start the new season—and the whole process over again. His comment: "The bull won't care what I did last week." Whether you're an untested rookie or a successful veteran, if you want to be a champion tomorrow, be teachable today.

V I S I O N :

Y O U C A N S E I Z E O N L Y

W H A T Y O U C A N S E E

A great leader's courage to fulfill his vision
comes from passion, not position.

—John C. Maxwell

The future belongs to those who see possibilities
before they become obvious.

—John Sculley
Former CEO of Pepsi and Apple Computer

N o   C h i p p e d   P a i n t   .   .   .
A l l   t h e   H o r s e s   J u m p

One of the great dreamers of the twentieth century was Walt Disney. Any person who could create the first sound cartoon, first all-color cartoon, and first animated feature-length motion picture is definitely someone with vision. But Disney's greatest masterpieces of vision were Disneyland and Walt Disney World. And the spark for that vision came from an unexpected place.

Back when Walt's two daughters were young, he used to take them to an amusement park in the Los Angeles area on Saturday mornings. His girls loved it, and he did too. An amusement park is a kid's paradise, with wonderful atmosphere: the smell of popcorn and cotton candy, the gaudy colors of signs advertising rides, and the sound of kids screaming as the roller coaster plummets over a hill.

Walt was especially captivated by the carousel. As he approached it, he saw a blur of bright images racing around to the tune of energetic calliope music. But when he got closer and the carousel stopped, he could see that his eye had been fooled. He observed shabby horses with cracked and chipped paint. And he noticed that only the horses on the outside row moved up and down. The others stood lifeless, bolted to the floor.

The cartoonist's disappointment inspired him with a grand vision. In his mind's eye he could see an amusement park where the illusion didn't evaporate, where children and adults could enjoy a carnival atmosphere without the seedy side that accompanies some circuses or traveling carnivals. His dream became Disneyland. As Larry Taylor stated in *Be an Orange*, Walt's vision could be summarized as, "No chipped paint. All the horses jump."

F L E S H I N G   I T   O U T

Vision is everything for a leader. It is utterly indispensable. Why? Because vision leads the leader. It paints the target. It sparks and fuels the fire within, and draws him forward. It is also the fire lighter for others who follow that leader. Show me a leader without vision, and I'll show you someone who isn't going anywhere. At best, he is traveling in circles.

To get a handle on vision and how it comes to be a part of a good leader's life, understand these things:

1. Vision Starts Within

When I'm teaching at conferences, someone will occasionally ask me to give him a vision for his organization. But I can't do it. You can't buy, beg, or borrow vision. It has to come from the inside. For Disney, vision was never a problem. Because of his creativity and desire for excellence, he always saw what *could* be.

If you lack vision, look inside yourself. Draw on your natural gifts and desires. Look to your calling if you have one. And if you still don't sense a vision of your own, then consider hook-ing up with a leader whose vision resonates with you. Become his partner. That's what Walt Disney's brother, Roy, did. He was a good businessman and leader who could make things happen, but Walt was the one who provided the vision. Together, they made an incredible team.

2. *Vision Draws on Your History*

Vision isn't some mystical quality that comes out of a vacuum, as some people seem to believe. It grows from a leader's past and the history of the people around him. That was the case for Disney. But it's true for all leaders. Talk to any leader, and you're likely to discover key events in his past that were instrumental in the creation of his vision.

3. *Vision Meets Others' Needs*

True vision is far-reaching. It goes beyond what one individual can accomplish. And if it has real value, it does more than just *include* others; it *adds value* to them. If you have a vision that doesn't serve others, it's probably too small.

4. *Vision Helps You Gather Resources*

One of the most valuable benefits of vision is that it acts like a magnet—attracting, challenging, and uniting people. It also rallies finances and other resources. The greater the vision, the more winners it has the potential to attract. The more challenging the vision, the harder the participants fight to achieve it. Edwin Land, the founder of Polaroid, advised, "The first thing you do is teach the person to feel that the vision is very important and nearly impossible. That draws out the drive in winners."

Where does vision come from? To find the vision that is indispensable to leadership, you have to become a good listener. You must listen to several voices.

The Inner Voice

As I have already said, vision starts within. Do you know your life's mission? What stirs your heart? What do you dream about? If what you're pursuing in life doesn't come from a desire within—from the very depths of who you are and what you believe—you will not be able to accomplish it.

The Unhappy Voice

Where does inspiration for great ideas come from? From noticing what *doesn't* work. Discontent with the *status quo* is a great catalyst for vision. Are you on complacent cruise control? Or do you find yourself itching to change your world? No great leader in history has fought to prevent change.

The Successful Voice

Nobody can accomplish great things alone. To fulfill a big vision, you need a good team. But you also need good advice from someone who is ahead of you in the leadership journey. If you want to lead others to greatness, find a mentor. Do you have an adviser who can help you sharpen your vision?

The Higher Voice

Although it's true that your vision must come from within, you shouldn't let it be confined by your limited capabilities. A truly valuable vision must have God in it. Only He knows your full capabilities. Have you looked beyond yourself, even beyond your own lifetime, as you've sought your vision? If not, you may be missing your true potential and life's best for you.

B R I N G I N G   I T   H O M E

To improve your vision, do the following:

- *Measure yourself.* If you have previously thought about the vision for your life and articulated it, measure how well you are carrying it out. Talk to several key people, such as your spouse, a close friend, and key employees, asking them to state what they think your vision is. If *they* can articulate it, then *you* are probably living it.

- *Write it down.* If you've thought about your vision but never put it in writing, take the time to do it today. Writing clarifies your thinking. Once you've written it, evaluate whether it is worthy of your life's best. And then pursue it with all you've got.

- Do *a gut check*. If you haven't done a lot of work on vision, spend the next several weeks or months thinking about it. Consider what really impacts you at a gut level.

What makes you cry? _____

What makes you dream? _____

What gives you energy? _____

Also think about what you'd like to see change in the world around you. What do you see that isn't—but could be? Once your ideas start to become clearer, write them down and talk to a mentor about them.

DAILY TAKE-AWAY

From 1923 to 1955, Robert Woodruff served as president of Coca-Cola. During that time, he wanted Coca-Cola to be available to every American serviceman around the world for five cents, no matter what it cost the company. What a bold goal! But it was nothing compared to the bigger picture he could see in his mind's eye. In his lifetime, he wanted every person in the *world* to have tasted Coca-Cola. When you look deep into your heart and soul for a vision, what do *you* see?

CONCLUSION

I hope you have enjoyed reading *The 21 Indispensable Qualities of a Leader* and have benefited from doing the exercises in the "Bringing It Home" section of each chapter. These assignments are designed to help you get a handle on each quality and start you on the process of continuous personal growth in your life.

I want to encourage you to keep growing as a leader. Review this book periodically to measure how you're developing. And put yourself on a regular program where you consistently read books, listen to tapes, and attend conferences that stretch you. If you're looking for resources to help you with that process, contact my organization.

We'll be glad to send you a catalog and current conference schedule. I also want to encourage you to find other leaders who will mentor you in person or through books and tapes. The only way to become the kind of leader that people *want* to

follow is to keep growing and learning about leadership. Good
luck in your journey.

> The INJOY Group
> P.O. Box 7700
> Atlanta, GA 30357-0700
> 800-333-6506
> www.injoy.com

BECOME THE LEADER YOU WANT TO BE— IN **3** STEPS

Carrying out the following three-step process will help you lift the lid on your level of leadership and transform your organization.

> Step **1**: **Spend 21 days reading** *The 21 Irrefutable Laws of Leadership.* Read a law each day to gain a better understanding of the principles of leadership.

The 21 Irrefutable Laws of Leadership Book

After more than thirty years of serving in leadership positions and speaking on leadership, John Maxwell is often asked, "If you were to take everything you've learned about leadership over the years and boil it down into a short list, what would it be?" This book is his answer. In it John outlines the essentials of leadership that transcend time, place, culture, and situation.

"I recommend this book to anyone who desires success at the highest level, whether on the ball field, in the boardroom, or from the pulpit."

—TOM LANDRY, FORMER HEAD COACH, DALLAS COWBOYS

Step **2:** **Spend 21 weeks teaching your leaders** through the *Learning the 21 Irrefutable Laws of Leadership* video series. Bring your leaders together to study one law every week. As you develop your people, you will begin to see a positive impact on your organization.

Learning the 21 Irrefutable Laws of Leadership Video Series

These dynamic videos will help you bring your entire leadership team together to develop a shared vision. John Maxwell will teach your staff for 25 minutes on each leadership law. A library of 21 lessons are yours to pull from each time you teach.

Package Contents:

- 5 interactive videos containing 25-minute lessons on each law
- 1 complete set of outlines and notes
- 1 copy of the book *The 21 Irrefutable Laws of Leadership*
- 1 bonus introductory video

B2143K: Video Package $99.95

*To purchase any of the **21 Irrefutable Laws of Leadership** materials, see your local bookstore or call **1-800-333-6506** 8:30AM-5PM, M-F, EST. Visit the INJOY Group web site at www.injoy.com*

Step **3**: **Spend 21 months working through the** *Living the 21 Irrefutable Laws of Leadership* **audio series.** To keep your organization growing, you have to keep growing. As you listen to one law per month and work through the personal growth notebook, you will assess your ability in that area, learn how to apply the law to your leadership, and follow an action plan making the law a part of your life.

Living the 21 Irrefutable Laws of Leadership Audio Series

Created to propel you to a new leadership level, this monthly leadership growth system can literally measure your growth each month. You simply listen to one leadership lesson, read one chapter, and complete one assignment each month.

Package Contents:

- 11 audiocassettes containing 21 lessons
- Introductory audiocassette by John Maxwell
- Bonus video of John Maxwell explaining the 21 Laws

- A complete personal development manual
- A copy of the best-selling book *The 21 Irrefutable Laws of Leadership*

B2143T: **Audio Package $189.95**

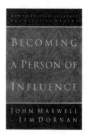

A B O U T   T H E   A U T H O R

JOHN C. MAXWELL, known as America's expert on leadership, is the founder of the INJOY Group, an organization dedicated to helping people maximize their personal and leadership potential. Each year Maxwell speaks in person to more than 250,000 people and influences the lives of more than one million people through seminars, books, and tapes. He is the author of twenty-four books, including *The 21 Irrefutable Laws of Leadership, Becoming a Person of Influence, The Success Journey, Developing the Leader Within You,* and *Developing the Leaders Around You.*

For more information on
John Maxwell seminars and resources:

Call 1-800-333-6506

8:30AM-5PM, M-F, EST.
Visit The INJOY Group online
www.injoy.com

Experience the Power of Partnership

INJOY Conferences
Empowering Leaders to Excel

These catalytic events can make a life-changing difference for you. Thousands of people are changed each year through more than ten different seminars. With many conference options, one is sure to be exactly what you need.

INJOY Resources
Equipping Leaders to Succeed

Known worldwide for cutting-edge books, videos, software, and audiotapes on topics from leadership and church-staffing to marriage and family issues, INJOY Resources equips people like you to lead more effectively.

INJOY Stewardship Services
Energizing Churches to Raise Major Funds

ISS was established to provide growing churches with strategic, innovative, and effective consulting for capital funding of projects. Whatever the challenge, we'll help you face it with confidence.

The INJOY Group
LEADING TO EXCELLENCE

www.injoy.com
1-800-333-6506

Also Introducing....

EQUIP Ministries
Encouraging the Development of Christian Leaders

As The INJOY Group partners with you, you can partner with other leaders in need. EQUIP is a nonprofit group that concentrates on developing leaders internationally, in urban ministries, and in academic institutions. For more information, call 1-888-993-7847.

down at it and immediately the rest of the liquid spattered the floor in front of him, soaking his feet, followed by the clang of the cup itself as it bounced across the stones.

Eskie laughed and walked back to him. "You must not get distracted by things if you're serving. You can't go studying your feet without dousing the entire clientele should you be supporting a full tray." She picked up the cup and filled it again. "Let's try once more, see if you can do it." She put the re-filled cup on the tray and walked off again. "All right, come to me," she called from across the room. The bald cook stopped to watch. Diverus cautiously walked across to Eskie without spilling the cup. When he reached her she said, "Now can you lower yourself so that I can reach the cup more easily?"

He thought about it for a moment before extending his back leg out, widening his stance to lower his torso. She took the cup. "Wonderful, Diverus! You learned that right away, faster than a lot of boys would've done."

The cook said, "Clever lad, innit," then went back to grinding.

She replaced the cup on the tray. "Now let's see how you do with a full tray."

After he had successfully walked the length of the kitchen twice while balancing a tray covered with cups, Eskie had the cook feed him again. She maintained that he was in need of extra nourishment. If Diverus passed out in the middle of the evening, a disaster would ensue. And while *he* might be forgiven, Bogrevil would certainly blame, and punish, her.

Once he'd eaten a cup of the soup that he would have again for dinner, she took him down to the lowest level of the paidika: the laundry.

This proved to be a large room at sea level with a square, shallow pool in its center. There were boys already at work in the laundry. They were different from the boys he'd seen above. A few were cruelly formed, with lumpish backs or twisted limbs, or heads too small for their bodies. Some of them were brutes, too large to be boys except that they were. They had dull faces, childish faces, faces expressing their inability to grasp anything beyond the work they were doing. The rest shuffled about with dirty or wet linens clutched in their arms. They seemed incomplete in some manner, like sleepwalkers, ignoring him and Eskie and everyone else. The ones in the pool plunged bedding and tunics into the water, sponged and squeezed and pounded the cloth, and every bit of their minds must have been focused upon the labor. One of the sleepwalkers noticed Eskie and Diverus, and stopped, gaping. His face looked old and wan; the eyes expressed a veiled panic, as if the source of his fear was inaccessible, and the lips were pulled back in a kind of rictus that drew the skin of his face tight across the bones. Diverus didn't comprehend what the look meant, but he saw in these boys his old life beneath Vijnagar, and what Bogrevil intended for him if he failed in his other duties.

Because of Eskie, he *had* other duties.

Across the pool a wide barred gate revealed a view of dark water. He circled the pool and walked up to the gate. His fingers curled around the vertical bars. The padlock securing it was nearly as wide as he was—a giant's padlock stolen from some other world. He pressed his face into the bars to see as much as possible. Where he stood lay at the very bottom of the span, looking out toward the pier of another tower on the far side of it. A boat with a single sail trolled past through the narrow channel, so close that he could make out the weathered features of the single occupant. If he could have gotten outside the gate, he might have jumped from the narrow ledge into the boat. Overhead he could see nothing save for the hint of an arch curving above the far pier. No platforms had been constructed in that space between the spans.

Eskie had come up behind him. He felt her press against him as she put a hand upon his shoulder. "It's the way out in emergencies, this gate. If we're raided. Which has only ever happened once or twice, because some of the magistrates are regular customers and they protect us. They don't think we know—they come in disguise, most clients do—but Bogrevil has an informative network, and he knows things he's not supposed to. He takes care of himself, which takes care of us."

He slid his hand down and fingered the keyhole cover on the padlock . . . a small keyhole for so large a lock.

She must have noticed, for she said, "Far too big for anyone to remove it alone. Some of the boys were street pickers before ending up here, and they surely know their way around locks. That one—even if they can work it, they can't get out without two more boys to help lift it."

He glanced back toward the pool.

She looked at the pool, too, seeing what he implied. "Oh, they're big enough, but they have no wish to leave. The paidika is the only proper home most of them have ever known. Many were horribly treated where they were before. You could never get them to help. In fact, they would probably stop anyone who tried to get out. Some of them sleep down here, in the corners. Like the demon sentinels of Nechron's underworld, they are."

He shifted his gaze, met hers with his brow furled.

"What, you've never heard the name of the god of the underworld? No. I suppose you wouldn't have, would you. Who would have taken the time to educate you? They would have considered it time wasted, but I think you're cleverer than they know, Diverus. You'll learn everything here—especially now as you'll be a server rather than a scrub boy."

He looked out at the water once more before turning away and accompanying Eskie back up to the higher level. The laundry boys watched him leave as though watching him walk out of their memory.

Eskie left him at the dormitorium after assigning him a pad to sleep on. She told him to sleep as long as he could during the day. Once the paidika opened for business, he would be on his feet the rest of the night.

She didn't lie to him: Diverus wandered through the three main rooms throughout that entire first night, weaving among clients and other serving boys, and the boys on display.

Most of the clientele were costumed and masked, as if arriving from a fancy ball somewhere else upon the span. He watched them descend the long, high stairway, dressed in loose pants and sometimes with sweeping capes. Bogrevil was often there to meet them. Many, he seemed to know despite—or perhaps because of—their costumes, welcoming them broadly and taking them immediately to one of the three chambers, where he would point out someone in particular. Most of the time, the guest agreed with his selection and allowed himself to be escorted into the narrow halls and the rooms beyond them. A very large boy—practically a giant—stood beside the base of the steps, with folded arms, still as a statue, though his eyes cast from room to room. Diverus he considered with disinterest.

The boys were costumed, too. Some had been painted in extravagant makeup and wore flowing garments, veils, and scarves. They could have passed for women. Others wore very little—short trunks or diaphanous robes. Some, especially muscular older boys, sported leather collars, and wide bracelets at their wrists, as if prepared for some combat. One of them strode from room to room, proudly naked beneath green paint. His hair had been spiked about his head like that of a sea sprite.

Those clients not swept up immediately by Bogrevil milled around, appraising the boys as they might have done a bolt of fabric. Their masks made them silent, somber, bestial. Beaks and snouts turned the liquid eyes above into wet stones, as if what lay beneath the mask would prove to be less recognizable even than the caricatured surface.

Whenever his tray was empty, Diverus returned to the kitchen for more. Initially Bogrevil clasped his shoulders and nudged him to let him know that it was time, but after a few hours he was able to sense from the weight of it when the tray was almost empty.

The first one he carried held cups of wine, the second, plates of finger foods. He and the other serving boys walked with measured strides in and out of the rooms, eyeing one another without comment. In the center parlor a boy sat cross-legged and played lamely at a stringed instrument with a curved neck. Diverus had never seen such an instrument and didn't know what it was called, but he knew from the dissonant notes that the boy was not accustomed to it. The clients all but ignored the performance until one young guest spilled a drink upon him, and the clustered entourage burst into laughter. That brought Bogrevil into the room so fast, it seemed he'd anticipated it. The young man smirked as if the matter was not of consequence and made a vague apology, insisting it had been an accident; but the trio who'd accompanied him still sniggered as he spoke and exchanged glances that, even beneath their masks, expressed cruel delight. Bogrevil asked them if they had any particular preference for the evening—"a particular essence you cared to sample." It seemed an innocent question but somehow conveyed the message that they must now either choose or leave. After fidgeting and shrugging among one another, they turned and departed back up the steps, with Bogrevil at their heels. He smiled and waved them along, but when he came back down the steps, his face had gone sharp and humorless. To the giant boy at the bottom, he said, "They never come in again, separately or together. The gate, if they do." The giant nodded slightly, though how he would distinguish them, Diverus couldn't fathom.

To the wine-soaked musician Bogrevil snarled, "At least tune the damned thing."

The remainder of the evening provided no excitement or diversion, and exhaustion replaced curiosity well before the end of the night. Sent off to bed, he slept so heavily that he likely could have been tossed into the laundry pool and wouldn't have noticed. He neither sensed nor cared who else shared the room, or who was missing.

In the afternoon, when he awoke, he found Eskie seated beside one of the pallets, feeding a boy as though he was ill; and he looked ill, too. He watched

Diverus through sunken eyes so asthenic that they couldn't maintain the glance and fell, unfocused upon anything this side of the grave. Eskie wouldn't meet his glance at all.

The nights thereafter were much the same. Over time he learned to identify returning customers well enough that if he was carrying their preferred drink or food, he would meet them at the bottom of the steps—an act that did not go unnoticed by Bogrevil, who reconsidered him, scrutinizing him as if to decide if he'd misjudged Diverus and, granted that he was a superb judge of flesh, been in some manner misled. He commented to the giant, "It's a shame that one's a mute, 'cause it's clear he's much more clever than what appears." The giant, who was *not* more clever than he appeared, stared at Diverus in perplexity.

The later the night wore on, the more the clients came in clusters, and by the second half of the evening there weren't but one or two individuals in any of the three parlors. The rest had retired to the private chambers. On his way to and from the kitchens he noticed some of them in the corridors, lolled on the settees between the private rooms; sometimes they were sleeping, but even the conscious ones appeared exhausted and muddled. Occasionally they needed assistance to manage the steps up to the span again, which task was assigned to boys who hadn't been picked, or to him and the other servers if no one more suitable was available. These people always smelled mephitic, as if some poison leaked from their pores. Diverus did not focus on what was going on in the paidika, or what it meant that boys who were chosen for a night the next day had to be spoon-fed, didn't leave their pallets, and often were given a second night off to rest. He didn't want to know. He listened to other servers gossip about it—tales of how boys who pried into the goings-on in those chambers disappeared. The boys who entered the chambers with clients refused to tell those who weren't chosen what happened to them.

Exhaustion became his excuse for not pursuing any answers. He slept through almost every day and worked through most of the night, with barely enough reserves to find his way back to his bed in the morning.

Then one very busy night, very late, one client in a purple cape and wearing a spangled mask arrived in the final minutes, and there were no boys left for him. At first Bogrevil tried to talk him out of his desire. "It's so late, sir, you'll hardly have time to enjoy yourself." He gestured to the hourglass in the corner, as if it somehow supported his argument. "Come back tomorrow

night—it's an anniversary, a celebration. We'll fête you better than anyone."
The client remained adamant, in the manner of a drunk who has made up his
mind. He demanded satisfaction, and Bogrevil finally suggested that the man
consider one of the servers. He called a coffee-colored boy named Abnevi
over. Though unattractively scarred with pockmarks, Abnevi was intelligent
and—Bogrevil assured the client—"brimming." The client, with obvious reluctance, accepted the offer, and Abnevi set down his tray to follow. His eyes
were round with terror.

When the three of them had left the parlor, the remaining server, named
Olk, nudged Diverus. Olk had a deformed, withered arm, and Diverus supposed that as with himself, superstitious clients feared that the deformity was
communicable. Grinning sourly, Olk said, "We're lucky, the way we are.
You're stupid and they don't want you, neither."

Before he could ask Olk to explain more, Bogrevil came back and dismissed them. As Diverus passed by, Bogrevil grabbed him by the arm and
whispered, "Another night, you'll be chosen, don't you worry, son. You're too
pretty to go to your death in servitude." Then he strode off.

The paidika closed up for the day, and the boys returned their trays to the
kitchen and slunk off to the dormitorium. Diverus hung back until the rest
had gone. Before that night he had avoided looking at what it meant to be selected, at what purpose a paidika served, because there was only one purpose
for such a place that he could imagine, and one use, finally, for all of them,
however kindly Bogrevil pretended to be.

He turned from the hall to the dormitorium and took a different corridor,
one that led to the private rooms Eskie had shown him.

Most of them were dark behind drawn curtains, but in a couple candlelight flickered, and in creeping to the nearest one he heard a slow, quiet
susurration that ebbed and flowed like waves rushing up to a beach.

Edging deeper into the doorway recess, he peeked through the space between the wall and the curtain. He could see the client, the one who had
chosen Abnevi, still dressed in his billowy costume and seated upon the tail
of his purple cape, cross-legged beside the immense brass water pipe. His glittering mask lay at his side. His blond hair hung over his eyes in an oily fringe,
and under it the stripe of a black blindfold circled his head, like a crown
fallen low. The rhythmic *whooshing* came as he pulled on the pipe, inhaling
and then leaning back to exhale, his mouth open, slack, drool glistening like
a snail's path from the corner of it down to his collar. Barely a wisp of bluish

smoke emerged from the chimney of his mouth. Abnevi was nowhere in sight
on that side of the hookah. Diverus touched a finger to the curtain and drew
it back farther. The tiered body of the hookah filled the middle of the chamber. A grayish fog emerging from its top led his eye around the curtain to the
far side.

Abnevi lay in the long, inscribed lacquer box, beneath the curious fingers
of bone. His eyes were closed so that he would not see what Diverus now
looked upon—what neither of the chamber's occupants saw. The fog con-
gealed above Abnevi, into manifest horror. Perched upon the bony tines like
a creature of prey, the thing was yet insubstantial—a translucent, ribbed torso
that glistened in the candlelight like a grub; it overlooked the sleeping boy.
A bluish vapor rose out of Abnevi's face toward it. The skin of his cheeks rippled as if seen through heat, and the body twitched once, twice, as if tugged
at from above. Diverus didn't think he made a sound, but the apparition's
head drew up abruptly. It faced him. Two horrible white orbs fixed upon his
position—milky eyes hard as alabaster. The jagged black hole of its mouth
spiraled shut, snipping the stream of vapor, which snapped as if sprung, back
into Abnevi. He bucked once more forcefully than before. The creature
trembled, fluttered, and with an outraged screech flung itself off the tines and
collapsed all in a moment, reeling into the hookah so fast that Diverus wasn't
sure if he'd seen it go in or it had simply evaporated.

Oblivious of any change in the situation, the blindfolded stupefied client
leaned forward again and inhaled from the hookah. He choked suddenly.
Then he dropped the mouthpiece, clutched his throat with one hand, his
chest with the other, and fell sideways. He pawed at the blindfold and drew a
dagger from his waistband, waving it as if to ward off something in the air
above him. He spasmed, gave one final creaking gasp, and lay still. A darker,
greasy smoke trailed from his mouth.

Diverus dropped the curtain and stepped back—bumping against someone else, who said "Oof" as he struck her.

He spun about, and there stood Eskie, glaring at him. "What do you think
you're doing?" she hissed. "Do you want to be drowned in the laundry?" He
might have answered, forgetting himself, if she hadn't gone on. "If you inter-
rupt the process, you could kill someone, the boy or the client. Afrits have
been known to turn and devour everyone in the room."

"Afrits?" It was a word Bogrevil had used earlier.

"That which resides in the hookah. A dem—but you spoke. You *spoke*!"

He hadn't meant to. Unaccustomed to his own voice, he hadn't realized what he'd done, but Eskie had.

"You've been able to speak all the time, haven't you? You kept this hidden, pretending to be the fool Bogrevil believes of you."

He cleared his throat. Having not spoken for so long, his voice was coarse, barely a whisper. "An idiot is what I was before I arrived here," he replied somewhat defensively. "He sees what he wants. What he was told he'd purchased."

"But you pretend to be mute."

He gestured his head as if to say, *What should I have done?* Then he asked, "What is an afrit?"

"A spirit, a demon. These ones are tied to water, the ones Bogrevil serves. And caverns—they are not accustomed to living in light."

He knit his brow. "He serves *them*?"

She nodded. "His very survival depends upon his service to their kind. I know nothing of how he came to be so indentured. That is something he never speaks of. But he provides them an essence to which they're addicted, and which in turn produces a vapor the clients crave."

"An essence . . . the boys?"

"Youth is powerful. The afrits thrive upon it."

His eyes widened at the enormity of what she was saying. "Doesn't it kill them?"

"Over time—a long time for most—it . . . alters them. But it's a pleasurable process for them."

"How can you know that?"

She gave him a look as if he *were* a fool. "Because they tell me so. What was I doing in this hallway just now, do you suppose? Did you think I was looking for you? Every morning I come as I do now in finding you. When the client emerges from the room, I go in. With Bogrevil or Kotul—the big one who guards the door—I assist the hired boys to their beds because they can barely walk afterward, and I serve them food to replenish them, usually soup, a broth, and often they sleep a full day through. It's then almost as if nothing has happened to them, as if they'd been ill with fever and I've nursed them through it. They tell me sometimes of the dreams they've had, which are like fever dreams. Wondrous places they've visited while they slept—it might even be that they journey to Edgeworld." She shook her head as if to dismiss her own observation. "But they do not see the afrit. They only know the dreamlife it gives them, for it sends them to sleep before it emerges. They are, I think, unaware that anything has been lost to them until perhaps toward the end, when their thoughts grow too confused to be unknotted. By then they are as addicted to the dreams as the clients are to the afrit's vapors. They cannot distinguish any longer between this and dreamlife, and the one often seems superimposed upon the other. I think they really don't know which is which."

"The boys in the laundry."

Her face screwed up at their mention, as if she wasn't prepared to think about them. "Some of those. But they don't know it. Nor much of anything else."

"That's my destiny, then. It's what everyone has intended for me. Even you." He looked her in the eye, expecting confirmation but seeing instead her alarm.

"I want nothing like that for you. You mustn't reveal to Bogrevil what you've shown to me, ever—that you speak, that you're aware."

He said, "Tonight he promised me I would find myself in here soon, that somehow it's better than serving."

"Listen to me. You must disguise your cleverness, and continue to play the mute simpleton. Otherwise . . . and for you it would be death because you know the truth and would resist, and if you looked into the afrit's eyes . . ." She glanced away from his. "If it saw you, it would devour your soul."

"You do this for him, knowing the truth." He tried to sound neutral, but the words accused her.

She burned scarlet. "I live, the same as you. I have the choices you have, maybe fewer. My family—" She stopped, shook her head. "I have nothing beyond the paidika, nothing to go to if I'm thrown out. Bogrevil takes care of me and I take care of the boys. I keep them healthy and alive. If I were to refuse, then they would begin to wither and die the very first time, and perhaps in great misery. You judge from the outside, Diverus, before you even know what you judge."

He had been trying not to judge but to understand. He apologized, secretly thrilled that she had instructed him not to become one of them. However she attempted to mitigate her own role, she nevertheless wanted to keep him from becoming the sort of boy to whom she ministered. He asked, "Do others know?"

"No one knows. Sooner or later most of the boys have been hired for a night, but none would ever dare intrude as you've done. One or two may have early on—or else Bogrevil invented the tale to scare the others off, of how those interlopers were never seen again. Those who aren't fed to the afrits are too simple to act upon such curiosity, and so must you be. If you had walked into that room, you would have been destroyed."

He recalled suddenly the aftermath of what he'd seen. "The client," he said, and turned back to the curtain. He opened it and heard her gasp behind him, but the afrit, as he knew, had fled into the safe haven of the water pipe.

The client was sprawled upon the floor, and even from the doorway Diverus could tell that he was dead.

Eskie pushed around him and ran to the body. He followed her, though watching Abnevi, who lay in a daze, his eyes darkly ringed, and unfocused as if no thought guided them. His head rolled from side to side. *It will devour your soul*, she'd warned.

"He is dead," Eskie proclaimed of the client. "What has happened?"

Diverus looked down at a face that was swollen as if the man were trying to hold in a lungful of smoke. The blindfold had been pushed up above one eye. Eskie removed it. His eyelids had not quite closed, and he looked as if his own death bored him. The dagger had fallen from his hand, and his open fingers seemed to be reaching for the brass mouthpiece as though he might yet drag it to his purple lips for a final draw.

"I'm the cause of this," Diverus said. He sank down, then explained how the afrit had somehow sensed him and retreated, and how the client unknowingly had continued to draw from the mouthpiece.

"Oh, gods."

"But what happened?"

"The water in the pipe must have become poisonous when the afrit withdrew. He was no longer smoking its vapors; it would have been the angry poison of the demon itself. What are we to tell Bogrevil? This man is dead, and surely someone will come looking for him."

"Surely, *I* will," came the reply from behind them, and they both turned to find Bogrevil holding the curtain up. "What has happened here?" He eyed the hookah, then Abnevi with a distortive repulsion before he entered the room.

Eskie stood and moved aside. As Bogrevil crouched down she gave Diverus a sharp glance and gestured *no* with her head. Then she answered, "I came to retrieve the boy and found this man in this position."

Bogrevil rolled his eyes nervously up at her; his glance flicked again to the brass hookah and back. "The afrit?"

"It had gone."

That seemed to allay his fears, but he pretended not to be concerned for himself. "Lucky for you. You wouldn't be telling me now if you'd met it." Then he acknowledged Diverus. "And what's *he* doing here?"

For a moment she hesitated, then said, "I enlisted him to help me. With the boys. Because he can't say anything. You and Kotul were absent."

He stared at her. It was clear to Diverus that he didn't believe her; but a lewd smile crossed his lips as he contemplated both of them, and he said, "*Enlisted*, is it? Well, it's no matter, and we'll need his help now. Now he *is* enlisted." He fitted the mask back onto the dead man's face, drew the cape out from beneath the lifeless bulk, and spread it over his body like a shroud, then stood, with the dead man's dagger in his hand, the tip pointed at Diverus's throat. "Khanjarli," he said. "Good craftsmanship." He tucked it into the back of his belt.

At that moment Abnevi stumbled out from behind the hookah. He leaned against the brass bowl, his legs trembling, and stared. "Where's my pen?" he asked. "I must write a policy and I've lost my pen. Oh, what's this, is this a different dream?"

"What's he talking about?" Eskie asked.

"An unfortunate accident," said Bogrevil. "The dream owns him." To Abnevi he said, "Your pen isn't here. I think you need to come along with us now. It's a long descent to the bottom and if anything falls out of this man's pockets, I want you to pick it up, yes? Maybe *he* has your pen."

Abnevi nodded brightly. Diverus felt ill, watching.

Bogrevil took the body by the legs, and Eskie and Diverus each took an arm as they carried it down the hall. The cape might have disguised the identity but not the substance of their burden. The body swung between them, the head dragging on the floor. No one was about at this hour, and no one else saw them.

The stairs were difficult to navigate, in part because the head struck every step, and even though the man was dead the *thock* of each impact made Diverus wince. Behind them Abnevi muttered, "Are we going to wash him? I want to bathe, too. Reasonable and customary cleanliness is a clause I put in every policy. It's healthful."

At the bottom everything was dim, although the early-morning light cast enough of a glow beneath the span that the checkered pattern of the gate was distinct. They lay the body down; Bogrevil fetched keys from a cord around his neck and unlocked the padlock. Abnevi broke away from them and clambered down into the washing pool.

By then one of the behemoths had awakened and lumbered over to see what was occurring. He was nearly bald, and his head was deformed, as if the skull had developed bulbs beneath the skin. When he saw Bogrevil he grinned stupidly and grunted. "Yes, yes," Bogrevil said, and patted him on the shoulder. "Good fella. We need to move that lock." The simple giant stepped over the body as though it were a log, and with Bogrevil's help raised the padlock. The two of them managed to hook it over one of the bars on the gate. The giant then pushed the gate open.

Bogrevil came back, and they picked up the body again.

Outside, the position on the ledge afforded a view in both directions. To the right the edge of the bridge pier was close enough that the joints between the blocks of stone were visible. It would have taken only seconds to reach the corner of the pier. Beyond it the surface of the sea shimmered with distant red splashes of dawn. To the left the ledge dwindled steadily, vanishing at last into the darkness of the span's underbelly. A bright semicircle defined the opening on the far side. Above them the air was filled with only darkness and the flitting brightness of a few passing gulls. No platforms, nor people—the underworld from which he'd emerged would be on the opposite side of the tower. There were no boats near enough to see them.

Bogrevil set his end of the corpse on the ledge. He got down onto his knees and plunged his hand into the water off the side. It took him only a moment to dredge up a large stone. This he dragged to the body, where he threw back the cape, pulled loose the man's trousers, and shoved the stone inside them. When he had done this three times, he cinched the belt again. "That's good enough," he said. Getting stiffly to his feet, he gestured his helper to come out onto the ledge.

The lumpish giant shuffled past the gate, round eyes darting from side to side. He made a whining noise.

"It's all right," Bogrevil said. "Nobody's tryin' to make you leave. You two, put down your end and come over here and take a leg with me."

They obeyed. The giant picked up both arms. "Now we shall swing him three times. Third time we let go. You understand?" He was asking the giant, who nodded, but kept glancing fearfully at the sea, as though something might come out of it at any moment.

"One."

"Two."

"Three."

The body sailed out over the black water farther than Diverus had expected. It hit with surprisingly little sound, and sank immediately. The cape floated for a moment then disappeared. A stream of bubbles trickled up to the surface. The exotic mask bobbed up, expressionless without eyes behind it; it swiveled about as if looking for something, and then drifted out toward the open water.

"Right, then. Back inside, everybody," Bogrevil ordered.

It wasn't until the gate had closed that Diverus realized he should have run then and there. The ledge would have taken him someplace, and neither the behemoth nor Bogrevil could have caught him. Even had he dived into the sea, it would have carried him away—to a boat, to the pier of the next span—but now it was too late and he was part of the paidika again. Why hadn't he run?

They slid the lock back onto its latch, and Bogrevil turned the key before turning to them. "Now, this did not happen. That gentleman, whoever he was, was never here, you never seen him, and you slept the whole morning through. Everyone slept."

Behind them, Abnevi splashed and splashed and tittered in the pool. His head lolled back and his eyes rolled up at the ceiling. "Oh, that's pretty," he slurred, but almost immediately he raised an arm as if to protect himself from something in flight, and dove, crying, "No, no! Get away!" He remained underwater only a moment, but when he came up he was laughing.

Eskie said, "What about him?"

"It's done sommit to him, hasn't it? Dunno what, don't care. He likes it so down here, I'd prefer he stay. Don't want him babbling—we don't know what he saw, do we? What he might tell if his mind were to come back. Down here, it won't matter. He can tell everybody. They're just like him." He reached out and caught Diverus suddenly, dragged him close.

"It's our anniversary tonight and we don't want nothing to spoil that. Nobody answers no questions. You want to have a little fun being 'enlisted' in the wee hours, I don't mind, see, 'cause *you* don't take away from no customers.

But no mistakes, pretty one, or what happened to Abnevi'll be something you'll wish happened to you."

Diverus shook his head and drew a finger across his mouth to indicate he would say nothing. Bogrevil nodded that he understood. "Oh, yeah," he said, "that's right, you can't say anything about *anything*." He released Diverus then, caught Eskie by the elbow, and started back up the steps with her in tow. "Can't say a thing!" he called out, and vanished up into the dark.

The sound of Abnevi's unmoored laughter followed Diverus up the steps like a curse.

Bogrevil took Eskie with him, so Diverus had no one to speak with, no opportunity to confess the terrible guilt he felt over Abnevi's fate. He returned to the dormitorium, where everyone was asleep, and lay down, certain that he could never fall asleep again. Abnevi's mind was shattered and it was his doing—he had interrupted the afrit at its feeding. He kept reliving the moment when the creature's head turned, severing its connection, the blue tendrils snapping back into the helpless boy: his fault. Those round white eyes seared him with accusation.

The next thing he knew, he was crawling from the depths of sleep and uncertain that the events had been real. Two other boys lay asleep in the room, sunken-eyed and pale. Afrit victims. Everyone else had gone. He got up and hurried past the sleepers to bathe and eat.

When he returned to the dormitorium, Eskie was feeding one of the weak boys. With the spoon she pointed to his pallet. A costume of red crushed velvet and white silk lay there beside a long white band of cloth. He dressed while she finished ministering to the other boy. The sleeves covered his hands, and strings dangled off the cuffs. She came and tied the strings to loops at the shoulders. The sleeves were so full that he could freely move his arms, but they looked like wings. Then she took the cloth and wrapped it around his head, forming a turban, efficiently, as if she did this every day. She tucked the end of the cloth into a seam, and then fastened a cheap jewel to the front of it. "That looks very good, you're becoming one of the more attractive boys here," she said.

The comment so appalled him that he stepped back from her. "How can you be so—" he snarled, but got no further, as the façade she had been maintaining collapsed. Her eyes filled with tears. She put her arms around him and whispered in his ear, "Remember what I've told you. Stay out of his way, stay out of sight. Don't do anything to call attention to yourself. He's dressing you for them and tonight he might do anything."

When she drew back and smeared the tears with her palm, he saw that her cheek was bruised and swollen. "He hit you."

"I—" She sniffled. "It was my fault."

If he'd had a knife just then he might have changed all their fates.

The celebration commenced. Corridors and parlors overflowed with guests, more than he'd ever seen. A trio of musicians had been given to Bogrevil as a gift for the evening. They stood back-to-back in the center of the middle parlor: One played a small drum dangling from a lanyard around his neck, another plucked a lute, and the third fingered a reed instrument called a shawm. The paidika's musician sat on the floor in the corner behind them, watching with envious eyes.

The side parlors had been fitted with long tables of food, artistic displays that were quickly turned into skeletal remains as if by a horde of insects and as quickly replaced.

The other boys like Diverus had been dressed in gaudier costumes than usual—feathers and glittering scales, splashes of color everywhere.

Diverus carried tray after tray of drinks—in his arms for a change, instead of on his head. Guests snatched everything off each before he'd even reached the parlors, some on their way to the afrits' chambers—as he now thought of the back rooms. The masked visitors gobbled and guzzled as if fearing they might be stranded without sustenance for days.

Bogrevil remained at the bottom of the stairs, dressed in regal violet embroidered robes. He bowed with great flourishes to each individual or group that descended, a sultan welcoming his guests. Initially people escorted their choices to him, but as the evening wore on and the guests came to outnumber the paidika's stable, they came to him with names written on slips of paper, which he wrote down on a small parchment on a podium beside his mammoth guard. They understood that they would have to wait to take their turns. Later arrivals might not have anyone left to choose from at all. He might send in a second client while a boy still lay in the afrit's perch, but not a third. Nobody could recover from three sessions in a row, and it wasn't as if he was going out of business after tonight.

Early in the festivities one guest clutched Diverus as he was retreating with an empty tray. He looked at the hand on his sleeve, noting the polished nails, and glanced up at coal-black eyes fringed by long lashes behind a gold mask. Dragged before Bogrevil, he listened as the guest said, "I'd have this one." It was a woman, as Bogrevil must have known, too. He expected to be let go.

Bogrevil closed his hand over hers. "He's lovely, you know. Your taste is uncommonly fine." He let this statement hang in the air for a moment—to tease, or to torture Diverus. "He is, however, of diminished capacity, and it might well be catching. Let me assure you, were he not, he wouldn't be serving food. Now, let me offer you something else tasty," and he led her away. Diverus didn't see her again for some hours.

One by one boys were purchased and taken off while others milled about waiting their turn. Each time he watched one leave the room, he wanted to stop him. Didn't anyone notice Abnevi's absence? Didn't they wonder what had happened? Could they read the guilt in his eyes?

He couldn't help thinking of each of them in their curtained and candlelit chambers, lying beneath insubstantial monstrosities as their life was drained, their souls served up as refreshment. How could Eskie suggest that they desired such a thing?

As the evening wore on, other guests considered him. Their eyes spoke their interest. He wondered what they got from what they inhaled, and why any one boy was more appealing than any other. And why was it only boys— a preference of the afrits or merely less problematic than if the genders mixed? Would there be paidikas full of girls, or was there another word for such places? He knew so little of the world, so little that was of use.

Each time his tray emptied and he escaped to the kitchen, he stalled as long as he could, staying at the back of the line, remaining as invisible as possible, remembering what Eskie had said. Perhaps the fourth time he had done this, the cook placed small brass cups upon the tray as he held it, then filled each with a green distillation. As he filled the ones nearest Diverus's body, he leaned across the tray and said, "Clever boy. Dressed so nice, have you become merchandise now?" At Diverus's look of shock, he laughed. "Can't dodge all night long, you know, no matter how you hang back. It'll be *my* turn to choose eventually, when they've all gone. He's saving you for me."

Diverus flung the tray at him.

Thick green liquid spattered the cook from head to waist, most of it running down his filthy apron. Diverus shoved past those waiting behind him. The cook yelled at him then erupted in the sort of laugh that promised punishment, but Diverus didn't stop. He ran out and into one of the back corridors full of afrit chambers.

A curtain parted, and the woman who'd earlier attempted to rent him stumbled out. Her dark eyes were slits, barely open, her features slack. A blindfold hung loosely about her throat on top of her gilded mask. So drunk on the essence she'd inhaled was she that she'd forgotten to put her disguise back on, or even all of her costume. She was barefoot now and bare-shouldered. The cape she'd worn must be in the room still. She kept to the wall to steady herself. As he passed her she called out, "Pretty boy," reaching limply for him, but then slid down onto the settee as if the gesture had robbed her of all energy.

He eluded her easily and merged into the cramped halls leading to the parlors, wriggling through clusters of guests and boys, realizing that he should have gone the other way, down to the laundry, where at least he might hide until the anniversary was over, even at the risk of never leaving it again.

Instead he emerged in the foyer before the parlors and ran right into Bogrevil, who was escorting someone from the main stairs. "Well, well, escaped from a harem, have we? Where's your tray?" He seemed to be drunk, but it only increased his malevolence. He turned to the guest behind him and asked, "May I recommend to you this handsome creature? He's very quiet, but you can tell just by lookin' that his essence is the stronger for it."

The guest considered him for but a moment, then nodded. "Definitely," he said, a deep, almost sultry voice.

"Good," Bogrevil replied, and clamped onto Diverus's wrist. "Time spent with an afrit will do you proper, my boy. World of good, take *you* down a peg and remind Eskie who she owes her life to." He started forward as the besotted woman with the gold mask emerged out of one narrow corridor, still lacking half her costume. She pointed at Diverus, the blindfold hanging from her hand. "Pretty boy," she repeated. Bogrevil turned to the client, grinning. "See there, he's very popular." He snatched the blindfold from her and snapped it to get the sentinel's attention. The huge Kotul took the woman by the shoulder and guided her toward the stairs. Bogrevil called out, "Be sure someone retrieves—ah, ne'er mind, I'll do it meself." Then with an exaggerated wigwag he led the way down the narrow hall. Boys and clients stepped aside to let him through.

In the afrit corridor Bogrevil directed them to the room the woman had just abandoned. He marched Diverus to the box in the corner and, by twisting his wrist, forced him to his knees. "Get in there. Now." He didn't let go, so Diverus could only crouch beneath the steeled tines and step both feet inside. Bogrevil released him. "If you try to come out of here," he said, "I'll drown you myself. You understand?"

The client, with obvious dismay at the tone of what was occurring, took the blindfold Bogrevil held out to him, and went around to the far side of the water pipe.

Bogrevil swept up the abandoned cape and boots; then, as if a signal had been sounded, he rushed out into the corridor before anything emerged from the hookah, transparently fearful. He might have been in league with the monstrosities, but clearly he didn't want to encounter them.

The curtain snapped shut.

Diverus lay in the box, watching the flicker of candles, listening to the breathing of the client. He waited, anticipating he didn't know what—Eskie had said that it put the victims to sleep before preying upon them, but how specifically he still didn't know. He didn't want to be awake.

Slowly he became aware of the candles growing dimmer, the light fading away. But the darkening room only made him more alert. Then on the curved ribs above him something slithered. Its grayish fingers ended in black talons, and it pulled itself along the tines as if climbing up a wall rather than dragging along horizontally. He was sure he was supposed to be asleep by now. The glowing orbs of its eyes became visible at the bottom periphery of his sight, and he squeezed his eyes closed so as not to see more. Shortly he could feel it directly above him, feel it staring down at him with such a magnetic pull that finally he couldn't help himself.

He looked up.

Gone was the white-eyed monster, gone the tines of bone and the room. Above him on a sharp outcrop of rock sat a beautiful sphinx. Her hair was plaited in a rainbow around her smooth and perfect face. Her full breasts rested upon her paws, and her paws upon a pink marble ledge. She watched him with such tenderness that his chest grew chilly with emotion. He wanted to climb up on the ledge with her, to rest beside her. She smiled to him, reading his thoughts. Then she raised her head, looking past him, and he turned to follow her gaze.

On the far side of him a strange black booth had been set up in the sand, with a pale blue screen in its center. The world about them darkened. While the screen began to glow, the shadows of two grotesque caricatures of people walked across it as if their joints had been broken, then began to talk to each other. One looked like Bogrevil. He could hear the shadows speaking, but it was gibberish. Somehow, though, he knew the story being told, knew what they were going to do. He watched, laughed at humor that eluded him, and was stabbed by sadness at tragedy he didn't comprehend. She spoke then, the sphinx, despairing. "You know this story?" He nodded, still watching, though he couldn't think of its name. "I played so small a part," she bemoaned. "But if my role were larger, then we should not have met at all in this place." He couldn't fathom that. "It wants music," she commented. "That will come soon enough, I know." Her voice broke.

He turned back to her, his heart wrenched by the sound of her weeping. Tears flowed to her paws, and dripped off the claws. He cupped his hands until they were full, and her image rippled in the held pool. He couldn't understand how, when everything was dark around her, she continued to glow as if in soft bluish moonlight.

He raised his hands and drank her tears as if he might absorb her grief. When he opened his eyes, she was receding, though neither of them seemed to be moving at all.

"Sleep, my darling," she said, and he knew the voice at last though he hadn't heard it for such a long time: She hadn't become a merwoman at all. She'd changed into this doleful manticore. "Sleep," she said again and though he wanted to run and embrace her and never let her go this time, he could only watch her shrink into the distance, a source of retreating light that filled in with black despair and was soon gone altogether.

He turned back to the play, but the booth was closed, the screen covered; then the remaining light dimmed and the booth also disappeared. Everything was dark now, and he was alone, floating, a mask on the waves, free of anguish, of pain, of the helplessness of his life, and he released himself to the will of the black water as it carried him away. Out to sea, he hoped.

When he awoke he didn't at first know where he was. His mind was confused, jumbled. Candles burned nearby, reflected in the white bone of the tusk-like tines above him, making them seem to dance as the candle flames flickered. He was in a bed, but the sides of it were higher than he. It was a box, really, a shallow box; and not far away stood a towering brass water pipe.

Then he remembered, and he knew what had been done to him, but he was so drained of emotion, of fear, anger, that he didn't react to the knowledge, only contemplated it as if the emotions belonged to some other person.

Eskie should be coming for him soon. She would help him back to the dormitorium, put him to bed, and later bring him some broth, something to revive him. That sounded very appealing. He realized that he was ravenously hungry. Now he understood why the boys let themselves be chosen, even fought for the privilege of service. Already he wanted to be with the sphinx again, to hear her voice, his mother's voice; he needed to tell her that he loved her and wouldn't let them throw her into the sea this time. No, he would cling to her as she moved into darkness, wrap his arms around her neck, and climb upon her back and ride her so that she couldn't disappear.

He licked his lips. They were dry, and licking them made them sticky. He remembered again that he was hungry.

After a while he crawled from the box on his own. No one remained in the chamber. The blindfold lay curled on the floor beside the pipe as if for the next client. He stood, swaying, and placed his hands on the belly of the pipe to steady himself. It was cold, and when he drew his hand away, his palm was imprinted with the designs etched in the bronze. He rapped his knuckles against it to listen to the sound echo inside. What did that do to the afrit? he wondered. Did it slumber after it had drunk of someone like him? Did it hear him? Know he was out here? He'd have liked to communicate with it, if only in the dream—if it *had* been merely a vivid dream and not a real vision of Nechron's world, of some manner of afterlife. What did afrits show everyone else? He closed his eyes and rocked his head. His existence was suddenly compressed, the whole course of a lifetime squeezed inside him. His eyes ached as if they'd seen too much.

He shuffled away from the water pipe, made it to the doorway and then out into the hall. No one was there, either. Candles still burned in a few of the chambers, but in most the curtains hung open upon darkened rooms. Perhaps even now Eskie was helping someone else back to the dormitorium.

He shambled along the hallway, looking into the darkened and empty chambers, wondering if everyone else was asleep and he the only one left.

The corridors proved to be confounding this morning. He would turn a corner but almost immediately forget what hallway he'd been in prior to it. In no time at all, he lost his way to the sleeping quarters. Down a corridor that should have returned him to the dormitorium, he found himself at the base of spiraling steps that he'd never seen before. What if they took him up and out of the paidika? Might there be an exit no one had been told about, that only Bogrevil knew? He had to see, because he couldn't imagine he would ever find his way back here again.

He climbed slowly, carefully, using hands and feet, and sometimes knees. He felt like a turtle. Each step took all his effort, and he tried to count them as he climbed but too soon forgot the number. He became aware of a noise, not voices exactly, but cooing and deep groans. He raised his head and saw that the steps ended in an open doorway. Dim light spilled down from it. He crabbed up a few more steps until his head was high enough to see through the opening into what he knew immediately were Bogrevil's private rooms. Neither of them saw him. Bogrevil was too focused on sensation, his eyes closed, mouth drawn back in a feral grin, and foam bubbling on his lips. Eskie lay with her arms out, head back. Her legs were locked around his waist. She moaned once, licked her lips, and turned her head, folding her arms around it in a gesture expressive of pleasure.

Diverus sank down and let his head rest on the cold step. He couldn't drown out the grunting and murmuring. Beyond that what could he do? He could barely crawl. If he intruded, Bogrevil would kill him before he'd dragged himself through the doorway—and for what? Eskie wasn't being harmed, wasn't performing against her will, not like he had done. Then he imagined that he saw the sphinx again, and he forgot his will.

He slid back down the steps, more confused than ever. Eskie had warned him, protected him against Bogrevil, yet here she was, his mistress, his lover if love was involved in the repulsive bargain. He wanted to feel betrayed but foundered in prying loose enough emotion. Why did he have to know this? He didn't want to know it. Better that the afrit should wipe away all his memory and return him to the imbecilic state in which he'd lived his former life. What good was knowing the truth of things?

He stumbled through the maze of halls again, and finally into a dark and unoccupied guest room, into the box, and onto his belly. Let the creature come for him, let it steal his soul and send him forever to live with the sphinx. He didn't care.

He fell asleep like that, but no dreams came, and if the afrit perched above him, he never knew. He woke only when one of the boys came to clean the room and found him. Thinking him dead, the cleaner ran out, calling Bogrevil's name and shouting, "Dead! Dead!"

Diverus pushed himself onto hands and knees. His joints ached. He was like someone who had been laid down by a fever and, having come through it, wants to get away from his illness. His legs held him as he plunged across the room. He was almost at the door when Eskie arrived. She'd run from wherever she was, and when she saw him her breath caught. She reached toward his face. "Thank the gods, you aren't dead. I thought . . . I was looking for you, you need—"

He slapped her hand aside. "I don't need anything from you."

"Diverus, what is wrong?"

He replied, "Get out of my way, please. I have to . . . have to eat something." He couldn't even look directly at her, but smoldered, his jaw clenched; yet he didn't move.

She read his inaction, his fury, and understood, though not how or when he'd found out. "Diverus," she said, "you can't be in love with me."

His whole face burned; his eyes scalded. "I'm not," he said.

"He *owns* me. My family sold me to give them enough money to live on. My father was ill; he needed things we couldn't afford. Medicines."

"Shut up."

"They sold me to him. I'm his *slave*. More so than you or any of these boys you live with." She twisted at the waist and pulled back one sleeve of her shirt and rolled her arm so he could see the dark crescent near her shoulder. "This isn't a birthmark. It's his sigil. It doesn't come off. I'm property. That's all I am, all I can ever be." Then she stepped aside and he pushed past her; he was not ready to hear explanations or excuses, least of all hers.

He shoved through the curtain and through a gathering of boys, then took one of the narrow halls that led to the kitchen level.

The cook was chopping turnips as Diverus entered. Glancing up, the cook said, "Well, well, come for your special treat at last, my little harem boy?" At the same time he set down his knife, placed both hands on the cutting board, and leaned forward. "Is it my turn finally, hmm?" As he reached across the board and tousled Diverus's hair, he smiled with vulpine connivance.

Diverus snatched the knife and drove it straight through the cook's other hand and into the board.

The cook shrieked to the ceiling. He clutched the handle but it had been driven hard into the board, and he had to rock it to loosen it, which made him squeal and squeal. His blood began to soak into the pale raw turnips. Diverus grabbed another knife, and this one he held to the cook's throat. The cook clutched the handle stuck into his hand and whimpered. He quavered, his face pale as dough and glistening with sweat. Diverus said softly, "Never." Then he laid down the knife and walked away. Behind him, the cook shrieked again as he finally freed his hand from the board. His cries rose and fell in waves of agony behind Diverus.

In the tight passage Bogrevil knocked past him, giving him a cursory but suspicious glance before hurrying to the kitchen. More boys followed; a few glared accusingly at him, others with a look more akin to worship. His own cored-out look challenged them all.

He went back to the dormitorium, to his pallet, and lay down. The others in the room were either asleep or too weak to do more than watch him lurch past. Kotul, asleep on his belly on the largest pallet, was sprawled halfway onto the floor.

By the time Diverus had fallen upon his pad he was shaking and feverish, and he drew his legs up, folding his arms around them, and waited for sleep that wasn't going to come. Strangest of all was that nobody pursued him for his crime. He expected them to pour into the room, Bogrevil and his legion of boys, to drag him against his will down to the laundry pool, there to drown him in the dark and toss his miserable, weighted corpse into the sea just as he had helped dispose of the dead client. Through the vents high up on the wall, he could hear distant noises from the underspan, from the world where he'd been a captive to his own helplessness. He'd escaped it only to be a captive here, no higher nor closer to the surface of the world. The difference was that he knew it now, but knowing improved nothing. Knowing was worse than being an idiot. He wished almost that the gods had never made him aware; he'd been better off when nothing stayed with him, when the abuses rolled off, one after the other, and he felt nothing more than the immediate pain, the anguish of the moment, forgotten soon enough. This—this thinking, feeling, knowing—hurt too much, demanded too much of him. He didn't want to die; he just wanted to lose himself once more. His brain whirled around the subject, and he closed his eyes to wring it out, to exorcise thinking, like a demon from his mind.

Eventually Eskie entered the hall. She carried a tray through the dormitorium, which she placed on the floor beside his bed. A large bowl and a fist-sized chunk of bread lay on it. She didn't expect him to take it from her. "You need to eat," she said, as if to the whole room. "If you want me to leave, then I will, and you can feed yourself."

When he didn't move, she nodded as if satisfied. "All right, then." She left the bed and walked with growing speed to the door and out again.

The bowl sat within his line of sight unless he rolled over onto his side, turning his back to it. Steam snaked out of it, and his stomach clenched at the smell. His eyes felt as if they would at any moment collapse into his skull; the sockets themselves throbbed. He had to order his hand to reach for the spoon. Once he had it, he had to concentrate to direct himself to lean up on one elbow, and then he had to drag himself closer to the tray.

The soup was hot and oily and thick. If the cook had made it for him, it must have been before . . . before the accident. Otherwise it would have been full of broken seashells or something else to kill him. Or maybe Eskie had made it. If only he'd spoken to her, said what he felt, she would have stayed, would have fed him as she did all the other boys. They didn't care that she belonged to Bogrevil, why should he? He was a boy, nobody at all. She wasn't his age. She'd never given him a reason to hope or even believe—no, that wasn't entirely true. She had warned him, had protected him, had in her way made him feel special and different from all the others. He didn't want to be just one more boy in the paidika, his body a source of someone else's pleasure and an afrit's meal until he was nothing but a husk, back where he began, stupid and helpless forever. Why would anyone desire that? But when he closed his eyes, he saw the sphinx again, alive and bright and loving, and he wanted her more than anything. He trembled with desire.

By the time he wiped the crust of bread around the bowl to sop up the last bit of the liquid, he felt newly born. He'd have crawled into a box for another client now—at least, he felt as if he could. It would turn off his mind, set him free from what he knew. Later. Let them ask him later.

He lay back and was soon asleep.

The paidika didn't open for business the following night. The events of the anniversary had taken a toll and required recovery. Some boys had indeed been subjected to the afrits twice that night, which Bogrevil never would have allowed any other time. The ones who weathered the abuse best needed to be carried to their beds; even when fed afterward, they showed little improvement. Recovery would be slow. One boy had, like Abnevi, gone mad, his mind scrambled. "One more for the laundry" was Bogrevil's glum response. It meant one less money earner among his brood, for which reason if no other he didn't punish Diverus directly.

The cook, with a hand swollen to twice its normal size, took to his bed, where he intended to remain for days, whining that he must be avenged.

Food became a matter of immediate concern, and Eskie had to take over in the kitchen. Without sustenance the exhausted boys would not recover, and Bogrevil needed them active by the second night. He knew perfectly well how the cook goaded and teased certain boys and that he'd repeatedly tried to have his way with some of them; in Bogrevil's opinion the bastard was lucky the blade hadn't ended up between his ribs. Nevertheless, Diverus had to be seen to pay for inflicting it. Such an act of rebellion could not be allowed to pass unchallenged, or soon the entire paidika would be out of control, stabbing cooks, snubbing clients, and most importantly disrupting the afrits. Those monstrosities would not take to being inconvenienced for long, and the price would be Bogrevil's to pay. His servitude to them had another year to run, after which he suspected he would be dispatched or, if lucky, merely forced to find someone to take his place before the ephemeral monsters released him. It wasn't as if he could escape them on his own. Where, in a world of ocean, could he hide from water creatures? He'd been young and insanely foolish, a ship captain's cabin boy emptying the slops over the bow, unaware that their ship had entered demon-haunted, seaweed-ensnarled doldrums, oblivious to the horrors swimming in their wake. And then when he'd befouled them, he'd laughed in their faces. It was a wonder they had let him keep his; but afrits did nothing but for a reason. They had wanted something from him. They needed a human agent for their purpose. Oh, to be a ship's mate again, to be free of these infernal tunnels, to breathe sea air and not worry about the likes of these misfortunate boys . . . which thought brought him back to the problem at hand.

The simplest solution seemed to be to rent out Diverus as often as possible from now on.

There is much in life that seems random, events for which no obvious purpose is apparent even though they may compound. In the aftermath only can a pattern be discerned—missteps lead to an inevitable conclusion, an inescapable fate, sometimes doom and sometimes triumph. We curse the one and pretend to be responsible for the other, while neither fortune is true.

The next evening the paidika opened for business again. Only two of the boys were still out of commission, and that was excuse enough for Bogrevil to recommend Diverus to some of the clients. Immediately this proved unnavigable: He had been too clever. Previously he had talked so many of them *out* of engaging the handsome "damaged mute" that the first time he proffered

Diverus like some newfound treasure, he got a look of such intense shock and loathing from the client that he made a great show of laughing nervously and proclaiming the suggestion "just my little joke," before sending the client off with a reliable boy at half the going rate by way of an apology. Then he sat on the steps with a blighted look about the eyes.

He could not recall which or how many of the various strutting peacocks he'd dissuaded from Diverus in the past. There had been so many. If he didn't refrain from promoting Diverus, he would surely see his reputation suffer—one could not habitually cover such an injudicious suggestion with a bit of laughter or soon the clients would decide for themselves that he was unreliable, and then he would find himself at the mercy of the afrits' smoke. However he looked at it, promoting Diverus spelled doom.

The result was that Diverus was demoted back to walking about with a tray strapped to his head, and Bogrevil chose the last remaining punishment available when he loudly ordered Diverus to clean the three parlors after everyone had gone. "An' before you retire, too—you don't sleep till these rooms is spotless!" He had to hope that such a bellowed exaction sounded harsh enough. At least until he could think up something else. Meanwhile, he discovered that he had a much more pressing—and annoying—problem: his musician.

After a night of blissful accompaniment provided by the donated trio of players, Bogrevil found the out-of-tune plinking of the household instrumentalist no longer tolerable. It was a shortcoming that needed remedy, or else he would assuredly strangle the talentless lad in short order.

The trio had left behind a shawm, bestowing it upon the paidika as a kind of lagniappe, for indeed they had been richly compensated by the lubricious crowd all through the night, more so than at any venue where they'd previously performed. Bogrevil had even petitioned to buy their contract from the guest who happened to be their owner, but the price proved wildly immoderate. Nevertheless, he couldn't—he just couldn't—go back to the discordant torture that had graced the parlors before then. How had he ever tolerated it?

In a moment of brilliance—at least, he thought so—he proposed a contest to all the boys in the house, that whoever was able play the shawm would be relieved of all other cleaning and serving duties and *elevated* to the position of musician, a proposal dependent upon their ignorance of the fact that *musician* was not a title currently deserving of any respect at all, and certainly not something to which one aspired given the verbal abuse their master and his customers had heaped upon the hapless boy and his tuneless lute from the very first night. For those serving, however, the prospect was so much better than their current station that, one after another during that slow night, they took up the shawm and tried to play it—with unsurprising if excruciating results.

If an untuned lute was a pitiful thing to hear, the squeals of a tortured reed proved infinitely worse. Many of the boys could produce noises on it, but no one was able to produce music. For the paidika the only consequent benefit was that arriving clients were quick to pay for and select a boy for the evening and go off to a distant chamber just to escape the teeth-grating cacophony.

Word of the contest spread to the depths of the laundry, and those with enough sense and a desire to escape their fate made the climb up and crowded the hallways. Abnevi was brought along, too, but unhinged as he was he could neither determine which end of the shawm went into his mouth nor tell when—as it happened, never—he was making music.

Watching each of his peers fail, Diverus found no reason to try it himself. He knew he had never held a musical instrument in his life. Instead he stayed away from the parlors and out of Bogrevil's way, even hiding in the stairwell to Bogrevil's chambers, where he managed to doze awhile.

Finally, late in the night, long after all the boys had tried and failed and retreated dismally to their inescapable duties and from there finally to bed, he entered the empty middle parlor to gather mugs and plates to carry to the kitchen. Some client's grubby hand had smeared a wall with an oily print, and he brought in a bucket from the kitchen and scrubbed at the mark.

Having cleaned the handprint, Diverus wandered over to the pillows where the lute and the shawm lay. For all their efforts no one had managed to coax a single musical strain out of the shawm. It seemed likely to Diverus that the hapless musician would have his job back tomorrow. Perhaps he would improve now that his position had been so threatened. Perhaps he would practice.

Diverus picked the shawm up to look at it more closely. The reed mouthpiece had been deformed by teeth biting it too hard, boys clamping and chewing on it in an attempt to accomplish what they could not through blowing. The tubular body was still gaily painted, though the lacquer was worn away around the holes from many fingers over many years. The wider bell had been chipped, but long ago. It now bore Abnevi's teeth marks, too. It had seen a lot of use before arriving here.

The instrument felt odd in his hands, soft and pliable, but he assumed that this was because his arms were tired. His palms seemed to slide around the shawm as if they and it were old friends. Without thinking he lifted it to his mouth, and his lips pressed tightly around the reed. His eyes rolled closed. The sound of blood roared in his ears; then, distantly, he heard a drone that rose and fell and swirled, catching him up. He felt as if he were approaching the place again where the sphinx dwelled—close, he was so close, and the swirl of the music took on added urgency as he strained, and failed, to reach that place. He could almost hear her voice again. *It wants music*—the whisper threaded past him in the darkness of his mind.

When he opened his eyes a client was staring at him. Perhaps the man had been sitting outside one of the private rooms, disheveled and drunk on the essence he'd smoked; he was pressed against the tiled edge of the doorway as though it were the floor and he had fallen there. His hands pressed to his face beneath a look of wonderment, or shock, as if what he'd heard had cut into some private and forgotten piece of his soul.

A few moments later Bogrevil arrived from wherever he had been. The disquiet of his features might have been rage, and Diverus, reacting to the look, quickly put down the shawm and stepped away from it. "I'm sorry," he said. Confused by what he'd done—not really certain what he'd done—he spoke the words before he could compose himself. He hadn't meant to speak, but he couldn't take it back, too late.

The master of the paidika then proved himself a master of the obvious. "You spoke," he said, and in those two syllables was an undertone that said he ought to have known all along.

"I—" He could think of nothing to say, and his voice sounded as raw and strange as when he'd spoken to Eskie. He cleared his throat, lowered his eyes. In the shadows behind Bogrevil, others were arriving, stumbling, shambling.

"Never mind the words now. Pick that thing up." Bogrevil pointed at the shawm.

Reluctantly, Diverus obeyed. "I meant no harm," he said.

"Put it to your lips again."

He needed no coaxing: Drawn to action by the very touch of the shawm, he tasted the reed again, tasted his own spit, and in an instant the sound emerged. He tried to watch his fingers close over the holes, to watch as a tune settled over him like a cape, coming from he knew not where; but his eyes rolled up of their own accord and he floated away, back into the dreamspace where she dwelled. His mother the sphinx was there, somewhere; he could feel her like a breeze upon his cheek, and in the distance that pale rectangle of light that he'd seen in his vision, and there, the pink slab of marble . . . Whether the song lasted one minute or ten, he didn't know, but when he returned to his senses he saw that the client in the front had sunk to his knees and was sobbing. Others—boys who should have been abed, other clients who emerged from the corridors— gaped at him, struck dumb. Weaving through the paidika, the sound had pulled them here, its magic so powerful that clients had come without their masks and costumes. Two women stood in their midst, having shed their male disguises; one was half undressed, as was the man with her, suggestive of the manner in which they'd been sharing the afrit smoke. And the afrits—had they allowed the people to escape? Did the music affect them, too, the way the flute of a snake charmer entranced a cobra?

With the tune ended, some of them looked at the others with a shock of recognition, as if they were acquainted outside the brothel and would never have dreamed of finding one another here. At the back, Eskie peered appre- hensively between two of the boys.

Bogrevil drew a deep breath. If he'd been angry at first, the wide-eyed look upon his face now wasn't rage at all, but something like ebullience. He en- tered the parlor and held out his hand. Diverus gave him the shawm.

"Why," he asked gravely, "have you kept this skill, this gift—for it's surely what the gods gave you upon that dragon beam—why have you kept it a se- cret from us?"

"I didn't know I knew it."

A moment longer Bogrevil stared at him. Then he laughed deep in his throat, once, twice. He turned to look at the assembled clients. "*This* is my anniversary present." He pointed back at Diverus, chuckling as he did. "I'm blessed by the gods themselves, am I not?" He seemed to become aware of the state of his audience, cleared his throat, and then to no one in particular stated, "Yes, it is not the policy of this establishment to cater to the female sex. It's not my prejudice, but the law of the span, which I'm sure everyone on the span knows. This being a special night, exceptions will be made . . . still, let's not be *advertising* our violation, hmm?" When no one moved, he added, "He's not going to play no more right now, so get off."

At that they did disperse, albeit with reluctance, some up the stairs, others to collect their masks and costumes. The boys looked their new musician over with a mix of resentment and reverence. Bogrevil had Kotul help the weeping client up and on his way, and then said to Diverus, "I can't let you have this back just yet. Got to get them all out the door and the rest of us to bed, or we'll be standing here all night. You could transfix the sun and hold the night with that reed." He bent down and lifted the untuned lute by its neck from the pillows, then handed that to Diverus. "Here. Amuse yourself with this instead."

He strode back to Eskie and presented her the shawm. "For safekeeping. We'll need it later, assuming—" He was interrupted by the strumming of the lute. Still out of tune, yet that had not kept Diverus from plucking a lilting phrase from it. Bogrevil wheeled about and watched him, amazed.

Diverus held the lute away from himself, and with his free hand turned the pegs one by one as though knowing exactly how much each needed to be adjusted. His eyes were strangely unfocused, as if he were listening to someone tell him how to accomplish this. When he strummed it again, the lute was in tune. The sound of it was as sweet as a zephyr, one that had never blown before through that sunken place.

Clients coming to the steps to leave stopped again and watched.

Bogrevil hurried to Diverus and covered the strings with a hand. Glazed dark eyes focused on him again, uncertain in their gaze. "Was I . . ." He saw the effect upon everyone and didn't need to finish the question.

A small hourglass drum lay on its side, and Bogrevil picked that up. He snatched the lute away and handed him the drum, nodded at it. For a moment Diverus caressed its shape as if by instinct, as he might have done the body of a lover. Seating himself on the pillows, he began to play an easy, loose beat, and shortly added flourishes, making it complex, intriguing. There was magic in the rhythm beneath his palms and fingers.

"You can play anything?" asked Bogrevil.

Diverus stopped. He didn't realize he had sat. He looked up at his owner. "I don't . . . I don't know where it comes from. I don't know how it happens."

"Well, don't you worry on that, 'cause I do," Bogrevil replied, and the look he wore was of a man envisioning great wealth.

Diverus became the celebrity of the paidika. The few who'd heard him that first night came back again the next, accompanied by a few more. While he played, the clients were transported, almost as they would have been by afrit smoke, and for far less investment—at least initially. They stood, leaned, sat, forgot their drinks, their conversation, even their established goal in coming here. One or two wept during a mournful passage he played on the shawm, and even Bogrevil looked stricken by the beauty of it when Diverus finally stopped—but not so stricken that he didn't jump up immediately and take advantage of the now pliable clientele. It turned out that the music weakened their resistance to Bogrevil's overtures. He easily matched them with boys, now also similarly docile, and sent them all off to the back rooms, even collecting a *higher* fee than he'd previously asked. His instinct for profit assured him that they would pay—he could smell their surrender—and they did, unhesitatingly. Either dazed by the music or magnanimous because of it, they met his price and went off to smoke the boys.

Almost immediately someone petitioned for Diverus's company; Bogrevil was ready for that with a fee that he would never have asked for any boy before. The client looked stricken by the figure, but Bogrevil justified it. "For you to have him to yourself deprives everyone else of his magic—the music stops, you see. The smoke sucks the will out of him this night and likely tomorrow. The cost has to compensate for that much loss. You ain't paying *me*, see, you're paying all these good people to deprive them of the serenity he provides. But if you're willing to cover it, he's yours, make no mistake." The client hastily declined and chose another, but that was all right. Bogrevil had his sights on other evenings. Word would get out, and someone would come along and pay it simply *because* the price was so exorbitant.

Meantime, word of the gods' musician spread across the span.

Weeks passed, with Bogrevil fine-tuning performances, limiting the shawm to a few minutes a night or whenever a fight threatened to break out. Diverus developed a sense of when to pick it up in order to quiet the customers.

The shawm soon became but one among dozens of instruments: As word of him spread, so did the story that he could play anything given to him. At the end of the first week someone placed a santur before Diverus and handed him two sticks. He set down his lute, accepted the sticks, and with almost no pause delicately hammered a plangent tune that made people shiver. The next night someone gave him a single-stringed fiddle with a bow, and he made it sing as if with a human voice.

Two nights after that Kotul at the bottom of the steps called for Bogrevil, who came running from the back, thinking that a great disaster had befallen them. What he found was a line of curiosity seekers that extended all the way up the steps; each person had brought an instrument, and each wanted to make Diverus play it. It was a disaster in the making. The business of the paidika was becoming the performances of Diverus.

Thinking quickly, Bogrevil shouted up the steps, "It's a condition of this establishment that if the boy can play your instrument, it remains *with* the establishment." The line of turbaned, masked, cloaked men and women roared with indignation, but Bogrevil waved them silent. "Look here, nobody's making you come down here like this—you have two choices. You either rent his time privately, in which case you can use him as you like, or you accept the challenge that he'll play anything you hand him. The boy don't come cheap, but that's how it is. He's blessed, and you pay for that."

The line broke up. Only a few remained to accept the rules and challenge the boy with their obscure instruments. They all went home empty-handed, but in most cases not until Bogrevil had packed them off to one of the rooms in back. Even losing, they were transported by the music.

Disaster was averted, and money flowed copiously. Bogrevil thought that if he could sustain this level of income for even a few months, he would retire from the brothel with enough wealth to flee to some large isle—oh, there were some big enough, he'd heard it from travelers, five or six spans on— where he would live far away from the demons, the ocean, and the children for the rest of his life.

The pile of instruments surrounding Diverus grew steadily, a testament to his magical skill. He would pick up the simplest ocarina and then a small harp, without hesitating, without thinking, and play. Bogrevil luxuriated in the attention as if it were all about him.

Then one evening, moments after they had opened their doors for business, Mother Kestrel arrived. She had with her three youths, and they shoved aside the boy on the door and went down the stairs together in a cluster, a four-headed dreadnought. Above them the boy at the door stuck two fingers in his mouth and whistled a signal to Kotul at the bottom. The group made it halfway down before he stepped into view like a barbican gate dropped in their path. Her boys drew up and eyed her nervously. One complained, "You didn't tell us about *him*."

"I couldn't, now, could I, being as how I've never been down this far."

Bogrevil, sent for the moment the alarm was sounded, appeared beside his behemoth. "Ah, Mother K, *lovely* to see you as always," he said. "Of course, you're not really supposed to be here during business hours, are you? I mean, there *is* a prohibitive policy regarding undisguised female clients. 'Course, maybe you'd be unaware of that, bein' as how you're no client."

She slipped down a few more steps while her escort hung back. "I'm not makin' a delivery this time."

"Well, there's a pity, because they look strapping strong, your youngsters. I can always use boys with good constitutions. They last so much longer."

"I'm here to talk about the idiot."

Bogrevil glanced around as if to identify the subject. "I'm afraid," he said at last, "I've got no idiot here at this time. My boys are rather more than that." A tune played on a lute floated up the stairwell, crisp as a chilled wine.

"That's what I'm talking about," she said. "The stories come to me that our lad finally showed his gifts, what he got on the dragon beam."

"*Our* lad? I wasn't aware we'd ever coupled, you and I."

One of the boys sniggered. Mother Kestrel came closer. "You know who I mean," she accused. "Word is, you're taking in a lot of coin on account of his gifts."

"Well, *some*, certainly. But you know, we struck a bargain, you and I, when I took him in—that all his gifts and the proceeds from those gifts were to be mine alone—"

"I spoke in haste."

"No doubt you did. You were aggrieved to have looked after him and took my recompense for your trouble. I recall that you were paid agreeably and that you discarded him with a great expression of relief."

She stood a moment longer. "So you won't cut me a share in him now that he's valuable."

"No," he replied. "I don't think I will. We concluded our bargain where he is concerned. Now, should you care to fob off another one so blessed by the gods, I'm sure I could be persuaded to pay less up front in exchange for what might manifest through divine intervention later on. It is a risk, isn't it?"

"Bastard."

"My dear, that's a given, so you gain nothing by pointing it out." He reached into a pocket and produced a gold coin. "Here." He tossed it up the stairs to her, and she caught it as efficiently as a hawk snatching a meal out of the sky. "Never let it be said I'm ungenerous."

She stared at the coin in her palm, then back at him. The coin was gold, and the fact that he could throw it to her so casually, dismissively, spoke volumes about the money he must have taken in on account of that creature she'd tended. For months and months she'd tended him. One coin only made her greedy for another, but she saw well enough that Bogrevil had no need to give her more. If she wanted her share, she would have to make *not* parting with it too dear for Mr. Bogrevil. She turned and started back up the steps.

"Very nice to see you again, m'dear," he called after her. "Always looking for some good strong boys." Her entourage parted as she pushed through them. One glanced down as if considering Bogrevil's offer, but they all followed after her. The boy on the door was speaking to someone just outside. Mother Kestrel poked a finger toward him, and one of her lads dragged him out of the way.

"A short figure in a gray tunic and domino mask stood outside the paidika that night, blocking Mother Kestrel's path," says the narrator. On the screen of the booth then, the puppet figure of the shadow puppeteer appears, its malachite eyes gleaming, and the audience chuckles as the joke spreads: The puppeteer has become a figure in her own story.

"That figure was a master of puppets, and was eluding the amorous intentions of her hostess on that span—a woman named Rolend, who'd fallen under the spell of the puppeteer and desired his embrace, for she believed the puppeteer to be a man. In that clever disguise the puppeteer had hired a mangy procurer bearing his own torch to take her to a place where women were not allowed entry, thinking that this would protect her from pursuit by Rolend. If her disguise could fool that amorous woman, it would surely serve to gain her entry into the paidika.

"Yet even as she allowed the crone, Mother Kestrel, and her gang of thuggish oafs to depart, the puppeteer saw, back along the alley, the light of a pole-lantern, proof that she had not escaped her passionate pursuer after all. She paid the procurer and stepped quickly through the doorway of the paidika. The procurer turned his attention immediately to the woman and her gang of boys. Waving his torch overhead, he called, 'Madame, good evening to you and your young fellows. If it's further pleasures you're looking for, allow me to guide you to them!' The puppeteer watched him scurry, rat-like, after the woman. Then the door closed and she was safe inside the paidika.

"There was no hint then that she was about to have a life-changing encounter . . ."

Outside, the procurer hung back behind the line of Mother Kestrel's thugs until they had passed the oncoming lantern, which turned out to be a guide and a statuesque woman in a cloak, whom he recognized as the mistress of Lotus Hall. The moment they'd passed, he wove around the trio and up behind Mother Kestrel, desperate to reach her before she exited the narrow lane. "You'll need light to find your way," he said. "Is there somewhere in par-ticular you might wish to see? I know everywhere on the span, the places that would invite you in, not like that *exclusive* place back there." He pronounced *exclusive* as if it disgusted him. While he babbled to her, one of her boys glided up and casually snapped a blackjack against the side of his head, re-lieving him of his purse even as he collapsed. The torch rolled and sputtered, but continued to burn. Mother Kestrel stopped and turned back. She sized up the situation. The lad tossed the purse to her, and she caught it as she walked back to him. "Good lad, Jemmy, I've taught you so well," she said af-fectionately, and tousled his hair. To his utter amazement she then dropped the purse into the lane beside the dazed procurer. "Right now, my dears, we need to be respectable, *terribly* respectable, which means we can't have the likes of him calling the law down upon us. No, no, no, for once we need those very forces ourselves. So, no more mischief. Not till I solve my little problem with Mr. Bogrevil." She walked on.

The lads stood around their victim a moment longer and only grudgingly left the purse there as they followed their leader.

Bogrevil made a sweeping bow and said, "Welcome, good sir, to the land where dreams o'ertake your other life. You would like a boy to smoke for the evening?"

The puppeteer hesitated and glanced from parlor to parlor, uncertain which one was providing the music. "I'll browse?" she suggested in a deep whisper.

Bogrevil stepped back and broadly waved his arm. "By all means." If he suspected at all that she was a woman, he didn't show it. She was disguised, and therefore following the rules. He said, "If I can be of assistance, or when you've chosen, don't hesitate to call upon me."

They made respectful half bows; she strolled past the left-hand parlor and drew up before the middle one. The icy music of a santur trembled behind the beaded curtain there.

Seated cross-legged upon pillows in the middle of the room and sur-rounded by musical instruments, Diverus did not react as she stepped through the curtain. A small boy wearing a tray on his head glided up beside her to offer a drink. She took it, but then turned back, fascinated by the ele-gance of the tune being played and contemplating all the instruments lying about the player.

The musician himself was under the spell of his music: His eyes remained closed and his head rolled, snaking back and forth. His fingers flicked the tiny mallets with astonishing speed and accuracy. He never looked at them once. He continued playing for another ten minutes before the piece found an end, and his eyes didn't open until the last tinny note was fading. Then his back arched and he inhaled sharply, suddenly, as if his spirit had plunged back into him from whatever dreamscape it had flown to on the wings of song.

Some of the others arose and made their way past her on unsteady legs. One was propped up by his rented boy. Outside the gauzy curtain, behind her, she heard Bogrevil directing them to various rooms. The beads hissed as he came into the parlor.

He stopped beside her. "Remarkable, ain't he?"

She nodded. "I wondered, how much . . ."

"For an evening? Don't misunderstand me, young sir, but I doubt you could afford him." Then he named the shocking price, almost apologetically. "You see, if I let you have him for the rest of the evening, then I deprive everyone else of his boundless talent. Thus he comes very dear. No help for it, I'm afraid."

"He plays all of these?" she asked.

"Oh, every single one. In more than a year nobody's yet brought an instrument to our establishment that he couldn't play, and with skill equal to what you just heard."

"The gods favor him then."

Bogrevil laughed. "Indeed, they do."

Leodora considered for a moment while Diverus rolled aside the santur and took up a teardrop-shaped ud. He seemed to shiver at touching it. She asked, "What if I were to wait until the evening was over? No one would be deprived of their music then."

Bogrevil's brow knitted. Nobody had ever proposed that before. The quoted price for the boy's services usually ended the conversation.

"That's hours from now. I mean, I *suppose*," he said, formulating, "the price would be a *little* more reasonable under those conditions. He'll be tired, though—don't know that he'll care to accept. And still higher, I'm afraid, than most of the boys, because the experience will still drain him and he'll still have to recover, and—truth is—nobody's had him like that. It might drain him too much to play *next* night. There's a lot to think about here. I must ponder it awhile."

Leodora nodded as if she understood everything he'd said. But knowing nothing of what actually went on in this paidika, she couldn't fathom what it was that might drain him. "I shall just listen then—if that's all right."

Bogrevil opened his mouth to object, but she touched his hand and a coin slipped between her fingers into his. He glanced at it, surprised and delighted by what he saw; and he wondered why he hadn't thought to charge for the pleasure of listening to Diverus right from the start.

"Listen to your heart's content," he said. "I'll see that he plays the shawm for you before daybreak."

"That's his best?"

"It stops everything in this place when he does it."

"Where did he learn? He surely can't be more than, what, fifteen?"

"Oh, he's a year or more older than you imagine, I'm quite sure. As to where he learned, it's the gods you'd have to ask about that."

The first few plucked notes of another song began. Bogrevil gestured Leodora to a nearby pillow, then withdrew before the spell from the double strings clutched him as well.

She listened, watching at first, but with eyelids soon falling shut as she was spirited away by the sound. She was imagining the song accompanying a performance; it would be the perfect marriage of music with her art. She could not help but wonder if the procurer hadn't been a god in disguise, who had led her to a destination she didn't even know she was seeking. It was the sort of thing a trickster might do, and wasn't the world full of them?

As the last note hovered and faded like a sunset, she opened her eyes and smiled at the performer. He nodded to her and she back at him. The room emptied out then—the remaining patrons going off either with their evening's choice or in search of one elsewhere. The serving boys pushed through the curtain again with their trays, but she waved them off.

"You have incredible skill," she told him. "You must have begun playing very young."

He tilted his head as if considering this. "Yes, I must have—before I was born, I think."

"And you can play them all?"

"So far." He set down the ud. "Is there one you'd particularly like to hear?"

Before she answered there came a distant shout and a loud whistle that abruptly cut off. Then a voice cried, "*Raid!*"

Leodora jumped to her feet. She poked her head through the beaded curtain. The clamor came from the top of the long stairwell. The immense guard at the bottom of the steps had taken a position blocking the way. Out of the other two parlors people bolted, most of them in disguise and all heading away from the steps; they fought one another to get into the narrow halls, where Bogrevil gestured them to hurry. His expression was sour.

"What do we do?" she asked the musician.

"Flee, I think," he advised. "This hasn't happened in all the time I've been here, but we've been instructed again and again so that when it happened we'd know what to do. You should follow me."

He picked up the ud and some of the other instruments. She reached out to accept one of the lutes and a double-reed instrument. "That's a mijwiz," he said. "I'm very fond of it. I'm called Diverus."

"Jax," she replied, and then they were in the foyer and past Bogrevil.

As they entered the narrow passage behind him, someone shouted, "There! Stop them!" It was a woman's voice, and Leodora craned her head to see. At the bottom of the stairs the woman who'd shoved past her as she was arriving was flailing her arms madly. She had four large uniformed men with her, but they were busy combating the giant of a bouncer behind her, and the woman charged after Diverus without protection. Bogrevil stepped in front of the passage then, blocking the way with his body. Behind his back a gleam of light delineated the double-curved blade of the khanjarli dagger in his hand.

It was Leodora's final view of him and of the events in the foyer. Diverus drew her out of the sloping passage and into a broad hall containing dozens of doorways and more passages leading off it. People were running about everywhere, some half undressed and many stumbling as if drunk or drugged. One sat on a small divan, head hanging between his knees, unable to rouse himself enough to take flight. She was surprised at the number of women scurrying from the rooms. Clearly they'd arrived disguised as men and only thrown off the disguises once they'd gained entry to these private rooms. Diverus dodged them all. She glimpsed some of the chambers they passed, each containing a giant water pipe, like a fountain fixture set in the center of the floor. Someone lay sprawled beside one, but most of the rooms were empty, the occupants already gone. In the last one, though, through the slit of the curtain she glimpsed or thought she glimpsed a face inhuman and insubstantial, with fierce marble eyes. She passed it so quickly that she didn't make sense of it, didn't register what she'd seen—a floating form, a ghoulish countenance—

except as an afterimage, like something you can only see when you close your eyelids.

She and Diverus fell in behind a line of boys who were flooding into one dark doorway in particular. It took them down another flight of steps, easily as long as the stairs from the street. Footsteps and voices below echoed back up oddly as off water, and sure enough the room they reached contained a broad pool in which a few boys were laughing and playing, as though what was happening in the paidika was a lark, nothing to concern them.

Beyond the pool an iron gate hung open. Most of the boys and the sensible guests were escaping through it.

Outside, a narrow ledge ran in either direction. They were under the bridge, at ocean level. A few lights shone across the water, where another tower wall loomed, seeming almost close enough to touch in the dark. The water stank of rot.

The ledge was hardly wide enough for the two of them to stand shoulder-to-shoulder. To the left of the gate, boys had lined up, shivering, pressed to the wall of the bridge pier as if this was as far as they were able to come before terror incapacitated them. Their line trailed into the blackness of the bridge. The clientele, on the other hand, had all turned to the right and even now reached the end of the ledge and vanished. Diverus hesitated for a second, but turned and pursued the escaping clients. No one tried to stop him. Encumbered by the instruments in his hands and tucked beneath his arms, he could have done nothing to defend himself if they had. From the other direction a woman's voice called out, "Diverus!" and he went rigid. He glanced back then, first at Leodora, and then beyond, into the depths of the darkness beneath the span. His face twisted up as if he was wincing in pain.

Under his breath then, he whispered, "Good-bye, Eskie," and turned away again. Leodora glanced back, but no one had stepped out, and whoever had called couldn't possibly have heard him.

The clients had disappeared where the ledge ended, as if they'd stepped off into the ocean and evaporated; but it was an illusion. The ledge wrapped around the corner, to roughly carved steps, which led right up the side of the pier. To be sure, they were cracked and treacherous, offering barely enough purchase for both feet placed side by side, but the customers from the paidika climbed briskly up, clustered bodies lambent in the moonlight. The musician and the puppeteer followed them.

Perhaps a third of the way up the side of the pier, the steps reached a landing of sorts. This landing, a broader platform with a rail around it, jutted off the
backside of the tower, and the two of them lingered there to catch their breath.
No one else was coming up behind them; Leodora gazed off across the ocean,
where a single lantern's light glowed distantly. She turned back to find Diverus
leaning far over the rail on the inside of the platform. She pressed around his
shoulder to see what had so captured his attention, and fell upon an astonishing view: the underworld of the span of Vijnagar.

Fires and embers glittered on dozens of levels, as far into the distance as
she could see. From the look of it, the place ran the full width of the bridge.
The glow from the fires suggested structures—an arch overhead and all manner of struts and supports on the far side of that arch, and even more platforms. She remembered that Ningle, too, had supports beneath it, columns
of stone that propped up the great boulevards and buildings. But she had seen
no one living beneath that span.

"That used to be my home," Diverus said.

"Where?"

"Somewhere in there. Someone else lives in it now. Or maybe they've
moved on, too. That woman who raided the paidika is from here. What do
you suppose she told them to get the authorities to act on her behalf? I should
have stayed behind and exposed her, shouldn't I?"

"I don't know how you would have done that," she replied. "She was after
you?"

"She wanted a cut of the profits I brought. I would have been trapped again
if I'd stayed. He wasn't ever going to let me go." He sighed. "Poor Eskie. She *is*
trapped." When she didn't ask him what he meant, he let the matter go. "I've
never seen it like this, not from below. I know where we are now, and there'll
be another landing above us, one that can be accessed from underneath—in
there."

As if to prove his point, a shout burst from above them, then another more
like a scream, which grew abruptly louder. A body hurtled past.

Leodora sprang back from the rail. Diverus didn't even flinch. "I wonder,"
he mused, as though the killing going on above them were a mere inconve-
nience, "if we might want to wait a bit. Let the two sides sort it out." Another
body fell past, this one silent. He leaned over the edge, followed the corpse
down, and then looked up. "The thieves are outnumbered. They couldn't
have anticipated so many all at once. They're used to couples sneaking off to

hide, or their own sort fleeing from officials up above with whatever boodle they've snatched. Easy marks." He tilted his head to one side. "I can't even tell you how I come to know that. I couldn't have known it back then, but someone must have said so, I must have heard it even though I was too dull to understand."

Leodora considered that they with their arms full of musical instruments would be "easy marks," too.

After minutes passed in silence, Diverus started up the second tier of steps, and she followed, wondering all the while why she inherently trusted the strange musician.

The second landing when they reached it was occupied only by a corpse. Though masked, he wasn't dressed in the finery of the paidika's clientele. Moonlight glinted off the hilt of a dagger embedded in his chest. Of the clients there was no sign. A small wooden ladder, nearly horizontal, reached from one of the inner platforms to the edge of the landing. Diverus shoved it away and it dropped, but swung below from ropes and clattered against a lower level. Someone shouted a complaint.

Without a word, he continued his climb up. By now Leodora's legs ached, and she would have liked to sit and rest for an hour. It hadn't seemed, she thought, anywhere near this great a climb down through the tower. The smell leaking out from the underworld grew more intense as they ascended—a greasy, sour stink it was, too.

As they neared the surface of the span, Diverus paused and pointed to where a makeshift platform butted up along the backside of the tower. They could have stepped off the narrow stairs and into the underworld from there. "This is where I used to climb from. My mother took me up, many times. And then Mother Kestrel, too, when she put me on the dragon beam."

"The dragon beam?"

"In the bowl—it's where I learned how to play all of these, though I didn't know it at the time." He continued quickly up the steps, as if to be quit of the subject, but she hurried after.

"How long ago?" she asked.

Over his shoulder he replied, "I don't know, really. A year or more. Bogrevil maintains that I'm seventeen, but he doesn't really know. When I arrived he thought I was twelve because I'd been starved so long, and I couldn't have told him in any case, because I don't know."

Then he rattled up the last steps and through the rail to the surface. She found him waiting for her, alone. The clients had dispersed back into the lanes and streets of the span.

"You must tell me," he said, "why you chose tonight to come to the paidika."

"I was escaping from a situation. I thought if I went there, I could elude someone."

"You're not addicted to the afrits then."

"Afrits," she repeated, and recalled the vaporous thing she'd glimpsed.

Her ignorance seemed to reassure him. He looked around. People strode past, in every case led by someone with a lamp. He and Leodora alone stood in the shadows. "I must impose upon you," he said. "I've nowhere to go, and I know no one up here."

Leodora said, "I can help. In fact, I can offer you employment of a sort that will make use of your talent." A lightbearer approached, and she gestured him over. "Lead us to Lotus Hall," she said, and handed him a coin in advance, in good faith for the distance he must cover. He lowered his lantern on its pole to check the coin, then tucked it into his tunic and directed them to follow.

As they walked, Diverus said, "Would it be a good idea for me to play music? They might be looking for me, or at least listening. Word will travel."

She nodded. "Yes, they might. On *this* span anyway."

"We're going to another?" The idea seemed to take him by surprise.

"Between your troubles and mine, probably the sooner the better. Have you never been on another span?"

He shook his head. "And what is it you do, sir, if I may ask, that you have a use for me?"

"I tell stories," she replied, "which seems to have become a far more complicated occupation than I'd ever imagined."

III
NEW SPANS FOR OLD

ONE

Soter knew that Leodora had eluded Rolend, the love-struck mistress of Lotus Hall, the previous night by fleeing from the hall after the last performance. And he knew she hadn't yet returned by the time he fell asleep; but he'd no inkling that she had come back with someone in tow, or that the booth now concealed a new member of the troupe.

Pushing his way through the curtain at the rear, he found a boy asleep upon the undaya cases and concluded reasonably that he'd come upon a vagrant who'd chosen the darkness of the unattended booth to sleep off his drunk.

"Of all the damned cheek!" he bellowed, and lunged.

The boy reacted by rolling away from the shout, and fell off the cases. Soter banged his foot against a lute that hadn't been there the night before and sprawled across the top case. The only thing he caught was the small nay flute that had been lying beside the boy. In pain and frustration he cursed and clutched his leg.

At that point Leodora pierced the entrance behind him. Soter glanced back at her, triumphantly waved the small flute, and cried, "I caught this little thief pilfering from the puppet cases!"

The boy stuck his head over the top of the case. "That's not true," he said. "I stole nothing!"

Soter swung back and started to grab at him again.

Leodora said, "He's not a thief, Soter. He's a musician. His name is Diverus."

Soter lowered his arm. "Yes, well. Well. I see now that he's dragged his instruments in here. But what are you doing, bringing him in here? We don't need a musician."

"Don't need one? Who is it complains to me every night that we won't be a troupe until we have a *real* musician, because the *smelly runt we've hired can barely play to the end of a single performance*. Aren't those your words?"

Soter recognized that he couldn't win an argument formulated on his own complaints, and changed his tack. "How do you know a scrawny street brat like this is a real musician?"

And so she told him the story of how she had eluded Rolend by escaping into a paidika in the leg of the northern tower of Vijnagar. "Their claim to fame was their musician, who could play any instrument ever made."

"Him?" he asked, the word dripping with skepticism.

"That's right. They were raided and I ran with him. We escaped the raid and the paidika both, and I promised him I would hide him. You won't find a better musician anywhere in Vijnagar. And for that reason I think we should leave Vijnagar now, before the paidika's owner hunts us down."

"First of all," Soter replied, "we're not leaving here till I say so. You're drawing bigger crowds every night. Second of all, please don't tell me you believed twaddle of that sort, and from a brothel, no less! It's how they get them in the door, that kind of story. *He's* some sort of magical musician? Lea, I am amazed at you."

"It's not—" she said, but Soter held out the nay flute and said, "Here, boy, play something. Right now."

Diverus accepted it. He glanced at Leodora. She nodded for him to proceed. He stood up and put the flute to his lips. His eyes closed and his face twisted as if some invisible entity slid beneath his skin. Even in the shadows of the booth, his transformation was evident. Soter tensed as though against an impending blow, though he'd no idea why. The song started softly, gently.

It was so seductive, so lovely, that Soter's eyelids fluttered as if he were about to fall into a trance. Then in horror he identified the tune. It was the one they'd played on *that* span, the one Leandra had danced to. He lunged again at Diverus, yelping "Stop!" as he tore the flute out of the boy's grasp. "What sort of treachery is this?" Betrayal filled his eyes like tears as he looked from Diverus to Leodora. "How do you know that song? Either of you. You've no right—"

"I don't, sir!" Diverus protested. "I don't know what song it was, nor where it comes from. It just . . . it just comes."

"It's a *divine* gift," Leodora insisted. "The music pours through him. I listened to him last night, I *saw* the effect his music had on the clients in that place. On me, Soter."

"Well, *that* song never pours out again, or he finds himself abandoned on the spot, do you understand?" Soter shouted. He made himself calm down, made his hands stop shaking by lowering them to his sides. He gripped the flute tightly. The choice of that song . . . how could the boy have known it? Leodora didn't know. No one left alive knew nor could have found out. It was just a song played by a blind old musician. It had no significance to anyone but him. No, they couldn't have known. But something did. *Something.*

His hand rested against the undaya case, and he snatched it back as if the leather had grown hot. For a moment he stared at it, his mind peeling back the cover, the layers of puppets, the false bottom, until he saw the chalk-white thing lying there. In his vision, it had eyes that opened to stare back at him— eyes that he recognized. The booth suddenly shrank. The sides closed in upon him and the ceiling of the hall was about to crush him flat. He didn't dare look up at it. He slammed the nay flute on the case, turned and dove past Leodora and out of the booth.

In the wide empty hall, he stood with his head back, gasping the air. The vision wasn't real, he chided himself. He was letting Leodora's complaints get to him. She was the one haunted by that figure. Ever since they'd left Bouyan she'd told Soter how she dreamed of being in that boathouse of her uncle's, of hearing a call as if from the whole ocean—that statue calling her name. There was nothing spectral in it—it was nothing but guilt and homesickness playing on her mind. He should never have consented to her bringing that piece of coral along.

He circled the booth then, putting distance between himself and the memory of the song Diverus had played. He had more than enough guilt to bear without that reminder. He barely noticed the cavernous room around him, the empty chairs, the tables, nor did he see the one figure in the hall: a squat gnomish shape seated at a table in the second row and watching him from under its lowered head until he had almost passed by, only then speaking up. "Stand me a drink for old times, would you?"

Soter stopped in midstep as if time had paused. It wasn't possible—first that song and now . . . He came about slowly, warily. Purplish eyes, amused and sharp, met his own. "Grumelpyn?" he said, and drew closer. "By anyone's gods you haven't changed a day—it *is* you, isn't it?"

"Well, if you'll recall, we age slower than your kind, we do. You've changed, of course, but not so's I wouldn't know you—I just never expected to find you traveling the spans again, old man. Not after—"

"Yes, not after that." He took a seat at the table across from the furtive elf. "I was more than happy to stay tucked away forever, but this puppeteer came along, needed managing, and, well, I wasn't doing anything at all but rotting. So I thought, why not, nobody's interested in old Soter, and here I am. But you, now, I thought . . . that is, that last day—"

"A terrible memory, I've blocked it from my mind, don't want to think on that when there have been so many other days worth the memory."

"Of course," said Soter. "Now let me stand you a drink for old times' sake." He got up quickly and wove his way around the tables and chairs to the kitchen, where neither Nuberne nor Rolend was present. He filched a bottle from below the serving counter and carried it and two cups back to the table, all the while speculating on Grumelpyn's motives. He was not so damaged from drink that he didn't remember how he and the elf had parted. It was no cause for camaraderie.

While he poured, Grumelpyn chattered idly. "So, you came from the south of here with this puppeteer called Jax and you're heading north toward my span. I would never have expected you to venture out again. This Jax is the new Bardsham, heh? And where'd he come from, I wonder."

Ignoring the questions, Soter raised his tin cup. The elf drew one hand from out of his sleeves, crossed in front of him, and took the cup. His nails were long and sharp. He clinked with Soter's cup. "This bottle's on me," Soter said. "All of it." He leaned forward on his elbows. "Truth is, since you've turned up, I need your help. We are going north, like you said, but I don't remember the half of it any longer. Been so many years."

"Well, well. You need a map." Grumelpyn grinned with sinister delight, revealing unnaturally pointed teeth. "Fifteen years ago you left me to fend for myself against the Agents, and now you think to buy me with a bottle of inferior liquor and to get my help in the bargain, you do."

"You know that I couldn't have done a thing for you. You don't think I wanted to leave you? For cat's sake, man, it was Bardsham's idea—the only way he could get away was to misdirect those Agents with a decoy. And afterward there was no sign of you or him, and I'd sworn to look after the child. I'd sworn!"

"Oh, yes, I'd forgotten. You never acted to save your own skin. You were thinking of Leandra's baby all the time. Dear, sweet Leandra about whom you could never say enough."

Soter nodded vigorously. "I was, absolutely, thinking *only* of the child. Why do you think I'm with her now?" Too late he realized what he'd said. There was no covering it up.

Grumelpyn tilted his head slyly. "So, then, 'twas a daughter, the baby. And Jax the magnificent puppeteer is she, heh? Bardsham's daughter, well, well. You should have delivered her to my span, let us take her for a changeling. Could have made a fortune. Your people wouldn't have known the difference, the parents weren't coming back, and the replacement child would've obeyed your every whim."

"Changelings are known to be cantankerous if not ungovernable."

"Lies," sneered the elf. "Lies and rumors put about by people who renege on their bargains." He showed his teeth again to ensure Soter got the implicit meaning. "She following in the old man's footsteps all the way, then, is she really?"

Soter lowered his cup. "Grumelpyn, she's better'n he was."

"Oh. My, my. You really should've swapped her, then. We likes a good storyteller."

"Yes, for *dinner*."

"More lies. Elves don't eat children. Generally."

"All the same, I didn't swap her, so wishes are air. I could have abandoned her to the spans and had done with it, couldn't I? And I didn't." He waved his hand about as if to wipe the air clean of rancor. "Look here, I'll pay you for your trouble, for a map."

The elf snorted and set down his cup. "As soon accept coin from a sea slug, I would. I only came here because I had to see for myself if you or Bardsham was connected to this phenomenon called Jax. And now I knows all about it. Wonder who the highest bidder would be for information on his off-spring, hmm? Think there's anyone left who cares? Might the Agents be about on the spans again?"

"Soter?"

At the sound of Leodora's voice behind him, Soter stiffened and his heart sank.

Grumelpyn leaned around him, smiling, to look at her where she stood. "My, my," he said, "I know whose daughter *you* are. Even with that mask on, I know. You've red hair beneath your hood, I'm certain."

Soter could feel her eyes boring into his back, but he remained hunched over his drink as if unaware of her. Grumelpyn rose and extended a hand past him—the one that had been kept hidden in its sleeve. It was shiny and hard as marble. Soter stared past it to the smile, almost a leer, on the little fiend's face. Grumelpyn watched his reaction.

"You're an elf," Leodora blurted.

Grumelpyn glanced about himself, at his torso and arms. "Why, so I am. Imagine that. I must have been transformed." He gave Soter a look of scorn. "Why didn't you tell me?"

Soter's frown curled with displeasure.

Leodora said, "I'm sorry, that was rude. I didn't mean—I meant only that we haven't encountered any elves before, on the other spans."

Grumelpyn waved away her embarrassment. "I'm surprised not at all. Few of my kind travel this run of spans. Except for your neighbors to the north, Hyakiyako, these spans are not partial to the elvish, they're not. And even Hyakiyako just wants us in their parade." He glanced around the room as if expecting to find some enemies. "If word of your extraordinary performances hadn't got out, why, I'd have never imagined old Soter was on the spans again. I was just saying." He leaned forward for emphasis. "Rumor has it you're the essence of an accomplished performer. I am so looking forward to a few performances, myself."

"Yes," Soter replied. "A shame we're not staying *longer*." He craned his head around until he could see her, then to the elf added, "Tonight's our final performance in Vijnagar. Heading north in the morning, in fact. To your friendly Hyakiyako."

"We are?" asked Leodora.

"My misfortune then," replied the elf, and he gave another sly look. All at once he brightened. "At least I'll have the privilege of seeing you once before you go. Do you know any elvish stories, by chance?"

"Some. Soter taught me them."

"Then they'll be corrupted, no doubt." He chuckled. "But still worth seeing, I'm sure, if you would humor an old troll like me and perform one."

"Of course. I'll put one in early." Soter could hear the confusion in her voice.

"And I thankee for it."

When she didn't move, Soter asked, "Is something the matter, Lea?"

"The musician—he really didn't know that song that bothered you. He wasn't lying. I watched him play last night."

"Of course you did, of course he wasn't lying." To Grumelpyn he said, "Auditioning."

"So, you'll let him be if I go off to sleep awhile. I won't come out and find him gone."

"Really, Lea. Where do you get such ideas?" He smiled at Grumelpyn, but the elf continued to smirk over what was being revealed in the conversation. "Of *course* he can stay. Didn't I say we needed a musician?"

"I—" She fell silent.

"What is it, child?" There was something wrong; he knew it but he dared not ask. He wished the elf would leave.

"I'm—I must be tired, that's all. I dozed after we got back this morning, and now it feels to me as if I dreamed this . . . this moment. Only your friend wasn't here. Someone else was."

He turned as far as he could then, to see where her troubled eyes looked; and though she looked where Grumelpyn sat, Soter could almost see what she was seeing. Her expression told him everything. The Coral Man again. He wondered if he could get her to cast it back into the ocean. "Well, as you can see, there's only Grumelpyn. Now why don't you sleep, dear? I'm awake and you need to be rested for the performance tonight. You can always call if you need something." He saw her smile, a sheepish grin.

"I was up all night."

There's the price of mischief, he thought, *no different from her father in that, either.*

"You'll wake me in time."

He knew that she knew he would. The tension in the question intimated more the fear of what might be awaiting her in her dreams. He said, "Of course, dear."

As she left, he watched the elf's gaze follow her.

"Remarkable," said Grumelpyn. "Under that tunic, is she built anything like her mother? That would be something. You should have swapped her for a change—"

"Enough!" Soter slammed his palm against the table. "You are too bold." Grumelpyn closed his eyes and sniggered. "Hate me all you like," Soter said, "but you leave her out of it. She's the reason things went the way they did, believe it as you like, or don't."

"Better than her father—is she really?"

Soter nodded.

The elf leaned back, stretching. "So . . . a map." He grabbed the bottle and poured himself another drink. "You waste your time, Soter, you really do. I mean, I'll do your map for a price. But you won't be able to linger anywhere. Word of her is spreading like blood in water. I wasn't even on this span nor the next and I heard about the Shadowplays of Jax. If I hear, then *they* will hear. Sooner or later. They travel everywhere, after all, and we know, you and I, that they're no myth. You've already lingered too long on Vijnagar for your own good. Or are you perhaps hiding out from more than one party? Someone else looking for her, is there? Did she run off to join the Mangonel Circus?" He held up a hand as if to ward Soter off. "Please, don't tell me, since you'll lie anyway." He sipped softly a moment. "Tell me instead about this musician and his troubling song? Is it something I'd have heard?"

"All I want from you is a map. No threads to link you to me, nothing to put you in jeopardy at all unless you're fool enough to sign it. I couldn't harm you if I wanted to."

Grumelpyn tapped his nails against his cup, the sound like a skittering cockroach. "You mentioned payment."

Soter glared, but when he placed his hand on the table, trapped beneath it were three gold coins. He slid them forward.

Grumelpyn reached out and patted the hand like a cook testing the plumpness of a chicken. At the touch of that petrified flesh, Soter snatched his hand back, leaving the money. "All right, then." Grumelpyn sighed. "For *her* I will do it. She is sweet despite who raised her, and I wouldn't wish to see her go the way of her mother. Do you think she screamed?" His smile widened, eager and repulsive.

Soter lifted his cup and drained it, closing his eyes and then avoiding Grumelpyn's. "I get the map tonight, then," he said.

"That's suitable. After her final performance. I would, perhaps, accompany you north myself, only I'm bound for southern spans. Emeldora, mayhap. Have you played there yet . . . for old times' sake?"

Soter blanched at the name of that fateful span. The taunt was too much for him. He pushed back his chair and stood. "We're done," he told the elf. He strode away.

"Don't forget to wake her," called Grumelpyn. "Or I could return one of these coins to you and you'd let *me* wake her, hey?" He chuckled.

Soter rounded the booth and pushed inside the back.

Diverus flinched and made to leap off the cases, but Soter waved away his fear. "I'm not here to eject you, so you can relax, boy. For now, anyway."

He moved to the rear corner and sat on the floor. He pressed a hand to his forehead. "Gods and ghosts conspire," he said, but not to Diverus, seemingly directing it at the floor.

The sordid conniving elf was, regrettably, right—they needed to move on. They couldn't afford to stay more than a night or two anywhere on this spiral. The money was good, better each night—and that was the trouble. He'd gotten greedy, remembering how things had been with Bardsham. He couldn't afford the luxury of staying anywhere. The troupe of Jax needed to catch up with the gossip, pass it by, stay ahead. Arguably he'd paid for a map when really he was paying for Grumelpyn's advice. The elf might hate him, but he'd told him the truth.

It wasn't until they were standing in front of Vijnagar's north tower the next morning that Leodora found out about the map. She was played out after a second night of little sleep, following a triumphal performance, and did not at first realize what Soter was doing.

The boulevard ended by dividing into three tall tunnel mouths—three oblique routes for leaving the span. She hadn't imagined there would be more than one. All the verges between spans she had seen thus far had provided only one portal. She'd no idea why this one should be different.

At the side of the road Soter set down the case he carried and walked off, leaving Leodora to look after their belongings and Diverus. She had dressed him up in blue robes and a turban encrusted with bright if cheap glass jewels, and darkened his face with a stain made for the puppets. He looked now like a member of a royal household and nothing like the boy who'd only escaped from bondage the day before; the stain made him look older, too. Nevertheless, by forcing him to stop in front of the lane that led to the very paidika from which he'd escaped, Soter had him all but crawling under the lid of one of the puppet cases: He crouched behind them and placed the knapsack containing his instruments on his lap to further obscure himself. Leodora recognized where they were, too. Soter had chosen the worst possible place to stop. She went after him.

He had his back to her and, as she came upon him, she saw he had unfurled a brown parchment with darker brown ink covering it in swirls and lines like veins across a leaf, but also in words, names, a few of which she recognized.

"Do you not know where we're going?" she asked.

He jumped. "I—" He swept the document from sight and turned defiantly to face her. "What do you mean, sneaking up on me like that? Of course I know where we're going."

"At what point did you begin consulting a map, then? You didn't use one before this, or did you? You made such a great show while in your cups of knowing the way across all spans."

It was exactly what he'd intended to claim, and her rebuke left him without a response.

She glanced back at Diverus and the cases. "We have to go now, Soter. He'll run away pretty soon if the paidika's master doesn't come upon him first. It's right at the end of this alley."

"You should never have brought him along," he squawked. The complaint wearied her even more, but she did not want to be drawn into another protracted argument. Instead she gestured at the three tunnels.

"Which one, Soter? If you don't tell me, I'll pick up my case and take whichever one I want and damn the consequences."

"The first one," he answered. She turned away with a dismissive abruptness, and would have been content with the answer had he not added, "Grumelpyn gave me the map."

She stopped. Without turning back she asked, "The elf just happened to have a map for you?"

"I paid him for it."

"Why?" She glanced darkly back at him.

Soter drew his arms against his body as if expecting her to assail him with her fists.

"Why?" she asked again more insistently.

"Because," he answered, then hung his head, "I can't remember." He brought the map into view again and smoothed it open. "We played so many spans, your father and I. More than once, some of them many times. I don't know any longer what comes next, whose establishment we performed in, who gave us lodging, even what sort of span it was. It's all jumbled up, you see. Grumelpyn—his elvish span is way to the north, dozens of spans out. So I knew he would be familiar with everything in between, because he's just traveled it. He drew this for me for the price of a few drinks before the performance." He gazed at her with wounded eyes. "You simply don't trust me enough."

"I simply don't trust you at *all*."

"Leodora, how can you say that? I brought you here."

"You complain that we need a musician, and I find possibly the most remarkable one in the whole world and you say get rid of him. You make secret appointments with old friends and acquire secret maps. You argue with the ghost of my mother as if she's in the room with you—what should compel me to trust you?"

He gaped at her. "How did you—?"

"I overheard you. I have my secrets, too, Soter." She continued back to where Diverus cowered and helped him up. Then she lifted her case, and Diverus his satchel, and the two of them entered the first tunnel, leaving the remaining case behind for Soter.

The tunnel had its own seigneur, who lived in a box-like house in the middle of the passage, from which he controlled the flow of traffic and collected a fee from every traveler. The fees for crossing varied from span to span. More ancient and decrepit spans often had no collectors at all any longer—it was a position that tended to be handed down through families, and families could die out—while on richer spans that considered themselves favored by the gods, the fees might be exorbitant. Soter had dreamed from time to time of being a seigneur. It seemed such an easy life.

Leodora and Diverus waited at the seigneur's booth for him to catch up. A few other people passed them without acknowledgment, paid their money, and kept going, in one direction or another, their footfalls echoing away. The far end was nothing more than a ball of bright light without details, as if the tunnel led straight into the sun.

Soter set his case down beside them and walked up to the booth.

The seigneur—his beaky, chicken-like head protruding from the window on a scrawny neck—named his fee. Soter put a hand to his chest and stepped back. "Outrageous," he grumbled. "That's twice what it used to be to come through here."

Observing this performance, Leodora commented, "I thought you couldn't remember this span."

"I didn't say I didn't remember *any*thing," he replied, using umbrage to disguise that he'd been caught out, but he could see that she was skeptical of all he said. When, he wondered, had she decided not to trust him anymore? And why? If she had heard him talking to the ghosts, that had to have been back on Bouyan, because they hadn't haunted him since. He wasn't sure— he'd never been sure—if his ghosts were real or just the manifestation of his darkest moods; but if they were real, he'd left them behind on Bouyan. Nothing was coming after him. It was what lay ahead that he feared. He couldn't tell Leodora without having to explain why, which he could never do, for she—like her mother—would steer straight for the heart of doom instead of turning away. A thousand lies were better than that. "I'm protecting her," he said to the darkness of the tunnel, as if it were a chant to ward off evil. As long as he adhered to that goal, perhaps the ghosts would leave him alone, let him be. He couldn't make her dispense with this boy. Certainly, he had said all along that they needed a good musician, but he couldn't have predicted she would find someone into whom the gods had fed their magic. Gods' magic was always capricious if not openly treacherous. She was supposed to be collecting stories on the spans, not *people*. Stuck, he was trapped by his own words, which hadn't seemed dangerous when he'd uttered them. The performances *did* need a good musician; but that was something for *him* to find, not her. He'd been guiding Leodora, cautiously, carefully. How had he lost control so easily? It was all the fault of that woman, Rolend, chasing after the great puppeteer, a celebrity she could bed. He'd made light of the pursuit when he should have helped Leodora fend the woman off. Such an insignificant mistake. He'd been in his cups; she couldn't expect him to be ready to offer advice on *every* little detail of their journey. So she'd run off, taken refuge in a paidika, and found someone . . . extraordinary, same as Bardsham had found Leandra. No, no, he didn't care for the parallel there at all.

He glanced up. They were staring at him—both she and the seigneur—and he realized he'd been tangled in thought for an eternity. With a show of resentment he paid the fee and then marched ahead, leaving Leodora and Diverus to catch up.

The dank, echoing tunnel smelled of salt and mildew. Whitish crystals grew like veins across the walls.

As he neared the end he set the case down again, then sat on the edge of it and waited. There was no point in petulance. He wasn't about to abandon her, after all. She angered him because she didn't understand his motives, and that was how it had to be.

Finally she came up beside him and set her own undaya case down next to his.

"This span—"

"Hyakiyako," he named it.

"You do remember being on it?" she asked.

He heard in her voice that she was trying to forge peace with him. He replied, "Most certainly. You can't go farther north without traveling through, therefore we played it."

"But you've no memory of it?"

"My dear," he answered with exaggerated patience from which he immediately retreated, "I tried to explain, we played *hundreds* of spans for *thousands* of audiences. They all bleed together after a while, and one is much like any other. You must remember that your father and I didn't start out from Bouyan, we didn't start out anywhere near it nor here."

"Do you know *anything* about this span at all?"

"I know my job," he replied. "Last night I asked Grumelpyn. He travels the spans much the way I used to, and he knows the best routes and places to lodge. Of course at first I thought I would have more time—a few more *nights* to buy him drinks, talk over old days, find out everything."

"Yet you made the choice to leave, after telling me we were staying. What did he tell you?"

He pretended with his answer not to know what she meant. "That there's some kind of parade at night here. Not every night apparently, but he couldn't say why or which nights or what it means that there's a parade, because he was strongly advised to stay inside while it was going on, or else never be seen again."

"A parade." She glanced back at Diverus. He sat with his head down. The bejeweled turban and the tunnel shadows made him look considerably older than he was. With his bag of instruments thrown over one shoulder, he might have been a wandering mystic guiding two travelers away from the fleshpots of Vijnagar. He glanced up and shook his head as if to say that he knew nothing of Hyakiyako.

Watching this interchange, Soter insisted, "I'm afraid that's all I can tell you. At least we should have a captive audience—I mean, if they can't go out, then they'll be wanting some entertainment while they're trapped inside. That can't be bad."

"Can't it?" she asked but more to herself than to him, as if she was distracted, and he imagined it was the story as the elf had laid it out that had her wondering. What sort of parade took place if everyone was dissuaded from participating? If people all stayed indoors, then who was marching in it? On the face of it, Grumelpyn's story made no sense. But whatever the answer, the three of them could not remain inside the tunnel. They were committed now to pushing on. As if she'd reached the same conclusion, Leodora stood, hefted the undaya case by its strap once more, and continued walking.

Groaning, Soter pushed himself to his feet again. Oh, that the world would let him lie down in the tunnel and never have to be anywhere at all. Yes, a seigneur's life would have suited him just fine.

By the time they came to the end of the tunnel, they were shielding their eyes against the light, like Meersh the trickster when he'd returned from the umbral land of the dead by popping out of his own chimney. And surely the world had presented no stranger sight to him than the span of Hyakiyako.

Vertical banners hung from poles up and down every street. The symbols painted on them meant nothing to him. Unlike the spans they had traveled since leaving Bouyan, there were hardly any tall structures on this one. The buildings were low to the ground, and wide, with double roofs—a smaller one on top of the main one, as if it were necessary for every building to represent itself in miniature above the original. Here and there even odder structures that looked like crookedly stacked cups poked up at the sky. Far down the span, probably in the middle, one great gateway dominated. It was a thing of two dark angled pillars and two curving crosspieces that ran the width of the span, the way most of the towers did. It was misty in the distance, impossible to tell what lay beyond the gate; but if that was the halfway point, then Hyakiyako was a very long span indeed. There would be no climbing that gate, either.

The view to the left revealed even more unusual aspects of the span: It abutted a hillside. The other two tunnels gave on to separate branches, boulevards running parallel at first, but slowly curving back toward the one on which they stood; the others were narrower than this one, too. Where they actually reconnected to the broader span lay somewhere in the distant haze, beyond the great gate. However, instead of there being nothing but ocean between the branches, there were hillocks rising above the level of the rails and then dipping down again out of sight.

Beyond the third branch the crest of a larger hill protruded and upon it a single tower—another of those crooked cup stacks.

It was the first span they'd come to that incorporated a landmass, although Soter imagined that she couldn't be too terribly surprised—he had taught her stories that could not have unfolded upon bridges, and thus implied the existence of the larger landmasses. She must have realized that Bouyan could not have been the only island linked with a span, else it would have been celebrated as a novelty instead of shunned as a backwater that nobody cared to visit. Of course, knowing that abstractly wasn't the same as seeing it.

He commented as if to himself, "The right-hand path *is* the main thoroughfare. Good, good. I guess we can trust this map of Grumelpyn's a little more."

Ahead of them on the streets, people milled about, dressed in jackets and robes of a finer quality than those worn on Vijnagar. A man who seemed to be acting as gatekeeper on this end of the tunnel bowed to them most formally. He wore a long dark coat, and he said something incomprehensible as he gestured for them to enter the span. Clearly, he wasn't asking for money, but was welcoming them. It was a completely alien gesture. And then, suddenly, it wasn't.

As had happened previously when they stepped onto a span, everything changed in a moment: The foreignness of the place evaporated like a sun dog. This, as he had explained to Leodora on the voyage out from Ningle and before they'd set foot on Merjayzin, was the magic of the spans. How it worked was something only the gods knew, but work it did. The symbols upon the nearest banner shifted from incomprehensible hatchmarks into easily discernible text, now reading quite obviously: THE SPECTER OF NIKKI DANJO. Diverus asked, "What does it mean, do you know?" Soter glanced back to confirm that they were staring at the same thing, but Leodora answered before he could.

"It's a story," she said, and then to Soter added, "You taught me a version of it."

"That's right. A ghost story."

"It means we have something to perform tonight. Assuming we can find a *place* to perform."

"We'll have a place. I'll find us a venue." He stared at the sky and with affected injury said, "The child does not trust my powers."

Leodora set down her case. "The *child*," she said, "has seen you drunk."

At this the one-man welcoming committee roared with laughter. Soter opened his mouth as if to tell the man to be quiet, but instead chuckled, too. He hefted the undaya case again and marched into Hyakiyako.

The banner over the door read, EAT THIS AND HAVE A CUP OF TEA, and beside these words was the drawing of a circle.

Soter reacted to it as if he'd been hunting for the very phrase, and lurched suddenly across the cobbled road to the wide steps up to the porch that appeared to girdle the building. A pedicab for a single passenger ran past, cutting him off from the other two. It slowed as the puller considered Leodora and Diverus, asking a question with his eyes. She shook her head, and the cab trundled on.

At the entrance beside the steps, Soter had left his case and removed his shoes, which sat next to a row of others, giving the impression that a dozen people had been lifted from their footwear and vanished upon the threshold.

Leodora placed her own shoes beside his, set her case beside the one he'd carried, and then sat upon the two of them. She stretched her neck and flexed her knotted shoulders. As her muscles found their limits and her vertebrae cracked, she groaned luxuriously. "We could use one of those pedicabs," she remarked to Diverus. "Put the cases in instead of us, and pull them along. It would have to be easier than these straps."

"We can trade if you like," he suggested. "My instruments aren't nearly so heavy."

Before she could reply, Soter burst onto the porch. "We have lodging!" he proclaimed. "*And* a courtyard in which to perform."

"A courtyard?"

"It's their custom here. The entertainments are held outside but inside." He clambered down the three wide steps, shooed her to her feet, and then grabbed his case by its strap.

"Would this have something to do with the parade?" she asked.

"I wouldn't know. I've no memory of the place, though we must have played here. Of *course* we played here." He stood with one foot on the porch, the other on the step, a majestic pose as he looked at the city around him and added, "I think."

"Maybe you went some other way?" she suggested.

"How? There is only this one span linking Vijnagar to other places north. Yorba to the south. I remember *it*."

"*You* said that you didn't begin at Ningle when you traveled with Bardsham. You began somewhere else, you said. Somewhere—"

"South," he interrupted. "Traveled for years, you understand? Years before we crossed paths with your mother. Took boats between spirals. Years and never the same span twice. That's how big, how vast, the world is. Maybe we sailed off after Vijnagar, didn't come farther north. Maybe we came back to Grumelpyn's span from another. His is the end of this one, I think. The final curl in this spiral. There were places down south that thought we were thieves, stealing part of their lives and like that—telling their stories was taking their souls, keeping them. You definitely don't want to go in that direction. Anyway, I have a map now. I'm your guide, Lea, you have to trust that I know what I'm doing."

"You know what you're doing but you don't remember what it is." She tried to remain irritated, but in the face of his ebullience this proved impossible. "All right," she said, and perched again upon her case, flexing her toes, and considered that his justification had inadvertently provided her with more information than he'd given her since leaving Ningle. Why, she wondered, hadn't he told her about those southern venues before? He'd told her so many things about traveling with Bardsham, but she realized now that they were only cursory things, events without details, as if he'd hoped she would take no interest in life on the spans. He'd answered questions when confronted, but he had never volunteered anything.

She wanted to know about the south. Had they gotten into trouble there? Had her mother been with them then? Had something happened on the southern spans that led to . . . led to—and once again, she didn't know. She didn't know the specifics at all.

She looked up to ask him, but Soter had left her and entered the building, disappearing into its depths.

She dusted off her feet, then wearily stood, lifted the case, and climbed up the steps. The slickly polished floor of the porch like unbroken water reflected the case and her upside down.

Diverus made no move to follow her. He stared at the rows of empty shoes as if they troubled him.

"Come on," she said, but in response he only shifted his weight uncertainly from leg to leg. "Diverus," she inveigled, "I'll leave you outside if you don't climb the steps right now." He slipped off his own shoes, placing them against hers, watching her as if fearful she might vanish in an instant. He climbed up beside her.

"I just play music," he said, as if that explained something.

"Tonight you do that in here." She lifted her puppet case. Side by side, they went in.

The glossy floors extended all the way into the depths, making the place seem huge, reflectively doubling the height of the translucent wall panels. The light melting through them rendered the interior into a state of permanent, golden dusk. People sat cross-legged on the floor at low tables, eating—at least it was her impression that they were eating—and drinking. They remained no more than shapes, lumps in silk tucked into corners and alcoves of which there seemed to be an impossible number. She wondered how they could see well enough to know what they were eating. Or maybe they didn't care. She couldn't tell if they were watching her, or even whether they noticed her. Perhaps not, if they couldn't identify more about her than she could of them. She might have been nothing more than the scent of barbecued eel, collecting for an instant above the tables.

Then out of the shadows the proprietor emerged, coming right up to them—a small man with crooked teeth and a sloping forehead, not much hair, and bright, eager eyes. Like two smooth white gems in that dusky light, his eyes glittered. "Yes, you come, you come," he said. He plucked at her sleeve, at Diverus. "You both come!" He tugged them still deeper into his establishment.

It hadn't looked all that impressive from the front, but Eat This and Have a Cup of Tea proved to incorporate more rooms in its depths than she might have imagined. She soon realized that they were walking around a central area, the source of the wan light beyond the screens, and guessed that it must be Soter's courtyard. At the point she decided she had been led through a complete circuit, the proprietor abruptly turned and pushed back a screen, revealing another room, this one with mats on the floor.

There, seated beneath a low table, Soter twisted around as they entered. He held a small cup in one hand, and a small pitcher in the other, caught in the act of pouring. "About time," he said. "I'm famished."

The meal proved to be sumptuous and exotic. Neither Leodora nor Diverus had ever tasted anything like it, and once sampled, she could not imagine never having it again. When she raised the question of the central space they had seemingly walked around, Soter confirmed that it was the courtyard where they would perform. "It is outdoors but protected from the parade. Oh, yes, Mutsu told me about the parade. A horrifying thing, to be avoided at all costs. Your very life could be forfeit."

"Mutsu. You remember his name?"

"Naturally." He sipped his tea under her critical gaze, which exerted a kind of pressure on him. He set down his cup. "The truth is, he came up to me, called out *my* name, and said, *Don't you remember me? I'm Mutsu.* So, there. He remembers *me*. All I remembered was the banner. Satisfied?"

"For once," replied Leodora.

They ate awhile in stiff silence after that, until Diverus asked: "What happens now?"

"Now," said Leodora as she stepped around a cart peddling fruit, "we hunt for stories. It's what my father used to do wherever he went. It's how he learned everybody's tales."

"Soter doesn't come?"

"No. He makes arrangements, asks questions, tries to find out if there are other places on a span we should play, promotes us to the local people."

"He angers you," Diverus stated.

She eyed him askance. They walked through a bazaar of stands, most sporting bright awnings. The smells of fish and confections mixed with more human, bodily smells. It all reminded her of Ningle and her childhood, back when her uncle had been clement. Those memories were intertwined with Soter, too. "He angers me because he lies," she replied. "I don't always catch him out, but the occasions that I do only make me assume he's lying the rest of the time, too."

He changed the subject: "How do you hunt for stories, then?"

"Well"—she glanced around—"you look for signs that stories are about."

"Signs," he repeated with evident confusion. The confusion wasn't his alone, either, for in truth she had little experience looking for stories. Prior to arriving on Vijnagar, Soter had been too nervous to let her go off on her own for very long, and when she could sneak off at all she'd climbed the bridge towers to escape from him. Yorba had been the first place she'd asked about a story and been given one, by a group of workers who'd been mortaring a building. That was the Dustgirl's tale.

A palanquin crossed their path. Four men hefted it by two poles, which rested upon their shoulders. A woman's silhouette was just visible behind the gauze curtains.

Leodora tilted her head at the passing vehicle. "There. Like them."

"The palanquin?"

"Not the palanquin itself—the carriers. If you could spend time with them, there would be stories in it for you."

"Why not the woman hidden behind the curtains?"

"First, she would be reluctant to tell a complete stranger very much. Second, her carriers would tell me all about her because they're paid to transport her but also to be blind and dumb about it. They'll have seen things. They would want to talk because they're not supposed to. They carry her *and* they carry her story."

"I see. That is, I think I see."

She grinned. "I'm making this all up." Doubt clouded his expression, and her smile grew wider. "The truth of it is, so far anyway, stories seem to find me."

"The way mine did?"

"Exactly. I didn't attend the paidika in search of a story, but I found an extraordinary one that even has elements in it from other tales I've been taught by Soter. Your life up till now is a story."

"So he *does* know something."

"He knows quite a lot," she admitted, and stepped through an open space between two stalls selling various aromatic kernels, the combined smells making her nose twitch as if she might sneeze. "But I think he withholds more than he tells. When he was training me, that was helpful because he forced me to knit stories together out of scraps. As a test."

Diverus was thoughtful for a while after that, and soon they passed the stalls and the crowd thinned, at which point he asked, "How can you be sure that the tests are over?"

She had no ready answer to that.

Ahead, there lay a park lined with intricately shaped trees and shrubs.

Some looked like exotic animals. Others were either abstract or imitations of things she had never seen. In the middle of the park, a group stood clustered beneath one tree, watching two figures in their midst. The two were engaged in a game of some sort, sitting opposite each other across a square board, with the rest ringing them as though they represented the height of excitement.

Diverus followed Leodora through the park. The group might have been her ultimate goal, but she took the most circuitous route to arrive there— pausing to contemplate the unusual displays of flora: One bush had been sculpted into a flock of pigeons just leaving the ground. The fronds that represented the outstretched wings even seemed to be shaped into feathers. The artist had cleverly linked them so that from any angle some of them looked completely separated from the rest.

Eventually she did make her way to the game. Members of the group glanced her way. One nodded in so formal a manner that it seemed a shallow bow. That man had a narrow spear-shaped beard growing off the point of his chin. He turned his attention back to the game immediately but as if his look had been a signal, the people to either side of them edged away to give them space to join in.

The two players hadn't acknowledged any of this. One was a small, thin man with a shaved head save for the wide stripe of red hair that hung from the back of his skull. He would have been the most striking member of the group were it not for the second player, who had the long-snouted head of an animal, completely white, and who sat beneath a strange ball of light. Fist-sized, it floated just above his head. Diverus touched Leodora's shoulder, his eyes wide. She understood his startlement, and whispered to him, "Kitsune. A fox-trickster."

The kitsune gazed intently at the crosshatched board and the array of small stones dotting it, as if the stones might change position if he looked away. If there was a pattern there, neither Diverus nor Leodora could fathom it.

The stones—some light and some dark—looked as if they'd been polished by the sea, like the little stones and shells that washed up on the beaches of Bouyan all the time; in fact, some of the white "stones" proved to be small shells. The aggregate of dark and light remained obscure to Leodora even as two more stones were laid, one by each of the players.

With the kitsune's placement of the next dark stone, some of the watchers exchanged knowing glances as if something significant had occurred. The fox-player picked up a group of the lighter stones from the board, placing them in the lid to a small clay pot at his side, and she gleaned that he had surrounded them somehow, and thus won them. Even as he collected the "dead" stones, she noted, his black eyes remained locked on the board, his expression hard and his whiskers bristling. She had the sense that he was not certain he'd made the best move. The excitement wasn't necessarily in his favor.

The other player picked a white shell from his pot and held it a moment while he pointedly assessed the arrangement of the remaining stones. As if following his thoughts, the fox's seemingly permanent smile fell with resignation. He muttered something that sounded like *shimata.* The light stone was placed. The fox nodded. Then he and his opponent eyed each other. The dark-stone kitsune waved a furry hand once—he would not take his turn. The other placed another stone, and the fox waved away his turn again. The group relaxed and began to talk to one another as if picking up from an earlier conversation that had been suspended by the game.

The two opponents clasped hands across the board.

Diverus leaned forward and asked, "What just happened? I couldn't see why they stopped—there are still lots of open lines."

"I don't know, either. Let's find out." She moved around some of the observers and approached the white fox. He stood now, stretching cat-like, his orange-furred arms above his head, the loose sleeves of his gown falling down around his skinny arms to his shoulders. In that position he turned to them as they approached. Leodora repeated Diverus's question to him.

He gestured to the board, where three of the observers were bent over and discussing, apparently, earlier moves in the game. "I arrived at the point where I could see the outcome. The battle is engaged where I removed his stones, and that and this other are the only two open areas remaining. But the most I will be able to do from this moment forward is expend more stones before he deprives me of them. If this were truly war, what a foolish general I would be to send more and more soldiers into a place where I know in advance they cannot prevail. Those already taken are lost, and I cannot have them back." He reached into his pot, raised a handful of black stones, opened his palm. "Should I not preserve these soldiers for another day and a better game? Only an idiot would do otherwise."

Leodora met his eye and smiled.

Diverus asked, "And you both knew this?"

"We both—" He sprinkled the stones back into his pot. "—both concurred." He looked at them critically. "This is your first game, then," he said as he stepped away from the board.

"We've just arrived."

"Then you've made good use of your time. And if you stay for another, you will discern how one arrives at such a crossroads." He gestured behind himself where two other audience members were seating themselves and removing the stones, which they returned to their respective bowls.

"What is your interest here then, young travelers? You don't know gō, so is it the park, the topiaries?" He scrutinized Diverus closely. "You need more stain for your skin, perhaps?" Diverus moved back behind Leodora.

"Stories," she said.

The fox tilted his head and considered her again. "How so?"

"I collect stories," she said. "It's my . . . calling."

"That is a *grand* calling. But tell me, how do you keep them? Are they in a satchel? Do you have them tied up somewhere? Because the ones I know are disinclined to sit still."

She laughed at that. Behind the fox, the new players eyed her as if warning her not to laugh while they were engaged in play. "It's quite true, they don't sit still and they like to change shape, one place to another."

"Exactly so," the kitsune agreed, and showed his prominent teeth in a smile. The player behind him made a shushing sound. "Ah," the fox said, "we must be polite and move away if we're to talk . . . or would you attend a game from the beginning? It is greatly rewarding, as I said."

She glanced at Diverus to find him leaning around her in order to witness the opening moves. "All right," she told the fox, "one game and *then* stories."

"Excellent!" the fox replied. Then he also turned to watch.

Unlike the previous game, the one they observed from the beginning ended with a definitive final move followed by the counting of open squares—or intersections, as the fox explained it—and captured stones. "Shells has won again," he proclaimed. "Next time, I'm going to insist on being shells."

Some of those nearest him laughed and slapped him on the shoulder. "You can't have shells, not with your white fur!"

He told Leodora, "They think I'd cheat. Imagine."

"Yes, ridiculous," she said, but she knew enough about kitsunes to side with the group.

As they were laughing and discussing the game with the players, the fox

waved his arms about and said, "My friends, my friends, these two are itiner-
ant story collectors and would like to add to their collection from our reposi-
tory. Does anyone have a story they would particularly like to tell?"

The entire group began to babble at once. She heard "ghost" and
"tanuki" and "When Oiwa became a lantern!" before the fox waved them to
silence once more. "Please, please, we can all tell our tales but not at the
same time, if they're to make any sense of it."

"Well," began the one with the sharp beard, "tell her about the emperor
who forgot about war. That has one of your kind in it!"

The fox waited to see if anyone objected to this choice. No one did. He
asked, "Do you already have that story?" Leodora shook her head. "In that
case, I shall tell it, and if there's time we'll pick another—or, better, you can
tell us one of yours." Everyone nodded enthusiastically and settled down to
listen. The fox strode around as he declaimed and acted the various parts.

THE EMPEROR'S TALE

Way over there our span touches land. You can see the hills and the tower
that stands high upon the tallest hill. We call that land Kochokana, and
legend has it that's because it looks so like the fluttering wings of a butter-
fly. The truth, however, is that we named it after a legendary empire. We
don't know where this original kingdom is now—some say it's sunk beneath the sea; others claim it lies at the farthest end of the eternal bridge.
Whatever the truth, at one time in our history the original land called
Kochokana was ruled over by a warlord. As this title suggests, he was a
man who came to power by violent acts, and who maintained his power
in like manner.

He had been trained in the strategy of war from earliest childhood.
This art he had taken to, proving to be the greatest strategist ever seen in
Kochokana. With his childhood full of political and martial matters, he
had never spent much time with women; and because of his position—
because he was being groomed to be, one day, an emperor—only two
women in the empire were considered worthy candidates for his affec-
tions. It is not overstating things to say he disliked them both intensely.
They were spoiled and shrill creatures, and he would have nothing to do
with them. Had his parents been alive, surely they would have arranged a
marriage with one of these harpies regardless of her shortcomings, but as

he was in charge of his life—ascending to the position of emperor at fifteen upon his father's death—he simply refused to choose between them, no matter how much members of his court wished to see him produce an heir. He determined not to marry a woman he did not love. And so his life might have been spent—in endless battles—but for an accidental visit he made to the royal gardens.

Now, it's often said by the most scurrilous of folk that we foxes are only out to trick humans. *Not so!* I tell you. We kitsunes are the victims of jealousy and bad publicity. It's not our fault that we are handsome creatures, and that humans who fall in love with us fall very hard. It's not as if we do anything to cause it.

So was the case here. There was a kitsune who worked as a royal gardener. She lived alone in the woods beyond the fortress, but she liked the company of people, and so every morning she assumed human form and came to work in the gardens. In this way she was part of the populace but outside and away from prying eyes, which suited her very well.

And then one morning while she knelt at her task, she sensed someone observing her, and turned to discover the emperor standing there. Recognizing him, she could not move, didn't even dare to breathe. Dirt and sweat covered her, but the emperor saw only a beautiful maiden. Even beneath the dirt, her fox-magic shone.

The emperor knelt beside her in the black dirt. So close, he became transfixed by the beads of perspiration upon her lip, and by the scent of her body. "I've watched you," he told her, "as you wiped your brow, as you dug a hole for this flower and placed it, filled it in. You were so intent upon your work that you didn't even hear me." Then he leaned forward and began to dig the next hole for the next plant, beside her. She sat stupefied. Here was her emperor ruining his silk robes as he clawed in the dirt with her. He held up his hands, admiring the moist dirt attached to them, and began to laugh.

"I did not know," she said, "that our great lord enjoyed gardening."

He sat back on his haunches and replied, "Neither did I. But that was because I didn't realize what a radiant blossom I would find here."

She blushed and lowered her face, but he put a finger to her chin and lifted her head until her eyes met his again. "Never bow to me," he said.

"But, my emperor—"

"No, no. Not emperor. Husband, rather, if you would allow it."

She stared at this handsome man, saw in his eyes the love he had for her, and fell in love with him in return there and then. She replied, lowering her head, "I would."

Because he was the emperor and she was his choice, they were married, and his advisers, as they wished to keep their heads, kept their opinions to themselves. But soon enough it became obvious to them that this was no ordinary affection. The daily reports delivered to the emperor went unread. When someone tried to read one of them aloud, the emperor, lying on a divan beside his bride, waved him to silence and ordered that those he'd put in charge should solve these matters, not bother *him* with them. The daily reports ceased, and soon only the chambermaids saw the emperor and his bride. They reported back to the advisers that he and his bride saw only each other, utterly moonstruck in their affection.

Now, among his advisers lurked two spies from the neighboring province of Maitake. They had infiltrated the court long before in order to look for opportunities for invasion. Delighted by the news that the emperor was completely lost in the fox-woman's charms, they'd no idea that she was a kitsune just as she had no idea that her love could doom a kingdom or rob her lover of his martial skills. The beauty of the situation was that, should anyone suspect them of plotting, they could blame the woman, even accuse her of being the real spy. The attack would appear to coincide with his bewitchment, and the minds of the men would forge the links to her.

When the weather turned warm, and the emperor and his court moved to his summer tower, far from the border with Maitake, the two spies sent word to their king that he must strike fast and furious. The emperor knew nothing of the attack when it came. His generals alone saved the empire from being overrun, and a border siege began.

In the summer tower the siege was but an abstraction. The emperor's every thought was of his wondrous bride. When the generals petitioned for his advice in the siege he told them, "Do what you feel is necessary," and then dismissed them. The greatest strategist their people had ever known had deferred to his generals and his advisers. The agents of Maitake gleefully reported that the empire must fall, and recommended more assaults on the borders.

The emperor's advisers held an emergency meeting. "Can we trust the generals?" one adviser asked.

"Their allegiance certainly. Their skill against this formidable foe is . . . untested, though. They've never had to concern themselves with strategy before. We cannot be certain of the outcome."

"We *need* him!" someone cried.

"He won't listen. We've implored, importuned. It means nothing. He moons over his lowly gardener and waves us away. What fools devised this enchantment? Did someone here provide some potion in the hopes of producing an heir? Well, he may well produce one, but shortly there will be nothing to inherit."

No one admitted anything but they all eyed one another distrustfully.

"There's no way to move him," said one. "The empire is surely doomed."

Then a young member of the entourage said, "Wait, there is a way I've just thought of."

"What?" cried the others—the two spies especially.

"If the empress were kidnapped by Maitake, then he would pay attention."

"Brilliant!" they all cheered, until someone said, "But how do we get someone from Maitake to do this?"

"Ha!" cried the young man. "We don't. We convince the empress to pretend to be kidnapped—for the good of our land."

"Brilliant!" they all cried again.

The difficulty was in approaching her, since she was rarely out of his company. Finally the advisers approached her personal bather and explained to the woman what she must say to her mistress. The girl complied, and finally the fox-woman understood the danger she had brought to these people. Yet she could not unmake his devotion any more than she could stop her own heart from adoring him.

She stole from the bath to meet with the advisers, and agreed immediately to go along with their deception.

The two spies, at some risk, hastily returned to Maitake and reported the plot. Seated before their lord and his advisers, they said, "Look at this opportunity! We can put our own men in place and kidnap her for real! Isn't that wonderful?"

The warlord of Maitake leaned forward and said: "Are you both idiots?" The two looked at each other. They didn't *think* so, but this was hardly the response they'd expected. "If we kidnap her," the warlord explained, "then her husband will bring all of his attention to bear upon our invasion and he'll destroy us, just as he will if he *thinks* she's been kidnapped. You fools must do everything in your power to *disrupt* this plot. She must not be taken by anyone!"

"But she's in on it," they complained. "She's going to help."

"Then," growled the warlord, "you have your work cut out for you. We launch our supreme attack in two nights, and he had better not be paying attention if you want to have a home to return to."

The two spies crept back into Kochokana and debated about what they should do. They knew they couldn't stop the plot from unfolding. The empress would steal away in the middle of the night to the gardener's shed in the royal gardens where the emperor had found her, and his advisers and generals would swear she'd been kidnapped. If they said anything else, their true allegiance would be revealed. "I suppose it could be worse," said one. "How so?" said the other. "Well, the advisers could just have asked her to ask the emperor to destroy Maitake as a favor to her." His partner pulled at his lip. "Let's not mention that to anyone, all right?" he said. "But I do have an idea how we might undermine this without implicating ourselves."

The "kidnapping" of the empress went off without a hitch. She withdrew to the hut in the gardens of the main fortress. Her disappearance was discovered by one of her women, and the alarm sounded. The generals importuned the emperor to gather his wits and help them destroy the enemy who had obviously taken her. But before they had even laid out their maps and battle plans, the emperor received a note from his queen, which told him to come to her at once in the gardener's hut, where she was safely awaiting him. "Oh, my heart's delight!" he cried, then raced from the tower and rode across his land to the royal gardens. Sure enough, he found his wife in her bath and was so overcome immediately with lust for her that they sent away the servants and made love there and then in the wooden tub. The battle plans remained untouched.

"How did he figure this out?" one adviser asked the group.

"He's too clever for us," replied a spy.

"No, she sent him a note. Didn't you see?"

"Why would she do that?"

"Maybe she's an agent of Maitake," one of the spies suggested.

"Is that possible?"

"What other explanation is there?" the other spy asked. "The spell must have been her own."

"What can we do? The enemy's at the very gates! We need him now."

"Maybe," someone said, "we could have the spell removed."

"We don't know if there's a spell."

"There must be a spell."

"Maybe we could kidnap her again. For real this time."

"We can ask her to visit us. Can't we? And then say she was kidnapped on the way here."

"Will he believe a second kidnap plot?"

"Do we have a choice?"

They couldn't think of an alternative, these clever men, and so they sent a message to the empress. To their dismay, she answered that she would not attend. Instead, she commanded all of them to attend *her* at the gardener's cottage. At least, they thought, they might confront her in the emperor's presence. However, when they arrived, they found her alone.

"Where is the emperor?" they asked.

"I sent him off to war."

"You what?"

"As we were making love, he asked me what I wanted most in the world, and I told him that I wished to see him victorious over his enemies." She unfolded a slip of paper and placed it in front of them. "He has more enemies than he knows. He tells me everything, you see. He keeps no secrets. He's too good a man for secrets. I wish to do likewise, yet I cannot help but keep secrets when such plans as yours are required. Such plans depend upon deception." She raised a hand to stop some of them from protesting. "Please, don't defend the need for subterfuge. The problem with your method is that it's quite easy to hide one deception inside another. This note, for instance. It's a note from me, telling him that I've hidden myself in this cottage in order to have an assignation with him away from all the business of the court, and that the kidnapping was merely a ruse.

"I wrote no such message. I was playing *your* game, gentlemen. By your rules. Therefore, one or more of you must be a traitor."

"Arrogant child! How dare you accuse us!" yelled one of the true traitors.

She stared at him, and the fox emerged from that black stare. The fox snapped its jaws at the spy's throat. He clutched his neck with both hands and fell back a step. His neck was unmarked, but he knew that what he had seen would happen if he said one thing more; pale, trembling, he took his seat again while his partner looked on, fearfully mystified.

The fox-woman made some slight gesture and suddenly four armed warriors stepped into the cottage. All of the advisers reacted with fear then; but she watched their expressions carefully for any that were more or less than they should have been. She already had the first traitor. And now the second one gave himself away as his hand slid into the folds of his robe, where his hidden dagger lay. But the soldiers merely blocked the exits. They made no move to attack.

"All of you are under house arrest," she said, "although I do now know the identity of at least two traitors in your midst." She made a point of looking at none of them, although they looked at one another.

"I love your emperor dearly, yet nothing he says to me can I trust, because it's threaded with magic, which is my fault. I told you that I would have no secrets from him, and I don't. He knows what you are about to know." Before their eyes she transformed then. Her sweet face became that which the traitor had seen. Her hands and bare feet changed shape and grew soft with fur. The advisers gaped; even one of the soldiers drew back. She continued to speak as if none of this had happened. "Because of my negligence, not one word could I be sure came from his true heart. The magic of the fox-people is such that we ensorcel you with our glamour whether we wish to or not. Now he knows my nature and when he comes back from this war, I will know his true feelings. In any case this siege is about to end, and there's no need for further trickery. He will blast the enemy."

"What if, when he returns, he doesn't love you?" asked one of the advisers.

"Then," she replied with bowed head, "I shall be no different from you."

She directed the soldiers to arrest the two spies she had identified. If there were more than that, she knew they would now flee for their lives.

She left the advisers and retired to the tower to await her husband's return and his answer. The execution of spies would come later. The guilt of those men meant far less to the fox-empress than the true heart of her husband.

The kitsune let the image of her in her tower hover in the air a great long time before he drew another breath and relaxed, so that his audience knew the story had ended.

"And what did he say?" asked Diverus. "What did her husband decide?"

The fox glanced at Leodora, who was beaming. "That," she answered, "is another tale."

"Just so," the fox agreed, and bowed his head.

"Beautifully told," she said. "I know no one who could tell it better."

"Ma'am." He bowed still deeper, his mouth curved in that slight smile that foxes wear. "We, all of us, have tales we could share with you if you care to hear them."

"I do," she replied. "Truly. But it's evening now, and we were advised not to be out after the sun set."

The fox shared a look with his fellows, and they all burst out laughing. But he said to her, "Quite right, you don't want to be caught out." More tittering accompanied the comment, though she couldn't see what they found so amusing. "I think it's best that you allow us to accompany you back to your ac-commodations, wherever they are. As a precaution against whatever it is you're fearful of."

"That's very kind of you."

"It's nothing. We can't very well sit here playing once the sun goes down, and it's just about to set, as you say."

She stood with the fox, Diverus at her side. The rest of the group folded around them like a shield, and they began to walk back through the park. "And what is the name of your abode?"

"I think it's called Eat This and Have a Cup of Tea."

"Ah, know it well, know it very well." He glanced at some of the others of the group with another meaningful look.

Leodora turned to the man beside her, intending to ask him . . . whatever it was, the question fell from her mind as she saw him. He was changing as they walked, no longer human. He had a great curling nose now, and his chin hung down as a beard might have on someone else. The man behind him was more grotesque still. His head had become part of his shoulders, flat-topped, and his torso funneled down into skinny legs and long-taloned feet, as if he were the child of a bird that had mated with a parsnip. He blinked back at her with round, inhuman eyes. The eyes all around her had changed: Some bulged, others had turned hard and black. Noses had reshaped, distorted, or vanished altogether. Likewise hair, which had disappeared or else sprouted in odd places, or transformed into feathers, reeds, seaweed. Only the fox, transformed before she'd met him, remained the same, although in the dark and among this company he looked more sinister and rapacious than before.

As they all walked down the seemingly deserted thoroughfare, more shapes emerged from the shadows or rose up through the pavement to double their numbers.

Diverus clutched her arm, all of his terror in his grip. He was staring behind them so intently that she looked back, too. A crowd had amassed, walking behind them, some thin and stalky, others squat and elvish, some slick and others furry. Two of the squat creatures held lanterns on long flexible poles and ran along the edges of the crowd to keep up. Behind the lights there were even more creatures, but in shadow, only now and then glimpsed between other bodies and in cast light. If anything they looked more grotesque than those nearby. It was a parade of monsters, and she and Diverus were their captives. Soter would say it was all her fault for not returning while daylight remained—that is, if he ever saw her again, he would. She wanted to speak to the kitsune, but he had drawn ahead to lead the parade. Two more lights on poles bobbed beside him.

Something cold brushed her shoulder, and instinctively she pressed against Diverus, away from the source, as a towering ghost drifted past. His mismatched eyes regarded her with surprise, as though he recognized her. He wore odd clothing—a black jacket over a white shirt with another strip of material hanging from his throat. She wasn't sure what manner of pants he wore because his legs faded below the knee into an ill-defined grayness. He floated past and toward the front.

Then all at once the parade came to a stop. Beside Diverus the creatures stepped away, and there stood the fox. He grinned. "Well," he said, "we've arrived."

Behind him lay the steps up to Eat This and Have a Cup of Tea. The fox waved them out of the parade. Holding hands, they moved toward the steps.

"I couldn't persuade you to come with us the rest of the way, could I?" the fox asked.

"Rest of the way?"

"To the end. The parade goes on to the very end."

"Of the span?"

"Of time," he said, as though surprised that she didn't comprehend this already.

"So, we . . . couldn't come back."

"Quite impossible. But we should love your company. You know so many stories."

Diverus was edging to the steps and tugging her after him. He said, "She can't. She has a performance tonight."

"Really?" the fox said.

"Yes, it's true," she replied.

"Oh, well." He sounded sincerely regretful. "You'd best go on, then. But come again to the park and we'll tell you another story. And you can share one of yours."

"That would be . . . I would like that."

"Good night, then, Leodora." He made shooing gestures at them both, then turned and took his place at the front again. The parade moved off behind him. Some of the creatures watched her and Diverus as they passed. Others stared straight ahead as if this world did not exist; those in the very back somehow did both at once.

"He said your name," Diverus noted.

"I'm sure I never told it to him."

"You wouldn't really go to the park again, would you?"

She made no answer. Gesturing toward the steps, she said instead, "We're probably late."

They climbed up and, after removing their shoes, entered the building. The moment the door thudded closed behind them, the noise and bustle of the front room died. All those within—every single person—turned from their meals, drinks, overtures, and conversations to stare at the new, and unlikely, arrivals.

Diverus and Leodora walked barefoot across the polished wood floor. With wide eyes upon her from every side, she felt as if she were still in the grotesque parade. The eyes tracked her closely as if expecting at any moment that she might transform. One man close by made signs in the air and threw some kind of dust at them that glittered as it sprinkled down, causing Diverus to sneeze violently, which in turn caused the man to dive for safety beneath his table. Leodora paused to brush the dust from her sleeve. When nothing happened, the man poked out his head, tittered nervously, and sat up facing his food, refusing to look at them. Diverus rubbed his nose. The crowd lost interest.

The proprietor entered then. He carried a woven tray full of covered dishes. "Ah-ha," he said, "there you two are. That Soter has taken to drink because he couldn't find you. He was sure you were gobbled up by goblins."

Diverus glanced askance at Leodora, who asked, "Are we late?"

"Not for my needs, no. You can see—they are all still eating. However, I am not of a nervous disposition."

"I understand. When is it we begin, then?"

"Oh, anytime you like, although if you would wait perhaps until those who ordered this food have had their fill, you'll be less likely to play to an empty garden."

"Of course."

"Grand." He hurried off to serve the food, leaving behind lovely smells.

The central courtyard was nearly deserted. Cut off from the street and the front room, the handful of patrons there did not react when the newcomers entered, apparently connecting them neither to the parade nor directly with the anticipated performance of puppetry.

At a small table beside the booth Soter sat alone, his head on his arms. Candlelight floated in a bowl by his head, illuminating his slack expression, telling her everything she needed to know of his condition. He stared at nothing, but then sensed her and shifted. When he saw her he closed his eyes, licked his lips, and pushed himself upright, swaying slightly.

"The vagabonds return," he muttered.

"We were collecting stories," she said sharply. "The way I do on every span. You know that."

"The sun set long ago. You were even warned about it."

"Our performance wasn't set to begin before this, and it looks as if it will have to go on without you."

"Nonsense." He bowed his head as if tired of the argument. "What happened to you? You could have been consumed by the monsters that walk these streets at night, the parade—"

"We joined the parade," she interjected.

"What? What happened?"

"They ate us." She had the satisfaction of seeing him dumbfounded.

"The good thing that came of it is, I have a story to perform belonging to this span, that we've never heard before, and perhaps more to come. Wasn't that worth it?"

"My girl, my headstrong mad girl. You are your mother's child, and like her you rattle the dark."

She gaped at those words. He had no way of knowing that Shumyzin had said the very same, and for an instant she stood in two places, atop the tower on Vijnagar and here, as if two moments had merged, folding over the events in between, as if to say that she had followed the correct path and reached the next clue, although toward what end she had no idea.

"You rattle it long enough," he went on, "and it'll rattle you back."

"So I shouldn't look for new tales?"

"I'm not saying that. I'm saying, be careful you don't *become* a tale." He poured his cup, but then pushed it at her. "Here, drink for stamina before we go on." She picked it up. "And don't worry about my condition. I could do my part roaring drunk, and you know it."

She sipped the wine and put the cup down. "I know you've tested the notion enough times."

He snorted, smiled. "I have, and even before yours. Now go get ready, and where's Div—ah, there you are, boy. Get in the booth. I'll go call us up an audience. You apply your skills, the both of you, to this story you risked your lives to get, and tomorrow night they'll be murdering each other to get in. We'll save Nikki Danjo's ghost till then." He drew himself to his feet.

Leodora pushed into the booth with Diverus behind her.

He picked up his lute. "We risked our lives?" he asked.

She shrugged at him. "Maybe a little."

TWO

Their performance of "The Emperor's Tale" that night proved so afflated that it was to the audience as if two demigods had manifested inside the booth to render the story. Diverus plucked a delicate tune underneath Jax's prologue, then switched to a small flute to represent the fox-empress, inventing a bittersweet theme for her on the spot. Even Leodora, in the midst of depicting the story, found her throat constricting with emotion. Every note was the perfect complement to the shadow figures on the screen. During an interlude, when she could glance back at him, she saw that his eyes were closed and his head was swaying as he played, as if while his body sat with her his spirit ventured into some other realm to bring back a music that no one had ever heard, yet all knew the instant it was played that it already lived in their bones, threaded through generations. Wherever he channeled it from, he was playing music that had formed the moment the story was first told—the music of the story's origin. She knew, even before she took her bow afterward, that they would be weeping as they applauded. She made Diverus come out, too, with his flute, and presented him to them. The ovation doubled. "Kitsune Jax!" someone yelled, and coins rained upon them. If Soter had an opinion of the musician at that moment, he didn't express it, but gestured, redundantly, to them both as if the audience needed instruction in where to direct their acclaim.

The next morning, with a mist hanging over the span, she and Diverus went back to the park, but the kitsune and his brethren weren't there. The benches on which the players had sat the day before were empty. No one played gō today. The strangely cut and shaped flora seemed different, too, but Leodora couldn't be sure if it was her imagination or if the topiary had been changed. She didn't remember the one cut like a huge bird with a fan for a tail, nor the one that looked like a giant depiction of her Meersh the Bedeviler puppet—and surely she would have noticed that one if it had been there the previous afternoon. Who was it cut these bushes, anyway?

People strolled through the park in leisurely fashion; some passing nearby stared at her curiously. Diverus noticed this first and pointed it out to her, and the two of them watched people watching her as they passed. Then one woman, rather than just watching, approached her. With her face hidden behind a small fan that she fluttered, the woman asked, "Would you sell me, young woman, some of your hair?"

"My hair?" She self-consciously touched the fall of it at her neck. She wore it unbound today, enjoying the freedom of anonymity.

"Enough to make a wig for me. I'll pay you well."

"I'm sorry, but no."

The woman made a slight bow of disappointment, then fluttered away.

Diverus said, "They must never have seen hair like yours."

"But it's just hair!"

"To us. We might want to leave this park, though, before she finds someone who's willing to take it from you."

"Take my hair?" Clearly she found the idea absurd.

"In the underspan of Vijnagar, if someone liked what you had, they took
it. If you disagreed with them, there was usually an argument, sometimes a
fight. Sometimes a murder."

"You saw this?"

"Not every day, no. Own nothing to feed someone's envy and you'll live a
good long time. Otherwise, you have to be willing to fight."

"You had something to steal?" she asked, thinking that he wasn't merely
reciting but spoke from personal experience.

"No," he answered. "I had nothing, less than nothing, so I was left alone."

They continued to wander idly through the park, which appeared larger
than possible. Beyond the benches and up a few steps the way was blocked by
a stand of bamboo grown so thickly together that when they at last located a
meandering path of small stones among the stems, they had to walk single-
file along it, weaving through an increasingly impeditive forest, so dense that
the clogged air hung motionless, while in branches overhead unseen birds
chattered shrilly. The world became green, crepuscular, and claustrophobic.

When it seemed the forest could be compressed no further and remain
navigable, the bamboo began to thin, until they were catching glimpses of
the world beyond it again. Soon only a single, random row of stems stood between them and the outside. The path ended at a few steps, leading down a
slope to a circular pond. In the center of the pond, water trickled over an odd
pile of stones that seemed to have been arranged to produce the most noise
possible—the trickling and burbling drowned out even the birdsong they'd
left behind. Orange fish with large sleepy eyes suggesting a jaded intelligence
swam lazily near the edge of the pond and followed them as they walked
around it. There were benches at intervals, but no one sat. This whole por-
tion of the park stood deserted.

The path led to a broad oval of sand, ringed by rocks. A solitary figure
stood in the sand, his face hidden beneath a low conical hat. He held a small
rake and, as Leodora and Diverus came upon him, he was carefully creating
a series of crosshatches. The sand had been worked elsewhere into swirls and
nautiloid patterns. In silence they watched him perform, and Leodora felt as
if she were watching the creator himself, making the world. He paused to
consider what he'd done, standing idly with one foot on his thigh and his

weight upon the rake. He seemed then like a statue, as if she had only imagined his movement. Quietly she and Diverus crept past him. If he was aware,
he didn't show it. He didn't move at all. On the far side and bordered by short
conical trees, a few steps led down from this strange plateau and across another area of exotically shaped bushes, and to a set of polished wooden trel-
lises that served as gates. Beyond them, people moved past randomly, as if
unaware of this enigmatic park.

Exiting through the gates, the two found themselves on a secondary
boulevard that paralleled the one they'd taken upon arriving on the span the
day before. Looking back, they found that they had walked beneath the oddly
canted central tower without noticing and viewed it now on the far side of
where they'd begun, halfway to the end of the span. "Maybe the bamboo forest hid it," suggested Diverus, as if reading her thoughts, but even to himself
he sounded unconvinced. He added, "Maybe we want to walk back on the
road instead."

"There certainly wasn't anyone to ask for stories," said Leodora.

"I think it won't be the same going back anyway." She looked at him ques-
tioningly, and he explained, "I think it'll have become another park."

What struck her as the most odd about his observation was that she both
understood and agreed with him.

This entire span seemed to be alive with elusive magic.

They walked along the avenue toward the center tower, passing other
pedestrians, fruit and vegetable stands, pedicabs, and shops. The shops on
their right hid the park from view, and when they did catch a glimpse, all they
saw was a stone wall.

The two of them had only just entered the shadow under the middle
tower's swaybacked crossbeam when a procession cut across their path.

It was nothing like the parade of monsters from the previous night. The
people—for they all looked human this time—wore white garments: robes,
pants, shirts, all white. Only one woman, near the front, wore color—a bright
red scarf upon her head. In the middle, lying upon a board but held up above
their heads on a series of poles, lay a body. It, too, was wrapped in white, from
head to foot.

Leodora turned and started after them. When Diverus didn't tag along
she turned back to him. "I have to see this," she told him. "I don't know why,
but I have to."

The street ran directly to one of the canted uprights supporting the swooping beam overhead. The street widened to circle the upright, and the procession flowed around it like water around a stalk of bamboo. On the far side the split road opened even wider, into a crescent at the span's edge. The funeral group spread out to fill the crescent. Leodora and Diverus remained on its fringe, slightly separate from the others so as not to intrude. They didn't know how they might be regarded.

The woman with the red scarf began a recitation: "There are two hundred levels to the universe. The higher we ascend, the hotter it becomes. The realm of the spirits would scorch us, and even they cannot reach the level of the fire and water gods, but are connected to it only by rays, as the sun connects to us."

A woman standing beside her and clutching the hands of two children began to wail. The children took their cues from her and added their voices to the anguish.

Diverus moved off from the clustered group, to the rail at the edge of the span. Leodora trailed after him, curious about his response. She could still hear the priestess's recitation, but the talk of levels made little sense to her. Through thin mist the other wing of the span was visible, separate but close enough that Leodora could make out the shapes of people in the nearest lane. As she approached the rail, she could see below them the darkness of the land that sloped out from under the surface of the span. A hillside. She leaned over and peered down into a deep valley that ran between the avenues. Houses on stilts dotted the lower slopes, and the ones at the very bottom stood in water, in a narrow stream that snaked through it. The course of the stream led back to a waterfall in the gray distance. On each side of the stream, the land had been flooded—a system of small gates and channels allowed water to be diverted from the stream, enough to cover the valley floor. Some sort of crop grew in the spread of water, and people worked there with hoes and other implements, with baskets slung over their shoulders, standing ankle-deep.

The funeral recitation had ended, and the body—still on its plank but now fastened to ropes—began a steady descent over the edge. She had to lean out over the rail to see where it was going.

The hillside below was cracked open, and inside the opening, directly beneath the descending body, lay a grotto. The sides of it were jagged; down in its depths lights flickered, like candles sparkling off faceted gems, revealing more white-robed figures. They stood awaiting the body, reaching up eagerly while it descended toward the open mouth of the hill.

Diverus said suddenly, "My mother died and they dropped her down into the sea." She glanced sidelong at him. He seemed calm, almost entranced. "There was no land under Vijnagar. Just water. They wrapped her up like that and then they sent her under the water."

"Diverus—"

"I came to believe she'd become a mermaid and lives now in a city at the bottom of the sea."

She found she could watch the descent of the body by watching his eyes. He tracked it until it was taken by the figures in the hole.

"It's the same, though, isn't it?" he said.

The priestess recited: "After the Storm of Raruro, comes a reuniting, and all spirits join. Shukkon and fukkon will join. Until that day he must remain separated from us—that is the order of things."

Diverus pushed away from the ceremony and through the many figures in white. Leodora followed after him. He didn't go far but sat down against a wall where a cart had been standing earlier—a few cast-off vegetables lay scattered there. He rested his face on his fists. As she came up to him, Leodora thought he looked like a little boy. She knelt, and then sat beside him.

"It's strange," he said immediately. "I can remember it all, but in the way you remember the stories you tell, the way I remember the story that fox told us yesterday. It never happened to me, but I can recall that emperor and his fox-wife now—as if I *was* there."

She said nothing, but considered that awhile. Idly she picked up a long-necked gourd and a taro potato and began toying with them, dancing them about. There seemed to be no answer, really. Diverus had been present, and yet from what she gathered, the Diverus seated beside her hadn't existed then. He was a creation of the gods. A Dragon Bowl had made him.

Meanwhile the funeral procession was returning from the burial. The wails of the two children at the rear of the group reached them well before the children passed by.

Without looking at him, Leodora said, "It isn't as if you could have saved her, Diverus. Any more than I could have saved my parents. They both died before I could talk." She met his angry eyes and held his gaze. "You think she died on your account."

His eyes widened with surprise and betrayal, and she knew that she'd guessed right. She spun the gourd around, then waltzed it to the potato. "There isn't a day when I don't miss my aunt Dymphana. I can't see her again, maybe ever." Her throat tightened and her face flushed. She'd thought she was saying this for him, not to express her own pain. She wanted to stop but had to go on. He had to understand. She willed herself not to cry. "It's not my fault I can't see her. I didn't make it this way, my uncle did. He made the rules, and what I've done . . . is because of that."

People were walking past now. She lowered her head, unable to look at him or anyone else, knowing that she might burst into tears if she did—and how stupid and pointless that would be—but she couldn't help it. She focused on the vegetables, on making them waltz about and pirouette upon the stones.

The crying children came abreast of her but she didn't look up, even when their noise was right on top of her. And then suddenly the crying stopped.

At that she raised her head slowly. The children stood directly before her. They were watching her hands in fascination. They might have been twins, both with black hair and almond eyes. Above, holding their hands, their mother, the widow, met her gaze and made a pitiful attempt at a smile, ruined by grief. Her tears had etched trails in the thick powdery makeup on her cheeks. The thought came to Leodora: *All of us are here on account of death.*

The rest of the funeral party moved on, but the mother couldn't work up the energy to order her children away, and so she stood there as if expecting Leodora to read her a future.

Quietly, Diverus suggested, "Tell them a story."

She glanced over at him. He seemed to have forgotten his despair. His eyes shifted from her to the children and back again.

She spoke what she'd been thinking. "We're all here on account of death," she said, and she spun the long-necked gourd about, as if it were turning to face the children. "Death is everywhere, but do you know that once upon a time Death didn't exist? No? Let me tell you, then, how Death came into our world." She raised her eyes to the widow. "I think you should sit down to hear this. It's not a long story, but it isn't short, either."

The mother knelt, and her children sat beside her.

"Now, does anyone here know who Chilingana is?" asked Leodora.

One of the twins said, "He dreamed Shadowbridge."

"That's right. He was the original dreamer." She walked the taro potato forward and hid the gourd from sight, then leaned over and picked up a small cluster of enoki and set it aside. She said, "One day a different dream came to him."

HOW DEATH CAME TO SHADOWBRIDGE

In those times the sun was called Lord Akema. He was a warrior god, terrible to behold, who would blind all those foolish enough to seek for his features. That's why there existed the second—the false mask of Akema— Nocnal, upon which everyone might safely gaze, and which they could petition when they wanted a favor from the war god. Behind the mask of Nocnal, the warrior would listen and sometimes answer.

It was under Nocnal's aegis that the fisherman Chilingana dreamed the bridges of Shadowbridge into place. Each night more bridges appeared— covered in structures, in houses and towers, in parks and alleys, but all of them were empty, lifeless, and still. Soon his dream stretched far across the world, and Nocnal observed it all as it unfolded.

By day, beneath the burning face of Akema, Chilingana's life persisted as flat as bread. He fished, he ate, and he dwelled with his wife, Lupeka, in his stilt house. Although he could have stepped across the gap onto the first bridge he'd dreamed, he didn't. He talked about going, almost every day, but each time he came to the edge of his own small world he hesitated, peered down the empty way until his eyes ached, and then gave up. He could not go traveling out upon these spans. To do so would have invited the unknown, and Chilingana, for whom everything had ever been the same, feared the unknown. He didn't understand that the unknown needed no invitation.

One night while he lay upon his seaweed mat, a chill wind called loneliness came floating down the empty spans of the bridges he had dreamed. It swirled about his house. It slipped into the sleeves of his clothing and fluttered the cloth against him. His mouth filled with it and he rose and went out and stared off into the distance, across the near-black sea. He looked for what he knew not.

Chilingana thought his wife was asleep inside, but she lay awake. The wind had filled his house, and she had breathed it in as well as he.

She was aware of him outside, yet did not call him. No distance had ever existed between the woman and the man before he dreamed the bridges. They stretched into infinity like the lives of Chilingana and Lupeka. This new distance touched her with longing. She wondered: When had she come to be, and who had built her house? She assumed Chilingana had done it, but he never said. She had never before thought to ask. The two of them wanted for nothing: All the food of the world swam through the ocean beneath their house. Why, then, create such things as bridges? What purpose could they serve?

Fear gnawed at her then, that her husband wished to travel away from her into an unknown so vast that he might never return. The distance opened like a pit beneath her, and her breath caught in her throat.

The wind of loneliness heard her and was surfeited.

She arose and crept out the back of the house onto the balcony that surrounded it on all sides. She gazed out across the sea away from her husband. Her eyes followed Nocnal's bright stripe upon the swirls and waves until she made out, just above the horizon, the black edge of a bridge's line, and in the middle of it the black spire of a tower, and her fear frothed and foamed. She knew in wordless fashion that these spans connected to some other place, although she knew no other.

Her fearful musings disturbed Lord Akema's rest, prodding the face of Nocnal to call down, "What troubles you, lady?"

"Well," she answered, and then fell silent before the immensity of what she wanted to say. What was still emerging inside her soul had no words. She'd never known anything but herself; how could she express something so much larger? She kept silent. If Nocnal had to ask, then he didn't understand.

Yet he continued asking her till finally she retreated inside where the walls were near, the territory small and safe. When her husband came in later and lay down beside her, she rolled over to clasp him and he held her tight. "I know," he said.

"What?"

"Something is coming."

The certainty in his words terrified her more than her own inexpressible unease. "What is? What's coming? Tell me."

"When it arrives, I'll know it." He couldn't tell her more, and they lay like that, tightly bound in unshared fear, too conflicted even to remember shared desire.

Chilingana tried to forget what he'd told Lupeka. He continued fishing as he had always done, but with uneasy glances over his shoulder, down the length of the adjoining spans, across the ocean to where they vanished over the horizon.

One afternoon the face of Lord Akema was particularly fierce. Chilingana lay on the shadowed side of his house as people still do to escape the god's fury, and he happened to glance up to find a stranger walking up the next span.

The fisherman who had created the world leapt to his feet. Other than his wife, this was the first person he had ever seen. Whatever he'd dreaded for so long, this had to be it.

The stranger was tall and gaunt. He wore robes that we would say belonged to a mystic. They were deep red and glittered with powerful designs woven with silver thread, thick as fishbones. The hood of his robe kept the stranger's features in shadow. All Chilingana could determine was that this traveler was very dark indeed.

The stranger came to the place where the dreamed bridge ended and stepped across the gap onto the balcony encircling the stilt house. The stilts groaned beneath him as if he weighed as much as the world. He walked right up to Chilingana, who huddled shivering in the shadows. It took all the fisherman's reserves not to cry out and flee inside. He stared into a face of sharp cheekbones and high polished brows, looked into bottomless eyes. "Who are you?" he asked.

The traveler replied, "I am Death."

"What sort of name is that?"

Death laughed. "One new to you even though you're the Dreamer. Your bridges have grown to encompass the world, reaching even as far as the land of the dead, which is a barren and uninhabited place I was happy to leave. Your creation invited me to walk the world, and I set out directly to find you."

The fisherman raised his shoulders. "You aren't making sense."

"I think you'll see that I am, once you've come inside me." Death opened wide his robes, and Chilingana saw a place so cool and inviting that the harsh rays of Lord Akema couldn't find him there. He must have fallen into those robes, for he had no memory of walking. Once he was inside the cool place his mind tumbled with memories. The robes that had been held open closed, and at the core of the darkness within them lay a red glow of life out of which came discordant noises he'd never known—crackling energies and devices that rang and then spoke, the barking of dogs, the canister rumble of machines as they rolled along an empty boulevard, the clicking of a metal thing that unfurled strips of paper covered in indecipherable symbols, and the voices of people—more people than he could hold in his mind—all speaking at once and shouting through objects in the sky that were nothing like Akema, lifeless creations, but spraying chatter out and down like rain in a million different tongues drowning him under their flow. He saw impossible blue-glass buildings across which clouds slid like oil, and lighted things that were not fish but traveled far beneath his perfect sea, and he knew that all of these things, however they were new to him, were also ancient, long gone, dredged up out of a collective silt of memory, from some other time and place before he and his wife had arrived. And he knew torment, for in all his new recollections, his birth was nowhere to be found.

He sank to the stones before the traveler. His head hung, too heavy for his neck to lift. Death spoke. "Now you know mortality. Now you'll live and age and cling to what memories you have, because you will always be falling away from them."

Then Death left the fisherman there and entered his house. Chilingana tried to crawl after him, to shield his wife from this terrible conjurer. Why should she have to know these things? She hadn't done this—she hadn't made the bridges. But she couldn't be spared, else gaze down upon a mortal man whom she no longer would recognize as her husband.

Death did not leave, but when the fisherman dragged himself feebly inside, the traveler had gone, and his wife lay upon the bed, naked and open to him. She had been made fertile, able to bear children. Thus did Death plan to people his realm.

Nearing her, Chilingana recovered his strength, and they folded together and slept, safe so long as they touched.

In the morning, when he awoke, he was alone and certain that he had dreamed the traveler. He stretched, to find that his body ached unfamiliarly.

As he stood, he kicked something from the mat. It clattered across the floor. It was a silver object, small enough to lie in the palm of his hand. Grooves threaded the length of it; at the top was a large single slot. He had brought it back from the realm within Death's cloak.

When he stooped and lifted the thing, Chilingana dropped to his knees with his fist closed, and began to weep because now he could remember his entire life and he recognized that each day would hereafter be different from the last, and farther away than the land of Death itself.

Time upon Shadowbridge had begun. Life had arrived, carried by Death.

Leodora laid down the taro and the enoki. The gourd she'd already hidden in one sleeve, and she let it roll slowly out. It came to rest sitting up, its "head" canted as if toward the children. For them it had become the figure of Death; and for their mother, as well. She smiled at the storyteller, and now that smile was proof against grief. Her tears had dried and those of her children. "Thank you," she said.

Some members of the funeral procession had stopped when they found the widow missing, and had wandered back. They'd clustered close enough to hear the story, and complimented Leodora by dipping their heads in an informal bow. The widow turned to her people and then folded the children back in among them, but the two kept glancing over their shoulders at Leodora and the gourds as they were drawn away, and then lost from sight.

She got up, weary, her legs stiff from all the walking followed by sitting awkwardly while she performed the tale. She saw the expression on Diverus's face. "What is it?" she asked.

"I—I've no words. I stand amazed."

Blushing, she lowered her eyes. "You've no call to be. You have a far more remarkable talent than mine."

"No," he said. "Mine was a gift from the gods."

"How do you know mine isn't?"

"But—" He stopped, thought. "You've never even set foot on a dragon beam—you said as much."

"Is that the only way one is granted gifts?" Her voice teased now.

The question being too enormous in implication, he could only laugh with her. "I don't know. I don't know much of anything, do I?"

A cloud passed over the sun, and the empty street became suddenly dusky and vaguely ominous. At the crescent, where the body had been lowered, nothing had been left to mark the spot. Every building appeared to be deserted. Leodora gathered herself up.

Diverus asked, "How did you know what story to tell them?"

"I had three vegetables. The tale of Death was the first thing I thought of with three characters." She faced him as a look of doubt crossed his face. She let it go. She didn't want to explain herself, didn't want to answer how stories found her or how she'd looked into the faces of those children and their mother and known what they needed to hear. She would have to admit that she didn't understand how it happened, either, as he didn't know where his songs came from. "Right now I'm famished. We have a long walk ahead of us still, and I wouldn't care to have to join that parade of monsters again—they might not let us go this time."

She offered her hand and drew him to his feet, and they walked off together.

After their performance that second night, Soter informed Leodora and Diverus that they would be journeying on following the third performance. "We need to spread your reputation far and wide, can't be falling into the trap of staying in one place too long, even if the audiences are respectable."

"Respectable?" Leodora all but laughed at the word he'd chosen. The central garden had been filled. People had crowded into all three entrances to see the performance.

Soter pretended not to hear the sarcasm. He rocked back and forth on his feet as though the matter they'd spoken of was closed. Judging by the look on her face, he could not have infuriated Leodora more.

"I understand none of this," she said. "We stayed on in Vijnagar even when the mistress of the theater very nearly exposed us by trying to have her way with Jax, even after I complained of it to you. We were going to stay on even when I told you we needed to go. In fact we would be there still if it weren't for your encounter with that elf."

"Grumelpyn."

"What did he say that has you pushing us along now, before we've even set down our belongings and drawn a breath? Even when we thought Uncle Gousier might come after us, we didn't flee where we had an audience. In fact, on Merjayzin you were willing to risk letting him catch up with us at the thought of a paying house. We stayed there for two full weeks!"

He'd stopped rocking on his heels by then, and focused on Diverus as if he might appeal to the musician and the two of them outvote her. "Those were early days," he explained. "We needed the reputation to build, to fly ahead, to do the work for us so that by the time we arrived upon the next and the next span, they had already heard the rumors of you and I could haggle over a larger percentage of the take for us than if we'd just come in off the street like two vagabonds who hoped to swindle them a bit before climbing out a back window and making off with our loot."

Before Leodora could respond, Diverus asked, slowly and thoughtfully, "So by the time she found me, her reputation had grown enough that now you don't need to worry whether the next span has heard of her, yes?"

"I—" Soter hadn't been prepared for that question. Why couldn't they just do as he asked for once, instead of requiring a more thorough explanation of why he expected them to do as he wished? The little musician was as bad as she was. "Of *course* we need to have her reputation spread. Of course we do." He tried to laugh, to make it all light and unimportant that they might not wonder at the tension that underlay every word he spoke—the tension of fearing that he might have to give up more than he wanted. "But you know, there are infinite spans, infinite peoples and tales, and don't you want to see more of them?" He knew, even as he spoke, that he'd taken a wrong turn, because the question itself offered her the power to decide—the very thing he wanted to avoid.

"I do want to see them all," she said, "but I also want to learn every story, and I can't do that if I leave each span so rapidly that I haven't time to *find* the stories, hear them, add them to what I know. You said my father did the same."

"Yes," replied Soter, knowing there was no other answer, and no way to distract her from what she would say next, which he heard as if it were an echo preceding the sound that made it.

"I want the time to collect the stories."

"Lea."

"No, don't grease your words to me. Don't make promises and don't explain my behavior to me when you can't account for your own."

"All right then." He hung his head. It was the only option left him. "How long do we stay?"

"I don't know."

"Yes, and that is because it's not your responsibility to know," he insisted, but carefully.

She shook her head in frustration.

"Three nights?"

"Longer," she said.

"Five then."

"I don't know."

He sighed. "Once again, Lea, it is my part, my *role*, to ascertain the best venue, and how long we can rely upon the people to attend, and who will pay us the most. This is a job I do well. I'm certainly no puppeteer, but without me, you would have no way to prove that you *are*."

She leaned forward then and said, "All right. Five nights on this span."

He nodded, and said, "Done!"

She got up heavily, as if the argument had worn her out. "I've two hours before the performance. I'm going to rest." The courtyard seemed to tremble at her passing.

Left behind, Diverus fidgeted, stealing glances at Soter as he commented, "I'm new to human interactions, but I wonder that anybody understands anybody." He, too, took his leave of the garden.

Alone, Soter toasted himself and, after downing the small cup of liquor, said, "Five, then. I can live with that. For now."

The next three days, Leodora collected stories. Each day she checked the park before looking elsewhere. On the first day she did find a group playing gō there, but it wasn't the fox and his friends, who never did reappear. "Maybe it takes a long time to go to the end of everything and come back," said Diverus.

"But they invited us to come back the next *day*." Even as she argued, she guessed the explanation, and before Diverus could say it she countered herself: "Days and nights aren't the same to the demons in that parade."

"That's what I think, too," Diverus replied. "What I meant."

She roamed the entire span, eventually crossing onto the split on the far side of the valley of stilt houses, seeking groups, clusters of people at leisure whom she could chat up and ask for a story. She even came across the same palanquin bearers she had used in explaining story collecting to Diverus, and as she'd told him they did indeed serve up a plethora of salacious stories about their mistress. None of these could be performed, but they contained images and ideas and moments she might borrow, retool, and fold into some unrelated telling to make it unique.

She received stories such as the tale of the priest who was so lonely that he created an artificial friend, but got the spell horribly wrong so that his friend wanted most of all to eat him—a story she performed the same night, provoking both laughter and gasps.

The courtyard filled earlier each night. People declined to take dinner until afterward in order to get close to the booth.

The final performance in Hyakiyako, she concluded with a repeat rendition of "The Ghost of Nikki Danjo." While the puppet of Masaoka pressed against the side of the screen and bit into her arm to keep from screaming, her son died in agony of poisoning. She dared not cry out, as the audience knew, else give away that she had discovered the identity of the real villain of the piece—Nikki Danjo himself.

Soter sat off to the side of the booth, both to watch Leodora's skillful performance and to mingle with the crowd. Once again the courtyard was full to overflowing. Mutsu would be deliriously happy, almost as happy as he had been furious when Soter told him that they could not stay beyond five nights.

The crowd booed when the evil regent Nikki Danjo slid onto the screen again. The body language of the puppet implicated him as he crept across the room to advise his lord, and the puppet of Masaoka, behind him, equally betrayed her fear. Soter, though he was used to Leodora's craft, found himself swept up in the tale. The puppets became real people. He could see the room that surrounded them rather than the shadow of doorways, screens, and lanterns. He heard not Leodora's voice, but the voices of the overlord and the woman and the evil Danjo. He shook his head as if he'd begun to fall asleep, and blamed the many cups of rice wine he'd consumed. It was powerful stuff, and he wasn't used to it. Plus, he conceded—if only to himself—Diverus's music made her voice seem to change, adding weight and depth to the male voices. Soter drifted into it, his head nodding.

He straightened up on his stool, then rubbed his eyes while glancing around himself at the crowd, all so riveted by the performance that not one met his gaze. He found himself similarly drawn back to the pale screen, glowing lightly red now as the story neared an explosive climax. She had learned to increase the colors subtly, slowly, so that the audience hardly noticed that it had gone from white to crimson by the end of the play. Gods, he was proud of her! She had no idea how proud. Why didn't he tell her? He ought to tell her.

Then, as he stared at the screen, it seemed to draw him in, growing darker the closer he came.

When he looked up, the courtyard had turned the color of blood, as if the light from her lantern had become liquid and smeared every surface. Soter dragged the back of his hand across his eyes. He looked first at the starlit sky above to confirm that it was still in place; but when he glanced down again the audience had transformed into puppets—giant, articulated puppets, their profiles translucent, features sharply drawn. He yipped and craned away in his chair, only to find that he was leaning into more puppets. The closest one swiveled its leathery head and gave him a nettled glare. He stared at the booth then, straight at the screen where Leodora performed. He clung to the identifiable shadows, denied the room. The performance continued, the story unfolded. In her fiction lay his truth. Without daring to glance away, he reached to the small table behind him and patted about for his wine cup.

A moist hand closed over his wrist and held it.

He stiffened. He sat paralyzed.

Close behind him a voice said, "So here we are at last." It was Gousier's voice and it was all Soter could do not to leap away screaming. Instead, denying the hive of panic whirling through his belly, he made himself slowly turn around, outwardly calm, his mouth fixed in a ghastly smile. Even that little resolve deserted him the moment he saw the speaker.

Behind and above him stood the Coral Man. It glowered down at him—he knew it though there were no eyes in its head, no distinct features at all. The grip on his wrist was some sort of clammy tentacle extending from beneath the table, as gray as the figure but alive and slick.

"Soter," it said, the voice no longer Gousier's, but distantly familiar—a voice from a void deep inside him that he wanted to deny. "Soter, you'll be found. Make no mistake. Found wanting."

He could not bear the force of the scrutiny, which seemed to split him open. It was as if all the wriggling creatures that had once lived in the pores of that chalky coral were burrowing into the wound and feasting their way through him. Soon he would be nothing but bones, enveloped completely, a husk. He had to break away, face the performance, the red screen—he trembled with the effort of dismissing the apparition—turning in time to see the fitting end of Nikki Danjo, haunting it was, yes, and *Remember the story*, he urged himself, it was a puppet ghost, but somehow he was in the story now, seated among puppets with a ghost of his own looming in their midst. He stared so hard at the red light and the shadow figures that his eyes burned with tears from not blinking. He squeezed them shut, then jolted upright in his seat again. His arm, twisted behind him, ached horribly and he moved it, clutching his cup. His hand slid freely upon the table. Only then did he blink and glance around, wiping again at his eyes, this time with the meat of his palm. He opened one eye while he covered the other, warily peeking at his neighbor who, sensing his movement, grinned at him and said, "Very good, yes?" A normal face—bad teeth, certainly, but a normal face, not one of her puppets. Soter knew before he'd twisted around on the stool that no Coral Man would be hovering at his back. Everyone wedged into the courtyard looked normal, joyous with recognition of the masterful storytelling they'd just witnessed. They raised their hands and applauded—a burst of noise that made him jump.

"I slept, that's all it was. I dreamed. Bardsham—" He rolled his wrist and saw it then, the one perfect circle, the sucker mark, purple where it had bruised him. Everyone else was clapping and cheering.

The screen had gone dark, the lantern extinguished. Instinct took over and Soter leapt to his feet, walked forward, clapping his own hands and calling, "Jax, my friends, the artistry of Jax!" while the crowd shouted and pounded their cups on the tables, and someone broke out a flute and began to play a frenetic melody above the din. The cheering flowed to follow and then accompany the flute, becoming a song.

After a minute Leodora stepped through the side of the booth, her head cowled, her face masked, and the song dissolved into a roar. She had played their stories and won their hearts. This was how it had been with Bardsham. The impeccable skill of a genius had overwhelmed the crowds. The energy of their pleasure flowed right through him to the artist. It was wonderful. Behind her, Diverus came out—it was becoming a routine now—and waved the shamisen he'd been playing; the audience cheered for him, too.

Here was everything they sought and he was making them leave because he was afraid. And the Coral Man had stood right there and told him it would do no good. Run to the next span, he would be found. If you wanted to remain hidden, you could not have great talent. Talent made noise; people would notice you, remember you. Jax—they would be speaking of the master puppeteer from one end of the span to the other tomorrow. A few more days and news of these performances would overtake the stories Grumelpyn had heard, louder now and more certain, the way it had been with Bardsham. "You'll be found"—he muttered the warning.

Why, he asked the air, why did she have to be brilliant? Why did she have to shine so brightly? Why had she made them leave the damned backwater of that island? He blamed her, knowing full well that she wasn't to blame. He made his smiles to the crowd. Then he realized she wasn't wearing the band that restricted her breasts. She'd forgotten to put it on after the performance. Someone would see, someone would fathom the truth. He thought to move, to step between the crowd and the object of their adoration.

Then Leodora did the unthinkable. She pushed back the cowl and drew her braid free.

Watching the crowd for any sign that they'd recognized her womanliness, he only glimpsed the flash of her hair. "No," he said, more in disbelief than as a warning, but no one heard him over the din of the song they were singing.

He faced her then, crying, "Don't you dare!"

But she'd already reached a hand in front of her face, and she pulled the black mask up and away. The crowd yelled louder. She tugged loose the cord binding her hair then shook it all free, a shining red fan, a copper waterfall around her. They simply went mad then.

She shouted her name and they gave it back. Cries of "Leodora!" drowned out "Jax!" Coins flew through the air and rained all around her.

Soter wanted to sear her with a look the way the Coral Man had crushed him with its regard, but her stance defied him, denying him the right to hide her any longer. *It's too late*, said her pose, *you may dictate the dates and the venues and the spans, but you'll not control my identity any longer*. He knew this story; he'd told it to her: How had he thought it would have a different ending this time? "Bardsham," he despaired.

Something broke inside him. He could not oppose her, he had no will any longer, no strength for the battle any longer. Chaos was coming after him, bearing down upon them all, and it would find him whether he hid her or not. It was what the Coral Man had been saying. He stared at the mark on his wrist.

There could be no going on to the next span now. No simple passage through a tunnel would disguise her identity, her name. That would travel, too, now: the skill of her father and the shape of her mother, the name so close.

She had unleashed herself, and now they had to flee.

THREE

"What do you mean, *by boat*?" Leodora asked Soter.

"I mean," he said, leaning upon the undaya case, "we have ourselves taken to another spiral of the span. We abandon this trip north along this arm of the spiral and begin again—"

"—where we're not known! It means everything I just did on four spans is for nothing. I go back to being Jax, a *boy*, because they won't know anything about what happened here tonight. The story of this will carry up the line, maybe even as far as your elf friend's span."

"Grumelpyn."

"I *know* his wretched name," she snarled, and for a moment he actually feared she would strike him, pick up a cup or a knife and attack him; but her anger, boiling up beyond her control, brought tears to her eyes, and despite her every effort she began to cry. "Daimons damn you, Soter, I won't do it!"

Diverus, standing uncomfortably behind her through it all, raised his hands as if to place them on her shoulders to comfort her, but seemed at the last to lose his nerve; he drew them back against himself like a mantis about to fall upon a victim. Soter saw it, registered the significance—that a bond had grown already between them that he would be foolish to try to sever—and bowed his head, pinching the bridge of his nose. His head hurt. He should have objected to such language from her, but he couldn't work up the false ire. He deserved every invective. Worse, he had no good argument to justify this change of plans. In that tense moment he could think of only one story, lame as it was, and only one promise that might convince her.

"You won't have to," he said. "You don't have to pretend to be Jax anymore—or, rather, Jax becomes a woman. We'll sail to a span where they won't mind. Colemaigne. We'll go to Colemaigne." It had been the span of choice anyway. "It's one of the oldest spans, and they have *no* restrictions about—"

"About women?" She might have been crying but her voice remained all threat.

"About much of anything. They're the epitome of the debauched."

"Like Vijnagar."

"Oh, my dear, Vijnagar is positively puritanical. It hides its predilections beneath its surface." He gestured at Diverus as living proof of what he said. "In Colemaigne there's no hypocrisy of that sort. And they'll welcome you. Perform a Meersh story for them first thing. They always loved him. Positively their favorite. I'll be surprised if they haven't erected a statue to him by now."

"I don't have to pretend?" She was wounded, but the anger had drained from her voice.

"No," he assured her. "No pretending. And we'll work our way around, you see, while the story of you spreads from two sources instead of one. By the time we play half a dozen spans on that spiral, the tales of you will have closed up, they'll meet with us in the middle. Then we'll have a circuit to travel. Maybe we'll even sail to a third one before then and spread your reputation farther. Why, by the time we return to Ningle, we'll be riding in on the shoulders of crowds, too esteemed for your uncle even to—"

"Ningle?" she said warily. "We're going back there?"

"Not soon, but, you know, it was part of the circuit in Bardsham's day, and there are many good venues on that spiral, but above and below it. We're just broadening our compass, is all, as well as our repertoire. You *wanted* to see the world and collect its stories, didn't you tell me that?" He waited for her reply, hanging everything on that reminder—the argument fabricated even as he was saying it.

She sniffled and made a weak smile. "All right. That is—" She turned about. "—Diverus?"

"Yes?" He seemed surprised that anyone cared to ask his opinion.

"Would you want to go? To sail to another span?" Behind her, Soter observed him coldly with a look that might have implied a threat.

He replied, "I've nothing to compare it to. I've never been on a boat." Then as an afterthought he added, "But if it takes me farther from Vijnagar, that's probably good, isn't it?"

"Well, there you are," Soter said.

She nodded. "All right, Soter. It's settled." He smiled but she didn't meet his gaze, wouldn't look at him as she parted the fabric and stepped out of the booth. He tried to listen to her retreat, but she tread silently like a cat.

Then it was just the two of them, with Diverus looking puzzled and uncertain. "You care about her," Soter said. "Well, so do I. I'm protecting her, though she's unaware of it."

"Protecting her from what?" asked Diverus.

For an instant he contemplated confiding, but as quickly rejected the idea as insane. "From everything," he replied. He stared at the open case and shivered. The Coral Man lay hidden in the bottom compartment. When that figure had invaded Leodora's dreams, he'd dismissed it, or at least pretended to. Now he appreciated what it meant to have something without a mouth, without a face really, speaking to you.

He'd have liked to open the case, haul out the boxed puppets, and confront the figure. In his mind's theater he carried the Coral Man to the edge of the span and tossed it into the ocean where it sank without a trace, for someone else to find. What he said was, "Be sure you secure that case well and then grab yourself some sleep, boy. We'll be up *early* tomorrow for us. Or, rather, today." Then he, like Leodora, stepped out of the booth and left Diverus alone to secure the lid and blow out the lantern.

From the stern of the ship, she watched Hyakiyako shrink slowly, steadily, rounding upon the horizon until the whole length of it and of the span north of it—which they would not know hereafter—lay upon the sea like the body of a great dark snake, with the towers that divided the two spans projecting like horns, but even this image dwindled and soon only the tops of the towers remained, illusively rising and falling, buoyed upon the choppy sea until, finally, they vanished and with them the sense of the continuity of her life. Disconnected, she could not mask the pit of terror this opened in her, that everything had now been abandoned and she was lost in a way she'd never been, even when turned from Bouyan and the haven of home.

When finally she pushed away from the lost view, the tillerman, seated beside her with one arm up and pressed to the rudder bar, looked her up and down as if not sure what he made of her.

She walked unsteadily toward the ship's prow—for all that she'd ridden a sea dragon and lived upon an island that fished for its livelihood, she had never set foot in a boat before, and this one seemed determined to throw her to her knees. It was a shallow-bottomed craft and felt much too small and flimsy to undertake journeys across vast stretches of open water—especially with no one but the tillerman seeming to pay the slightest attention to how it sailed.

In the middle of the deck and butted up to the mainmast stood the only shelter the boat afforded, a small shack—at least, that was her opinion of it. The crew called it a "house." Soter had ducked into its dark recesses before they'd even left the span, along with the remaining three crewmen, and he hadn't come out since. He'd been unusually reticent this morning, mostly nodding or shaking his head in response to questions, and more than once as they'd waited to cast off she had caught his gaze at the other boats moored along the two quays that projected from the side of the span, as though he expected something to come from them. When she looked, the boats were empty. No one was paying them any mind at all.

Like Soter, Diverus sat in the shadows of the shack. He had his arms wrapped about his knees and was trying very hard not to be ill. She would have liked to have confided in him, asked him what he thought of Soter's behavior, but clearly he was in no condition to discuss anything at the moment.

The two undaya cases were secured to the side of the little shack, surrounded by more crates and baskets of amphorae packed in straw. She steadied herself against them as the ship abruptly lurched. Then she took hold of one of the sail-control lines and swooped beneath the woven main sail and toward the second mast. A control line ran from that smaller sail to the side of the boat, and she caught it and swung beneath it with her feet up and was a child again for a moment, free and untethered. She let go and landed beside the mast, almost kicking what she took to be an enormous yellow cable, as big around as her waist, that encircled the base of the mast. The cable flinched, and Leodora caught herself against the mast, leaning forward precariously over the cable. In the middle of it an eye opened and a thin reed of a tongue flicked into the air. The cable's color changed then, yellow becoming brown, darkening to viridian. It was not hemp rope at all, but an enormous snake. She backed away from it, then scurried to the prow of the boat, and once there glanced over her shoulder. The snake hadn't moved. Its color was blending with the deck again, until she was looking once more at a coil of rope that had no apparent eyes or tongue. The snake had gone back to sleep. It didn't care about her.

In the vee of the prow, ahead of the lugsail, a small step boosted her high enough that, gripping the side tightly, she could lean over the stem head of the boat to look down into the water as it parted beneath her. She saw a fragmented reflection in the ripple, a face split into shadowed halves topped by a burnished cowl of hair that flared with the late-afternoon light. The water was a deep blue, almost violet. She felt that if she'd leaned down far enough to dip her hand in, it would have come out dyed.

Ahead lay only more ocean, and no hint of any other spiral. Gulls wheeled around them, probably hoping for some food, and that suggested to her that nothing else lay anywhere near, for surely gulls would find better feeding off a span or even an isle than from a single small boat where no one was eating.

If the world was infinite as Soter claimed, then how far might Colemaigne be? The way he'd described the world when she was small, she'd imagined that one span led to the next, and wherever you were you could look out over the rail and see the nearest spiral just across the way. That was certainly not the truth, however. The world might contain infinite spirals, but they could also be infinitely separated. And so, no longer able to assume that what she assumed was true, she wondered about the truth of Colemaigne. It was a much-celebrated place, the subject of endless fables and tales and, most likely, lies. A locus for hedonistic delights, they said, where wine flowed from a huge central fountain and through a thousand capillaries, so that no matter where you were, you had only to dip your cup to sample it. Streets were paved with a crust of hard rock candy, and glazed pastry shell houses leaned over them. No one ever went hungry and every pleasure was indulged—no worries, no desires left unfulfilled. She might have been amazed by such tales once, but now—and especially after rescuing Diverus from the paidika—she understood that for one person's pleasure to be indulged, another must submit to indulging it. Pleasure had its price, even when paid by another.

In any case the stories were ancient, as old as those of the storyfish and Meersh, according to Soter. What Colemaigne might have been in its past said nothing of what it was now. Look at Ningle, a decrepit, crumbling span that had once been new and glorious and blessed by Edgeworld, and which was surely much younger than their proposed destination.

Colemaigne by implication had to be on an ancient spiral. How else could a span so old exist? Every span linked to it must likewise be old, mustn't it? Or did bridge spans spring up suddenly after long intervals, the way that spans had appeared night upon night in Chilingana's story? Another span, called Valdemir in one of the Meersh tales, had fallen into the sea because it was so old. Would another span have replaced it, then or later, or was there a permanent gap where it had been? She hadn't seen enough of the world to surmise much less know the answers to such questions. Besides, every span on every spiral had its creation story; many were alike, but just as many contradicted the rest. While Chilingana's was nearly universal—at least it seemed to be so far—it didn't account at all for the unseen gods of Edgeworld, for Dragon Bowls or the myriad creatures and cultures she knew existed. How could one fisherman have dreamed it all? Finally she doubted she knew anything about the truth of the origins of Shadowbridge and suspected nobody else did, either. It didn't bear contemplating. She was part of this world. The truth of its creation and its being, whatever that was, wouldn't make her less or more so. Nevertheless, she wondered if she could ever unravel the mystery. Maybe, someday, if she ever found the mythical Library and it contained all the works it was supposed to—maybe *then* she would discover the truth; but not here, not in the company of a drunken old liar and a boy her age whose memory barely stretched back beyond a few subterranean months. So she focused her thoughts on their destination and let herself be excited by the notion of setting foot on one of the most ancient spans no matter what shape it was in now, for such a span must know the oldest stories, the earliest versions of all the tales she already knew. With luck Soter would let them stay awhile on each of *these* spans, giving her time to soak up everything while Jax's reputation spread.

She stood at the prow until sea spray showered her, then jumped back, but too late, already drenched. The lugsail slapped against the back of her head.

"The price of curiosity," hissed a low voice.

She crouched and looked beneath the sail. Nobody else stood on the deck; but the snake, against the mast, had raised his head. Although his body was yellow, the head had darkened again to green.

She pushed her dripping hair out of her face and walked halfway to the second mast. "And what's *your* price?" she asked, just to be certain who was speaking to her.

The snake's head rolled from side to side. He said, "That would depend upon what you're purchasing."

"What sort of snake are you, then?"

"Do you mean, am I the sort who would sup on you?"

"It would be useful to know."

"Your drenching hasn't done a thing to curb your curiosity, has it?" He sounded amused.

She walked closer. Her bare feet left wet prints across the deck. "I'd rather know than not know, if that's what you mean."

His head bobbed back and forth as if he was weighing her answer, then suddenly he stretched toward her. She leaned back but otherwise didn't move. She'd judged that he would have to unwind one coil to reach her; but close, she could see the remarkable blue and yellow facets of his eyes. He opened his mouth wide in a yawn. There were no fangs.

"If you must know, I'm an Ondiont."

"Ondionts are water snakes."

"So you know something then, after all. Yes, we are water serpents, my people."

"Then what are you doing on a boat?"

"Being lazy. Actually, I'm supposed to be a sentry to protect the cargo these creatures shuttle back and forth from one span to another. I've been sentry now for months, and so far I haven't had to do more than stick out my tongue to send off the occasional scavenger. Eventually, I've been assured, they will ferry me home."

"Do Ondionts have a span of their own?"

He snorted. "A span? What would we do with a span? How would we get up the stairs from the sea?"

"I've no idea."

"Nor does anyone else. No, we have an isle, mostly rock, full of caverns— very nice, cool caverns out of the sun to sleep in."

"So, what *do* you eat?"

"Everything. Same as you." He rubbed the side of his head against the mast, his eyes closing ecstatically. "We squeeze it to death first. If necessary." His narrow pupils settled on her again. "Now, what is it you're buying, story-teller?"

"How do you—?"

"I listened to all you were saying to one another when you boarded. People will tell you everything if they don't realize you're listening. Stillness is a great skill. I'm sure you know this. I'm sure there are moments when you hold your puppets absolutely rigid to draw in your audience, and then *strike*." She thought if he'd had teeth he would have been grinning at her.

"If you know what I am, then you must know what I'm seeking."

"You would like a tale of the Ondionts, as different from your own people as I am from you." When she nodded, he said, "My price for this is that you must sit beside me."

"So that you can squeeze me to death before you eat me?"

His tongue flicked in irritation. "So that you and I have a pact of trust. You must trust that I won't crush you."

She rubbed the bottom of one foot against the other ankle. "That would seem to put all the trust on my side of the bargain. What are you trusting me to do?"

"I am trusting you to honor the story every time you tell it on the spans of men and other creatures, by telling it true. Mine is the greater trust, because if you break it, there's nothing I can do about it."

"There's nothing I can do about it, either, should you choose to crush me."

"That's quite probably true. But you might attract the sailors and your comrades, who are inside, and they could certainly kill me before I could finish my meal. And anyway, they would see. It's not as if you would be easy to hide once I did eat you."

They faced each other in silence then, and if the snake was thinking anything at all, she couldn't tell. Yet she sensed that, like the kitsune who'd led the procession of monsters, the snake meant her no harm.

She walked boldly up beside him and sat down cross-legged on the deck. "What story then pays for my trust?"

The snake opened his mouth wide and hissed. She tensed to flee until she realized that he was laughing. "You've steel in you, storyteller."

"Maybe not as much as you imagine."

"Oh, the contrary. I'm a judge of such things. But now to your reward. Here is a story you do not know." He lowered his head and, very delicately, laid it upon her lap. His crystalline eyes swiveled to look up at her as he spoke. "There was once a serpent woman who collected souls."

THE STORY OF MISSANSHA

Her name was Missansha, which means "the lonely one" in the Ondiont speech. She was born blind, and this is very rare among my people. Perhaps because of this, she schooled her other senses. We have a strong sense of smell, but hers was superior. She could flick her tongue and tell you what lay beyond the horizon, picking up its scent long before anyone else could.

However, as she came of age, she developed one particular talent that no other of us has—she could sip life itself. When she came near anyone else, she drank from them. She surely didn't know this was unusual. It was how she was. Nor could she control it, any more than the living can control the urge to breathe. Inadvertently, like a basilisk, she drained the life from two playmates.

We have elders among us in whom we place our governance, and she was taken before them for this crime; but even as she was escorted into the room, she was draining those guards who accompanied her. One collapsed at her side; the other slithered away for his life. No one, nor especially her family, could come near her. The more she cared, the more absolutely she absorbed.

Now, we do not slay our own, least of all for things they cannot control, and Missansha bore no responsibility for this. She wept for those she destroyed. We could not harm her for it.

The elders chose the only solution they could imagine. They would commission a tower for her, high enough that she would never again come near them. As you can imagine, for snakes such an undertaking was near impossible, and so we sent out messengers to the bridges, to ships, to other islands, asking for assistance. There were few who accepted our very generous offer to come and erect our tower. Serpents have an unsavory reputation among other species, most of which we've done nothing to earn. We're simply distrusted for our appearance and stories concocted about us, our decency dismissed. But I digress.

There were humans who deigned to set foot on our island. They were paid handsomely for their masonry skills, their talent, and their labor—we have much gold in our caverns. And there were no unfortunate incidents of the sort that can spoil a relationship . . . that is, until the tower was complete and it was time to place Missansha in it.

Some of us there were who speculated that Missansha's powers might only hold sway over her own kind. The long, ascending rampway that spiraled around the outside of the tower, though it was built for snakes, still posed a burden to us. We asked that these foreigners would escort her to her chambers. None of us wished to be close enough, and we could not have her slither off the edge of the narrow ramp.

We made another generous offer, and two of them volunteered. The rest waited alongside us.

Only one of the volunteers returned. The other died as he reached the top. His body became as glass, transparent and stiff. The survivor managed to lock her in before he stumbled back down the spiral to safety. We offered to nurse him back to health—we had much experience by now with the effect of her—but, no, the foreigners did not trust us after that, these alien creatures. They departed our shore and never returned. The tower they'd built was solid, well constructed for the ages, and we left her there, banished with us but never among us.

Once a week someone carried food to her, leaving it where she could reach it. At least for a long time this was so. Over time, the act of delivering food became a ritual. To be chosen was an honor. Because it was codified as ritual, no one asked if the food was taken, if there was a sign she still survived. She surely had long since died. The ritual continued nonetheless.

And so it was for centuries, the lonely one isolated safely above us. We congratulated ourselves that we had found a benign solution to her existence.

What happened then was that Death paid us a personal visit.

Death as you know looks like anyone. When he is among you humans, he looks like one of you. Among the Ondionts he was a serpent, and yet dissimilar. Obsidian of eyes and sheathed in bone. Unlike us, he had arms, thin as reeds and supple, down the sides of his body. We knew him the instant he arrived, and he did not dissemble, but came right to the point.

"I want to know," he said, "how it is that you have all stopped coming to me."

The elders, who had been unborn when Missansha was sent away, shuffled meekly up to him. They replied as one, "We don't know what you mean."

"There are rules," he explained. "I for my part must adhere to them, as must you. Else what sort of a world would we have? You, for your part, seem to have ceased to die, and I wish to know how you have done this—

what magic or art now protects you. I've traveled a long way for the answer and I will not leave without it."

Now, none of them understood Death's accusation. Ondionts had been born and had died as always. Our insignificant island would have become surfeited otherwise, and our caverns jammed with wriggling tenants. Death saw this for himself even as they protested their innocence. He noted the tower rising in their midst—something no snakes had built—and his sinister arms pointed at it.

"Why is that erected?" he asked.

Before they had even finished reciting the now mythic story of Missansha, Death gestured them to silence.

"You think then that by placing a problem out of sight, you resolve it? That is your notion?"

"But how could we punish her?"

"Forgive me, did I suggest you should have punished her?" answered Death. "And yet you are of the opinion that she relishes her imprisonment. That placing her in a tiny room in the sky is not a punishment to her?"

"But . . . but she wasn't put to *death*!" exclaimed one of the elders, who immediately regretted his outburst and shrank away. For a moment he had forgotten to whom he spoke.

"No," agreed Death, showing his teeth. "She was not. Not to *death*, but surely to madness have you condemned her. You are not people who fare well when isolated, and she began life more isolated than the rest of you." With that Death passed through the crowd. One by one they lay down before him. At the tower's base he stared up into the sky, to the very tip of it. He imagined himself there and a moment later he stood at the top, for that was how Death traveled.

His hands pressed that barred door, and it opened to him. Inside, it was dark and cobwebbed. Spiders had busily taken over the space. They dropped from their webs as he passed beneath them.

Deeper into the chamber, Death saw tiny lights burning—an entire wall of them. This struck him as unlikely. The lights sparkled. They were round like the eggs laid by Ondionts. They *were* eggs, in fact, and the fire in each was a spark of life. He reached the wall and pried one loose from the mucilage that held it. He held it in his hands, and with his needle-like fingers, he cracked it open and let the light escape. Like a flame it leapt up at him, and then through him. He heard it, saw it, experienced its life in a burst, because that is what the soul is—every moment of the life that was known, compressed into a flame of existence. It sang to him as it passed from this plane of being. And from the darkness behind him, a voice unused to speaking croaked, "What was that? How did my little song escape?"

Death turned and there she was. Impossibly alive, thin and ancient, and yet to him unutterably beautiful.

"I let it go," he said.

Missansha gasped. She uncurled and rose to his height, the height of his voice. She'd learned to do that as a child, as a way of protecting herself. "How did I not hear you enter?"

"No one hears me enter, just as no one can surprise me. And yet you have just done that impossible thing."

She didn't need eyes to identify him. The sense of him burned her like heat.

"These," he said, and turned back to the wall.

"My songs," she replied. "Long ago they began to come to me here in this chamber, I don't know from where. They entered me, pierced me, and then I birthed each one. So long ago that began, I can hardly remember the time before it."

"Another impossible thing, I think." He could still taste the essence of that soul he'd freed; he understood now how she had lived for so long. The lives entering her had passed to her a little of their being, each one rolling back her age. "Once upon a time, you lost your wits. You had already a power, a great and fearful power that frightened your people, and in the madness of isolation this gift transformed. It grew. You became as I am."

He drew beside her. His hands embraced her, and for the only time in her life Missansha felt what it was like for others to stand near *her*. There was no pain, but she was sundering from the world. "Am I dying?" she asked.

Death answered, "No. Something else."

She could not think what to say.

When it was done, her metempsychosis, they opened the eggs together and let Missansha's songs fly. It was orgasmic. The songs swirled and swept through her. She leaned back her head, and her tongue flicked at the sky. She moaned and would have swooned but Death caught her. "You're not used to it," he told her. "So many at once is dizzying."

She would have agreed had she been able to speak, but her voice failed her. She looked into his empty eyes and realized that she could see. He, as if apprehending her confusion, said, "Your corporeal eyes could not see; but you no longer have need of them."

Soon the last of the souls had been released from where Missansha had collected them. She had been preserving them—though she hadn't recognized it—as a dowry for her groom.

When, after some days of speculating, the surviving people climbed the tower, they found the room at the top abandoned. No trace remained of Missansha save for her cast-off skin. Her body was missing and the floor covered with shattered eggshells, dry and empty; covered also with the bodies of a hundred spiders, curled and desiccated.

Of Death himself there was no sign, either.

"And that," said the snake, raising his head from her lap, "is how my people met Death. In return for providing him with a bride, we were given very long lives. And we've never been sure if that was his blessing or his punishment for how we'd treated her. What do you think?" He leaned over Leodora; the sun had all but set now, and the penultimate orange glow glittered in his eyes like hunger.

"Both," she answered without hesitation, and the snake tilted his head thoughtfully and then gave a small nod.

"Ssseeyash," he said and placed his head on her shoulder.

"What does that mean?"

His tongue darted. "It's not translatable; you don't have the concept in your language. It references the shedding of the skin, the death of the old shell and the life manumitted beneath, the balance of the two coexisting being true existence, and so it is a word that expresses ultimate truth."

"That's a very complicated way to say you think something is true."

"Yes, which is why we have a simple word to hold all of it."

She reached up and stroked his nose. He sighed and closed his eyes. After a moment he muttered, "You're dangerously brave, Leodora."

"Foolishly so?"

"That has yet to be determined, and won't be by me. You imagine that stories protect you, and that makes you brave. But it doesn't mean it's true."

"Is that a warning?"

"Advice. Nothing more. Death comes looking for everyone eventually."

"I'll try not to invite him."

"I suppose you *must* take it lightly," he replied. "To do otherwise is to admit your fear."

"If I let it stand in my way, I'll never get off this boat. I wouldn't have gotten on in the first place. I wouldn't have ridden a sea dragon. I'd have married the choice of my uncle."

"All concrete objects of fear, real and tangible," said the snake, and she knew by the way he said it that there was another kind of fear he didn't speak of.

She would have asked him, but at that point one of the crew members raced past to the boat's prow, and she turned to look where he did.

Riding the horizon, a black sail protruded against the sun's ember. It was tiny, but clearly a ship.

Soter walked up beside her. She looked at him, and saw abject horror on his face. His gaze flicked over the water to where the crewman was looking, then down at her as he said, "You have to come inside. Now."

"Inside?"

"In the shack, the house, here."

"Why?"

"For safety. Please, don't fight with me, just come inside till that boat out there has gone."

"What about my friend the snake?" She turned, to find that the snake had retreated, his head down, eyes closed, back around the mast so that he looked like a rope again. His was the perfect disguise.

"What are you talking about, a snake?"

"Nothing," she replied, and got to her feet. He grabbed her arm and drew her along beside him. As they hurried clumsily into the shack, one of the crew came out from it, carrying a large lit lantern. He carried it to the starboard side and hung it off a hook there. It dangled out over the water.

"Why not in the bow?" she asked.

"In case someone hostile comes, they'll see the lamp, but from a distance they can't tell if it's fore or aft, or port or starboard, and so can't gauge where to board till they're close upon it. Every ship, every boat, puts the lamp somewhere different, and the only reasonable thing you can do is steer a wide berth around 'em."

How, she wondered, did he know the way things worked on board ships? "Hostile?" she asked, but he didn't answer.

By the time the new ship neared, the sun was gone, the sky black; the breeze had died away. For a while Leodora had watched the ship's inexorable approach. One light split into two—two red glows like mismatched eyes of a behemoth slithering silently toward them. Soon the ship came close enough that she could make it out—at least the places where it glistened. It was black as the night around it. The red running lights were strung upon ropes, one off its nose and one off the stern. As it overtook the tail of their boat, Soter pulled her back into the blackness of the house. Where he sat behind them, Diverus looked up at the commotion. The nose of the black ship pushed into view.

The ship had a high foredeck that dropped off before the mainmast. It was a deep-bottomed craft, and its ropes and tackle creaked as it drew alongside. The red lantern on the prow rocked back and forth. The ship slowed.

Soter's grip on her shoulders squeezed tight, and she almost cried out before he released her. She could hear him slide deeper into the darkness, his fear like an oil sprayed upon the air. The forward light glided past, and the side of the ship hove into view. It seemed to be lined with odd pillars. Then all at once she realized that the pillars were people, figures standing motionless along the side—she counted five of them, their bodies dark like the ship, edged only in the rolling red lantern light; their pale heads smooth, gleaming, hairless, their eyes seeming to welter in deep sanguine sockets. Their fixed stare like a braided force sliced through the protective shadows. Red light splashed along the deck ahead of her, doubling and bending the shadows, penetrating the depths of the three-sided house, steadily, rhythmically, like a pendulum as the forward lamp swung. She watched, hypnotized, as color flowed toward her feet and away, cast back again, closer, away and closer, away and closer. Then Soter snatched her into the depths of the shack, and the light splashed across Diverus where he sat staring at it, either unafraid or too ill to move. It lit the room, hooks and gaffs, ropes and tackle, all along the wall where Diverus sat. Soter pressed Leodora against the starboard wall and out of the light completely.

Yet for all that his dread was palpable, nothing happened. The black ship glided on into the night until the light from its rear lanterns had merged into a single spot, a cinder cooling, shrinking, until it went out altogether over the horizon.

"What was that?" she asked without turning to look at him.

"Nothing. Nothing at all," was his answer. Then he pushed past her and strode to the stern, where he appeared to strike up a conversation with the tillerman, but too quiet to be heard.

"Could they have been pirates?" asked Diverus.

"I don't know," she answered, but in fact she was certain that the explanation lay elsewhere.

"Would the snake know?" He glanced up from where he sat; in the lantern light, his face devoid of anything she might call wry.

"How do you know about the snake?"

"I walked around the house before, to try to feel better. He was speaking to you about a tower. You had the same look you had with the fox, and so I knew you didn't want to be interrupted and I came back here to wait."

She thought a moment, then said, "You know about pirates."

"Only from things said in the paidika. There were two boys, and they'd been stolen off a boat by pirates, far from Vijnagar, and brought to market there. I know no more than what they said, and so the black boat *could* have been pirates, couldn't it?"

"I think it's something else."

"What?"

She shook her head. "Something that scared Soter."

"Pirates would be enough to scare me."

She replied, "Me, too."

Stars smeared the sky overhead. The boat sailed on and Soter stayed beside the tillerman, while Diverus and Leodora hunkered down inside the house. Tension and the motion of the boat worked upon them, and they fell asleep against each other.

In the morning the light of dawn woke them, and they walked stiffly onto the deck, to discover that they were docked below an astonishingly high wall. It must have been twice the height of Hyakiyako. Pennants flew from its top. The wall was rough, the stone uneven, and scattered across its surface were small star-shaped objects, like medallions, that glinted in the early light. Farther along, away from the jetty, the wall opened into a dark and uninviting arch that wouldn't even have accommodated their mast. Any ships wanting to pass to the far side of this spiral would have had to sail on to the next span up or down the line. The rest of the span repeated the pattern of massiveness broken up by low arches. The steps and the jetty appeared to be dead center along its length.

One of the crewmen, red-bearded, came up behind them, carrying a basket on his back. He passed them and, climbing up and over the prow via the step Leodora had used to look into the sea, he walked down the jetty to the wall. A platform attached to ropes lay there, with another of his shipmates standing by, and he set his cargo carefully in the center of it. Then the two of them gave two of the ropes a tug. The ropes snapped tight; the platform lurched slightly, then began to ascend. They steadied it until it slid from their reach. High above them but beneath the top of the wall, beams jutted out, and between the beams was an opening, another arch. The sound of a squeaking pulley echoed distantly down like a bird's solitary cry.

As the crewman returned, Leodora asked him where Soter had gone.

"Up," he said, and gestured his head at the wall. "First one of us out, he was."

She turned, anger infusing her until she saw that the puppet cases were gone, too, already uplifted. Soter had accompanied them. She was chagrined then by her own overhasty judgment. Behind her, Diverus set down his bundle.

"Time to go," she muttered, then looked around for the snake. He was nowhere to be seen. The mast he'd girdled was empty, the sail drawn down and wrapped in loops of rope.

The bearded crewman and another came lumbering around the house now, carrying one of the larger crates. The platform was still ascending, so they set the crate down and watched it from on deck.

"The snake," said Leodora. "Where did he go?"

The two men looked at her, then at each other, then at her again. "Snake?" asked the bearded crewman.

"The snake who guards your cargo. He was wrapped around that mast there last night."

The other one said, "She seen it, too." They remained facing her, their faces tight with worry as if weighing what to do with her, and she thought that perhaps she shouldn't have said anything, that the snake was their secret.

Abruptly, the bearded one said, "He weren't crazy then. He were tellin' the truth."

"And we trussed him up for nothing," said the other. The morning sun glistened off the stubble on his face. "This snake, he speak at you?"

She nodded uncertainly. Behind her, Diverus said, "I saw it, too. Talking to her." They all looked his way then. "Last night. It was telling her a story."

Said one to the other, "But why can't we see it? Why these two an' not us?"

"Does it matter? It's real. That's all, that's what matters. We have us an avatar on board. We been blessed."

An avatar. She'd spoken to an avatar before that no one else had seen . . . and Soter hadn't seen the snake, either. But Diverus *had*.

The bearded sailor grabbed her by the shoulders. Close up, he smelled of sweat and brine. "You brought on us luck, girl, you and your friend. You ever want to venture between spirals some more, we're your men. We'll take you."

"Thank . . . thank you."

He let her go and lifted his end of the crate again. To his partner as they carried it the rest of the way off the boat, he said, "We go back to Merjayzin and get him released first thing. We've committed a crime here, we have to make it right. Make it right with the avatar. Bring that poor sod back on board and let him talk all he likes . . ." They climbed onto the jetty, their words fading.

Diverus asked, "We saw an avatar?"

"Apparently."

He stood still a moment before asking, "What *is* an avatar?"

"A spirit of the gods. Or a god made flesh."

"Or snakeskin." He smiled a little sheepishly and hefted his bundle of instruments.

"Yes, snakeskin." With a final glance back at the mast, she followed him up and off the boat.

From right below, the stairs looked even more imposing than they had from the boat, impossibly steep. At least, she thought, they were wide.

Responding to the same view, Diverus drew a breath and started up. The sack of instruments rattled on his back.

As she ascended, the two sailors waved to her; they grinned as if the oyster girl, Reneleka, had arisen from the water and handed them her pearl. And, thought Leodora, perhaps she had. Perhaps the snake did indeed herald great good fortune.

Twice on the climb up the steps they had to stop. The second time they stood parallel to the pulleys that lifted the platform, still a dozen steps below the top. Turned around on the steps, they could see that the ropes securing the platform ran from the pulley in beneath the opening in the wall, and as they watched, hands reached out to grab the goods and drag them off the platform, out of sight into the darkness there. The workers remained ill defined in the shadows. Clearly a large space existed beneath the surface of the span—possibly nothing more than a place to store goods; but with the memory of their climb up Vijnagar still fresh, they both could well imagine a much more extensive underworld. The semicircle out of which the pulley beams projected was itself an ancient opening, the lip of pinkish stone grooved as from years of ropes cutting into the face of it as cargo was raised, perhaps from a time before beams and pulleys had been applied.

Down below, the sailors had become no bigger than gnats and the boat a toy in a crystalline harbor. Off to one side of the boat, something serpentine floated upon the surface. It might have been nothing more than the ridge of a reef. Farther out and to the south, a cluster of small islands rode the horizon. Leodora wondered if fishermen lived there.

Above them threadbare pennants snapped in a strong breeze, which buffeted them as they came up the final few steps.

If, as all the tales claimed, most ancient Colemaigne had once been made of spun sugar and other confections, then centuries of rain and wind had eroded the hard façade of the buildings, exposing and aging more traditional materials underneath—crumbling mortar and stone. The skinny buildings had lost their flat surfaces, their precise edges. Rooftops dipped, and tiles coexisted with thatchwork while the frameworks leaned askew. The roofs and the top floors had collapsed in most of them. It was as if monstrous claws had swung down from the sky and scoured them of their skins, leaving them to rot. The buildings were chalky ruins, their cracked beams like broken bones. The wounds looked old, and yet no one had repaired or rebuilt the houses. That seemed odder still.

The steps opened onto a wide square of broken flagstones, off which half a dozen streets branched. To the supplies being hauled in below, there was no apparent direct access.

Small ramps ringed the steps, wedges with their apexes facing in toward the square. At some time in the past carts would have met travelers here and whisked them away across the span in either direction. She could see them in her mind, the carts backed up to the little ramps, accepting trunks, crates, whatever people brought. She could hear them, too. The excitement of that time crackled up into her through the broken street. The sense of displacement lasted a few minutes, then evaporated as if blown apart by the wind; after that she was fluent in the language of Colemaigne.

In the center of the square stood the remains of a fountain, with figures in the middle of some sort of animals, four of them facing four directions. The waters of the fountain trickled darkly from their mouths and down their bodies, leaving a dark stain, like blood. Soter was seated upon the edge of it with the cases beside him. His head was down, arms resting upon his thighs and his hands holding a cup between them. The stones of the street between the ramps and the fountain were pitted and cracked. Some were shattered or missing altogether, and difficult to walk on.

At their approach Soter glanced up, then lowered his head again, as if they weren't what he'd been waiting for.

The fountain did contain wine, although if she'd stood in it, it wouldn't have reached her ankles. It looked black, but Leodora remembered the stories he had told her and knew that it wasn't. It seemed that at least one part of the myth was true. Small earthenware cups like the one he held dotted the lip of it.

She and Diverus flanked him and sat. Without looking up he said, "It didn't used to be like this. When Bardsham came, they had banners flying. A welcoming crowd. They knew us, they cheered us. This place was *alive*."

His words slurred appreciably. This was not his first cup of wine. She asked, "What's happened then?"

"Blight," he said. He gestured with the cup toward an open stall selling vegetables and fruits. She noticed that his hand was trembling as if the cup was heavy. "I asked there, and they told me," he said. "Terrible. Cut a path the length of the span, years ago, but the place has never recovered. Chaos. The richness is gone, washed away. Your father and me, we entered this very square once in triumph, and it was everything I said it was, a confection of a span. Good days, those. Good days."

She didn't understand what he meant—his description of the maelstrom made it sound as if something like a water spout had descended and smashed across the span. *Chaos*—he used that word too freely to account for too much. He blamed everything on chaos, as if it dogged him wherever he went. He seemed inordinately affected by the state of Colemaigne.

"So, what do we do? We're here and we're surely not climbing aboard that boat again and going back."

"Back? Gods, no. Not an option, going back. Anyway, it's not blighted everywhere, according to them, or not so badly anyway. There's another square on the opposite side, a mirror to this one. We can look. Things are better over there, they said. The whole span might not be so bad. Depends on how far . . . how deep." He lost himself in some thought then, but came out of it quickly. "And it's early, you know, barely past dawn, so there's not much of a crowd out yet." In fact there was nobody anywhere save for the two vendors behind their stall. He twisted about and dipped his cup. "The fountains still run, I'm pleased to say."

For once she was inclined to let him have his fill, although his rambling about the blight upon Colemaigne told her very little. It was a span that had been great but had fallen upon hard times since he'd last seen it. Between that and the small stand selling produce, she thought again of Ningle. Someone brought the produce, someone caught the fish. She understood better than anyone the complicated processes that no one saw—and no one cared, so long as what they wanted was available.

"The other side, then," she suggested. "It's not that far, is it?"

"Not far," he agreed. He stood, an unsteady moment. Prominent veins mapped his left calf and, although she'd noticed them before, it was only now she appreciated that he was an old man, strong and proud and unwilling to bend, but old nevertheless. Perhaps it was the remaining magic of this span, or the result of meeting with another divine adviser, but she seemed to be experiencing an array of epiphanies today. She found herself feeling affectionate toward him despite everything that pitted them against each other time and again. She got up and kissed his cheek. Diverus could not have looked more shocked, while Soter's bewilderment had to swim through the muddle of his brain.

"All right," she said. "Let's see the rest of Colemaigne. We have to find *somewhere* to perform."

She hefted one of the cases and ducked under the strap, then started walking. After a dozen steps she turned and looked back.

The other two were eyeing each other distrustfully. Then Diverus, as though taking a cue from her, offered his lighter bag of instruments to Soter and shouldered the second undaya case. "You can't imagine what this place was like," Soter said to him as though he hadn't described it. "It was so magical."

Diverus traded a look with Leodora that said he was pretty certain magic was still afoot.

The far side did prove to be in better shape. Whatever tumult Soter had been describing, its effects hadn't blanketed the whole span. Some of the slender houses near the opposite square still maintained their surface coats, which were hard like stone, shiny and carved, like sculptures, with all manner of swirls and motifs. In one lane Leodora wetted a finger and wiped it across a bright green wall before sticking it in her mouth. "Sweet," she said around her finger. "It really *is* sugar."

"No one in the world knows how they do it, either," Soter told her. "They've a guild, sworn to secrecy. Can't even catch them working if you try."

More people were gathered in this square, too, the span now awake for the day. They milled about shops and stalls. It was exactly like a market day on Ningle, if not as busy.

Soter inquired at the shops about some places and names, and was given directions and information. "Yes," said one purveyor, "that old theater is still standing. No performances there anymore. The owner died, oh, years, long time back. Probably can find you a place to lodge, though. They got lots of room."

Soter strode into the lead, along a seaward lane so narrow that they had to go single-file with their luggage and press up against the buildings if someone needed to pass by, which happened every few minutes. He regaled them all the while, in love, it seemed, with his own voice. "Oh, yes, we played there for months. People were coming from half a dozen spans away to see, not thinkin' or maybe they just didn't care, that we would be moving on to theirs eventually. 'Course in the end we didn't, we got on a ship and sailed off to Re-morva." He stopped talking. A look of puzzlement pinched his face as if he couldn't decide quite how he had drifted into that part of the story. In a more subdued manner he added, "I guess they were right to journey all that way for Bardsham, after all, 'cause they wouldn't see his like again in a generation — not before now, in fact." He turned about and shook a finger at Leodora and Diverus. "They'd better let us play here or they won't know what they're miss-ing." He bumped into someone coming the other way. Apologies were made, and thereafter he focused on the direction he was walking. "Better let us play," he muttered to no one.

Carrying a load that was lighter than usual, Soter didn't notice that he was in-advertently putting more and more distance between himself and the other two. Approaching the dragon beam of Colemaigne, he thrust a finger at it and called back, "Look at it. That thing hasn't seen a visitation in your life-time . . . What am I saying? In *my* lifetime, which is much more considerable.

Of course, used to be nobody much minded, since the span had everything." More quietly, he added, "My gods, it's lost its edge, hasn't it? Gone quiet. You see this, you bloody coral ghost, you see what happened here? This is *our* doing, sure as I'm walking here again. We sucked the life out of Colemaigne, and the gods of Edgeworld forgive us. I ought to know what happened here."

He pressed against the buildings to let a woman in a dark purple wrap scuttle past, saying "Begging your pardon" as she did. She kept her head down and gave barely a sign that she'd heard him. "Not very sociable, are you," he muttered to her back, but if she heard that she didn't respond.

Passing the opening, he gazed out along the curve of the dragon beam.

It *did* look as ragged as if it had been gouged out of the sky. The sides were crumbling, and it was so thin across the middle, it was a wonder the weight of the Dragon Bowl at the end hadn't caused the whole thing to snap off and plunge into the sea. Soter hastened to pass it by.

Diverus and Leodora progressed more slowly. The cases made passage along the lane difficult. The corners kept bumping against the uprights in the railing. When the woman in purple reached them, they had to set down the cases and step back into a doorway to let her pass. A cluster of three more people came along behind her, and so they waited in the doorway for the rest to pass, too.

Leodora asked Diverus, "Was the bowl on Vijnagar as decrepit as this before your transformation?"

Diverus peered at it ahead. "It might have been. The beam was crumbling and the walls of it had fallen away like that one. On Vijnagar, the bowl had broken tiles in the bottom, you couldn't even tell what the mosaic had been. I can't see from here if this one's like that, too."

"Would you dare me to go out on one?" she teased.

He turned to face her. "You've never stood in a Dragon Bowl?"

She shook her head. "I've meant to. The first spans, Soter argued it was too dangerous. Too public. Someone might notice, and if my uncle came along looking for us, they would tell him. Now that I think on it, that makes almost no sense. Soter's so protective, even when there's no reason. I don't know why. Jax is out in the public and I'm to stay hidden from sight. Even now, you'll notice, and there's no chance Gousier's hunting us here."

"I thought you said your uncle was dead."

"I said he might be. I don't know for certain." She leaned around him. "As for the beams, Soter wouldn't allow me near one. I suppose I started climbing the towers to defy him without stepping out on a beam. Your story is the closest I've gotten to one."

The impeding pedestrians had walked on, and the sea-lane was now empty. Soter had moved far ahead. Diverus slid the strap over his shoulder and hefted the undaya case. "Well," he said, "I think I wouldn't dare you. Unless it was the *only* way to get you on one." He gave her a puckish smile and walked off clumsily with his burden.

They shortly reached the opening onto the beam, and their regard traced the curve of its route that, tentacle-like, nearly surrounded the hexagonal bowl at the end. Not a single person sat or stood anywhere on it. The Dragon Bowl was likewise empty. This was a span where the inhabitants had long since stopped believing in the capricious gods. Diverus and Leodora paused and stepped back as two more people emerged from an intersecting lane and came toward him. They looked at them sidelong as they passed, but neither so much as glanced toward the Dragon Bowl.

Up the lane Soter came to a point where everything looked like the square where the trio had first arrived. The building beside his shoulder, the nearest one, was a ruin. Half the quarrels in its windows were missing. There were one or two places where bits of glossy façade remained, but most of the front of the house revealed an underlying structure of irregular stones and gray, gritty powder. He touched one stone and it crumbled in his fingers. Above, the last story and the roof looked to have collapsed into the building. It was like a house that had been consumed by an attic fire, except that no traces of fire remained, and the rest of the houses as far down the lane as he could see shared its state of decay. Seabirds appeared to have nested in the upper reaches of some of them. The surface of the lane stretching ahead comprised nothing but flinders. The sea rail had disappeared, too, reduced to stubs where the posts had been, making the route more precarious.

Under his breath, Soter said one word: "Tophet."

He edged forward cautiously, and had only gone a few steps before Diverus caught up with him. Diverus set down his case and scanned the damage much as Soter had. Then he stepped out and peered over the side at the ocean below. "It's a ruin down there, too," he said. "Looks like pieces of the houses fell off. There must have been a quay once, but it's just rocks now. What happened here?"

Soter set down the instruments again. He shook his head at first, but then said, "I wager that, if you followed this line of damage street by street all the way back, it makes a straight line to that square where we climbed up."

Diverus squinched his face. "Like a path, you mean? Like a giant smashed them all?"

"Not a giant," Soter replied. "Like a curse."

"You sound as if you know what it was."

Soter blinked. "What? Why, no, of course I don't. I just . . . now, where's Leodor—" His eyes swelled with horror. "Oh, gods help me, no!"

Diverus turned, following his gaze, not up the lane but to the Dragon Bowl.

Leodora left her puppet case beside the opening and walked out onto the crumbling beam and onto the Dragon Bowl.

She considered that the beam's condition made it slightly perilous, but not more so than climbing up a tower. She didn't fear the height at all; she embraced the thrill of it.

What had Diverus felt? she wondered. What was it like to stand within the hexagonal bowl, hoping for some sign that you were exalted, chosen? A thriving span, covered with people, and only one or two would ever be blessed by the gods in such a way, and no one able to predict who it would be or when it would happen; no one sure it would ever happen at all. Spans like Ningle eventually forgot the bowl was there at all. There must be stories in that—of course there were, and she knew one: the tale of the two brothers. Soter had taught it to her years ago.

This bowl was in worse shape even than what Diverus had described of Vijnagar. There were almost no tiles remaining. If he hadn't said, she wouldn't have thought it had ever been covered with them.

She turned around and looked back along the ragged beam. From the narrow lane Soter was waving, and she waved back. The buildings behind him were osseous husks, like the ones on the far side they'd seen. It looked like the rest of Colemaigne all the way to the far support tower was a ruin. Before she could wonder at that, her attention was drawn to the underside of the span, visible from where she stood at the entry into the bowl. Unlike the opposite side, this one wasn't hidden behind a solid wall.

What she saw beneath Colemaigne was utterly impossible.

There were houses in a kind of mirror image of the city above. They hung upside down off the bottom of the span. She crossed the bowl and leaned over the lip, astonished.

The wind gusted at her back, then swirled around her. It blew back her hood. Soter shouted something, but she couldn't hear him over the wind. He was hurrying back. He'd left Diverus's instruments in the lane.

Diverus was calling to her, too, from between his hands. His words were drowned out by a rumbling in the sky overhead, and she tilted her head back.

Above the Dragon Bowl the sky was roiling as if throbbing with heat; the blue had darkened to greenish black as though the substance of the sky itself were scorching. Lightning flicked from this mass like the tongue of the Ondiont snake, transfixing her in fascination. She wasn't even aware that she had stepped away from the edge, back into the center of the bowl. The air crackled. It pulsed with energy that tingled right through her. She held up her hand, and a blue fire surrounded it. She had the presence of mind to think *I should be frightened.* Instead she spread out her arms as white lightning shot down from the middle of the overhead darkness, straight into the bowl. The world evaporated in light. The light stung her like a thousand bees and she screamed. The bowl, the beam, the span, and her friends upon it all disappeared in an instant. The pain released her and she fell into oblivion.

THE BLACK SHIP

Upon a deep-bottomed black ship well on its way across the sea to Vijnagar, beneath a thick, striped awning, a bony, bald-headed creature saw a bright flash just on the horizon whence they'd sailed and inadvertently in response said, "Ah?"

At this utterance of surprise, another, who might easily have been his gaunt twin, poured from the darkness behind him to see what had elicited the sound. On the horizon there was nothing now to behold. The morning sky was untroubled by so much as a single blemish. Not even a bird flew, as if even birds knew to keep far away from that ship.

The two creatures stared and stared at the horizon, unblinking, until one looked into the other's sunken eyes and both shrugged together. "Enh," said the first.

"What did you see?" asked the second.

"Nothing, Scratta."

"This *nothing* caught your attention."

"It was—"

The second one, Scratta, reached over and pressed a fingertip to his nose to cover a spot of calcitic gray showing there; when he withdrew his hand, the spot was gone, the nose pale and fleshy. He gave a satisfied nod at his handiwork. "Nothing to do with us," he said, "unless it's the one called Jax."

The other shrugged again, dismissing the idea.

"No," agreed the second, and he flowed silently back into the raven recesses of the ship.

The other turned to survey the untroubled distance behind them once more. A flash of light, he thought, most probably lightning over the horizon. It couldn't possibly be relevant.

The black ship sailed on. It would reach Vijnagar by nightfall.

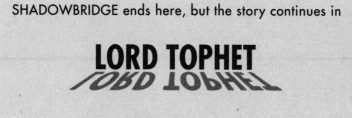

SHADOWBRIDGE ends here, but the story continues in

LORD TOPHET

coming from Del Rey Books

GREGORY FROST has been a finalist for nearly every major award in the fantasy field, including the Hugo, Nebula, James Tiptree, Theodore Sturgeon Memorial, International Horror Guild, and World Fantasy awards. He is the author of five previous novels, as well as the critically praised short-story collection *Attack of the Jazz Giants & Other Stories*. Greg is currently the Fiction Writing Workshop director at Swarthmore College. He lives in Merion Station, Pennsylvania.